JOURNEYS INTO EMPTINESS

JOURNEYS INTO EMPTINESS

Dōgen, Merton, Jung and the Quest for Transformation

Robert Jingen Gunn

PAULIST PRESS
NEW YORK / MAHWAH, N.J.

Library of Congress Cataloging-in-Publication Data

Gunn, Robert Jingen.
    Journeys into emptiness : Dōgen, Merton, Jung, and the quest for transformation / Robert Jingen Gunn.
       p. cm. — (Jung and spirituality series)
    Includes bibliographical references.
    ISBN 0-8091-3933-2 (alk. paper)
      1. Asceticism. 2. Spiritual life. 3. Dōgen, 1200–1253. 4. Merton, Thomas, 1915–1968. 5. Jung, C. G. (Carl Gustav), 1875–1961. I. Title. II. Jung and spirituality.

    BL625.G86 2000
    291.4'092'2—dc21

                                               00-028570

Published by Paulist Press
997 Macarthur Boulevard
Mahwah, New Jersey 07430

www.paulistpress.com

Printed and bound in the
United States of America

CONTENTS

For my brother
BILL
and my daughters,
ALLISON and LARA,
WARRIORS ALL
in the
EXPERIENCE of EMPTINESS

In Deep Gratitude, I Bow

First and unendingly to Ann Belford Ulanov, Christiane Brooks Johnson Memorial Professor of Psychiatry and Religion at Union Theological Seminary in New York, who responded to a movement of psyche and spirit within me and gave so generously to me of her time, heart and mind, as each piece of this book sought its shape. Her ability to see gaps and ask questions, her sense of what needed to be said and her willingness to enter into the material and respond personally sustained and encouraged me throughout this process.

From the Catholic Community:

To the late Robert Daggy, Ph.D., director of the Thomas Merton Study Center in Louisville, Kentucky, who gave me personal time, some of his own writings and a welcome to the Center's library for my research.

To Brother Patrick Hart, O.C.S.O., of the Monastery of Our Lady of Gethsemani, Kentucky, Merton's last secretary, for his conversation and constructive comments regarding the living Thomas Merton.

To Jonathan Montaldo, Merton scholar, editor of volume 2 of the Merton Journals and acting director of the Thomas Merton Study Center, who gave unstintingly of his time in the reading of the manuscript, offering important corrections and additions and talking through various issues as they arose.

To Anthony Padovano, Ph.D., Merton scholar and professor of American literature at Ramapo College, for generously taking me into his home and guiding my own encounter with Merton, and for supporting my research at the Thomas Merton Study Center in Louisville, Kentucky.

From the Buddhist Community:

To Roshi John Daido Loori, abbot of Zen Mountain Monastery, Mt. Tremper, New York, and my teacher.

To Bonnie Myotai Treace, Sensei, vice-abbess of the monastery and resident teacher at Fire Lotus Zendo, the New York City branch of the monastery, and all the members of the sangha. Without their practice, my own practice would never have begun.

To Robert A. F. Thurman, Ph.D., Jey Tsong Khapa professor of Indo-Tibetan Buddhist studies, Columbia University, for his guidance in the formulation of the chapter on Dōgen and Zen within the larger context of Buddhism and for his continuing commentary as the chapter developed.

To Kazuaki Tanahashi, creative artist dedicated to peace, noted translator of Dōgen into English, for his marvelously light-handed support and comments.

To David Noble, who edited my Japanese and offered valuable responses to the work.

To Konrad Ryushin Marchaj, M.D., of Zen Mountain Monastery, for his reading and commenting on the first chapter.

From the Depth Psychology Community:

To Harry W. Fogarty, Ph.D., instructor in psychiatry and religion at Union Theological Seminary and faculty member at the C. G. Jung Institute of New York, for his comments and suggestions as each chapter unfolded.

To Jonathan Goldberg, Ph.D., my Jungian analyst, and the members of his Wednesday night group, without whose support I would never have ventured into my own experiences of emptiness.

To Jo League, Ph.D., friend and colleague, whose unswerving support helped me believe in this work.

To Ruth Dombrow, Ph.D., friend and colleague, whose great combination of gentleness and toughness evoked my own.

Further bows of gratitude are due to numerous other people who were essential to the writing of this book:

To Barry Ulanov, Ph.D., McIntosh Professor of English Emeritus at Barnard College, Columbia University, through whose classes I had the opportunity to revisit my Columbia education in an entirely new, in-spirited way, for his verve and encouragement.

To Frederick C. Collignon, Jr., Ph.D., professor of urban economics, University of California at Berkeley, my best friend from Columbia College, for first believing in my ability to use words and for funding my first computer.

To Jane Greenlaw, who gave generously of her time, expertise and support in research at the New York Public Library.

To Jacob Miller, whose assistance in the organization, expression and editing of this material was another sine qua non to the completion of this study. His ability to join in my aspirations and work through raw material helped make this work a happy task.

Whatever mistakes remain in spite of so many generosities are mine alone.

Finally, I bow in the ten directions for having been given this great opportunity to engage this topic, these people, and their work with so much support from so many people. The writing of this book has been for me a powerful and meaningful encounter with the True Self, a work of joy and deep satisfaction. I hope others will also find it so in the reading.

SERIES FOREWORD

The Jung and Spirituality series provides a forum for the critical interaction between Jungian psychology and living spiritual traditions. The series serves two important goals.

The first goal is: *To enhance a creative exploration of the contributions and criticisms that Jung's psychology can offer to spirituality.* Jungian thought has far-reaching implications for the understanding and practice of spirituality. Interest in these implications continues to expand in both Christian and non-Christian religious communities. People are increasingly aware of the depth and insight that a Jungian perspective adds to the human experiences of the sacred. And yet, the use of Jungian psychoanalysis clearly does not eliminate the need for careful philosophical, theological, and ethical reflection or for maintaining one's centeredness in a spiritual tradition.

The second goal is: *To bring the creative insights and critical tools of religious studies and practice to bear on Jungian thought.* Many volumes in the Jung and Spirituality series work to define the borders of the Jungian and spiritual traditions, to bring the spiritual dimensions of Jung's work into relief, and to deepen those dimensions. We believe that an important outcome of the Jung-Spirituality dialogue is greater cooperation of psychology and spirituality. Such cooperation will move us ahead in the formation of a postmodern spirituality, equal to the challenges of the twenty-first century.

Robert L. Moore
Series Editor

(See back of book for a complete listing of titles in this series.)

PREFACE

To embark on a psychospiritual journey is to engage in a search for truth that is simultaneously larger than oneself, yet inextricably intertwined with the details of one's personal life. Our quest for transcendence, our urge to be grounded in being beyond all beings, is fraught and freighted with our bodies' desires, pains and limitations, as well as the cultural, familial, intellectual and emotional particularities of our lives.

This is as true for our heroes as it is for ourselves, and thus we look to their lives with more ambivalence than when we look at their work. On the one hand, we want to see them as human, as like us in our limitations, frailties and foibles, so that we may feel that we, too, are capable of greatness. On the other hand, to the extent that we acknowledge their humanity, the very stuff out of which they drew their achievements, we grow suddenly timid, for we are left without excuse to take responsibility for our own actual, creative possibilities.

We are nevertheless emboldened by the promise of both the lives and work of the three men we meet here that perseverance will be rewarded and that those who continue knocking at the door of the unknown will find it opening onto a vast field of liberation, a heavenly feast, the infinite, richly textured wholeness of the Self of which we are a part.

Toward that end, we will be looking closely at Dōgen, the thirteenth-century Japanese Zen master, Thomas Merton, the twentieth-century Euro-American Catholic monk, and Carl Jung, the nineteenth-and-twentieth-century Swiss psychiatrist. We want to see in what ways the experience of emptiness was for them not merely a passing hurdle to be overcome nor a mere theme of study, but a way of living, of being fully alive, productive and creative.

For each of them, the experience—not the concept—of emptiness was considered a necessary stage in the process of self-transformation. The meaning of emptiness, as well as the understanding of the process and goal of self-transformation, are different for each. Yet all three would agree that by confronting and working with experiences of emptiness, a person undergoes a fundamental change in the direction of becoming more real, more truly oneself, including a heightened sense of what one has uniquely to offer to the human community. All three men would also agree that attempts to bypass experiences of emptiness ultimately compound suffering, creating confusion and illusion, while attempts to accept and work with the experience of emptiness lead to an enriched appreciation of life.

Our focus is on experience as subjective awareness, consciousness, knowing that one knows. Such awareness, consciousness, knowing is in contrast to things happening to one, including thoughts and feelings, without one being really aware of them. Such inattention is common on one level. At other levels, one is simply unconscious, in denial, experiencing dissociation, or what Robert Lifton has called "psychic numbing." Each of the traditions to be examined here values consciousness as primary. Awareness, being awake and alert to what one is experiencing, regardless of whether it has to do with any of the senses, memory, imagination, thoughts, feelings or dreams, is a value in itself, a barometer of vitality. Lowered awareness of what one is experiencing means one is just that much less alive, just that much less in one's actual life. Such consciousness comprises the essence of presence. Not to be aware of what one is thinking, feeling, experiencing in this very moment is not to be present, not to live in the here and now.

At a later stage in spiritual development, one moves beyond the self being aware of itself into experiencing that transcends the separation between experiencer and experienced, the knower and the known. In each of these traditions, such awareness, such consciousness, accelerates the realization of the true self. Alternatively, lack of consciousness limits one's ability to change, to grow, to become fully one's self.

Additionally, and importantly, each of these men asserts that ordinary consciousness is a relatively small part of human potential and that we are largely unconscious of the deeper dimensions of reality, whether understood as Buddha nature, God or the unconscious. Though their methods differ, they agree on the spiritual and/or psychological imperative to increase consciousness of that larger reality that ultimately underlies and influences our ordinary lives. For all three men, the experience of emptiness is seen as a door to a different dimension of consciousness, a dimension in which the deepest levels of being are encountered that enable personal transformation. Attention to the experience of emptiness is thus part of that larger on-going work of increased consciousness that leads to transformation.

As we walk through these men's lives, we will be paying attention to the subjective side of each writer's experience of emptiness in detail. This emphasis will be necessary because self-transformation, which involves a multiplicity of levels of consciousness, forces us into the realm of subjective experience. Thousands of people die every day, but if it is *your* child, your child is not a number. Pain and suffering abound throughout the world, but when it is *your* back or head or lungs or tooth, the experience has a meaning for you that is entirely yours.[1] Similarly, the experience of emptiness is not some thing or object that can be put out on the table for all to view; it can be known only by being entered into, absorbed, reflected upon and gleaned for whatever it may bring of meaning. Each of our participants intentionally spent long hours in self-reflection through writing, prayer, meditation, and/or psychotherapy.

Both physics and psychotherapy teach us that we, the observers, also influence what we are observing. In this way, attention to what we experience as a participant/observer in emptiness brings us that much closer to understanding the process of transformation. Put another way, the focus of knowing is not external or outside the self, but is the self's most acute awareness of its own experience or process. Therefore, we will need to look at how each of our speakers dealt with his own subjectivity as he sought to study himself in the experience of emptiness.

Each of these men was bound up in a tradition that we, on this side of their lives, may tend to take for granted. In order for them to achieve what they did, each one struggled long and hard against what they experienced as the deep inadequacies of the tradition they inherited: Dōgen found Zen practice in his contemporary Japan deplorable; Merton found most Catholic monastic life vapid; Jung was a psychiatrist who refused to accept the limits of what was known in his field, not only in psychiatry, but in the newly emerging psycho-analysis of Freud. All three had to let go of the best and most revered in their respective traditions in order to bring new life into them.

Each chapter will therefore weave three aspects into each writer's journey into emptiness: the traditions in which they were working, Zen Buddhism, Christianity and depth psychology, respectively; the par-ticular events of their lives; and the experiences of emptiness as con-necting links between their lives and their work.

My copies of Jung's *Memories, Dreams, Reflections,* Merton's *New Seeds of Contemplation* and Shunryu Suzuki's *Zen Mind, Beginner's Mind* are all more than twenty-five years old. It took that long for me to be ready to see and hear what they had to say. But then, I am a slow learner.

I commend them to you, dear reader, in the hope that, however slow or fast your own journey, you will find riches here, as I have, and great encouragement.

Robert Jingen Gunn
New York City, 2000

INTRODUCTION

About the Experience of Emptiness

Whether it is an experience of loss of things outside oneself, as depicted in the story of Job, or an inner experience of having no purpose, or even self, or of life lacking any meaning of satisfaction, the experience of emptiness most commonly thought of is an experience of being without, of not having: not having answers, not having property, not having love or power or hope.

In the process of self-transformation, the nature of the experiencing changes, as does the nature of the emptiness experienced. In very broad terms, what begins as a negative experience of emptiness ends as a positive, or perhaps beyond that, a neutral experience.

This is a study of the self in transformation—a process that begins with one kind of experience of emptiness—often equivalent to the Buddhist concept of *dukkha*[1]—and moves through various changes to another kind of experience of emptiness that is seen by each of the men studied here as the *telos* or goal of the transformation process.

The circumstances that trigger the *initial* experience of emptiness are as varied as our life situations. On a personal level, they may be triggered by the experience of death, divorce, depression, abortion, illness, bankruptcy, failure, success, addiction and recovery, loneliness, identity confusion, loss of community, an unidentifiable inner discontent, loss of meaning or the end of a life script or stage. On a larger scale, the initial experience of emptiness may be triggered by a sense of the persistence of injustice; the ravages of war, disease, poverty, starvation; mass destruction and pollution of land, trees, air and water, fish, plants, animals and mountains; the monotony of collective life without the serendipitous and idiosyncratic; the loss of any valuing of the personal amid bureaucracies and faceless decision makers.

Such experiences raise basic life questions: Who am I? Why am I here? Why are there suffering and evil in the world? Whom shall I marry? Shall I stay married? What should I do with my life? How can I stop the pain? Why is this happening to me? What is death? What is life? Is this all there is? Where is my community? Where is the force for good in our society?

These are disquieting questions. We would prefer to forget about them and simply fill up the emptiness with—something—anything. This experience of not having peace, comfort and pleasure is contrary to every natural impulse of body and mind. Every bit of common sense says it is better to have something good than not to have it, and whether it is about relationships or identity or status and power, most of us would easily prefer having to not having and will go to great lengths to insure it. To have implies, or carries the hope of, stability, security, solidity. Not to have is to be unstable, unreliable and at sea. Facing emptiness and letting go of the familiar and secure is terrifying. Much of human conflict and destructiveness derive from the terror of the experience of emptiness and our attempt to achieve and sustain what we think is its opposite: a fullness of life. Paradoxically, however, it is precisely around the urge toward fullness of life that the experience of emptiness often enters.

Not all experiences of emptiness are negative. Some are mixed, such as the pang of missing one's beloved when one can neither see nor touch him, or a father giving his daughter away at her wedding. The Zen-related Japanese arts all carry this poignant juxtaposition of life and death, affirmation and negation in their work: *haiku* (poetry), with its central emphasis on *wabi*,[2] expresses it in the form of words; *ikebana* does it with flowers; *shodō* does it with ink, brush and paper. Some experiences of emptiness are actually positive: an experience of religious conversion; standing by the seashore or taking in a star-studded night; witnessing the birth of one's child.[3] Thus, even experiences of great beauty or love can be experiences of emptiness when the beauty or love is acknowledged as foreground and the inevitability of change is in the background.

Each of the examples above *can* be an experience of emptiness. What makes a particular experience an experience of emptiness rather than simply another experience of pleasure or pain is the impact and effect that event, thought, dream or object has upon us and our response to it. To *experience* emptiness is to pay attention to the impact of the event on one's feelings, especially in the body, and to be moved to a deeper level of consciousness than is ordinary in at least two ways:

1. It is experienced *in the body*: often in the lower abdomen, the *dan tian* (in Chinese, hereafter abbreviated to Ch.) or *hara* (in Japanese, hereafter abbreviated to Jp.); sometimes in the genitals, as a lack of sexual energy or as a hole that needs to be filled; sometimes in the "pit" of our stomach, which involves a sense of having one's "breath taken away" when experiencing awe or overwhelming beauty and being made aware of one's tininess or insignificance in contrast to the sea or stars or, when it is negative, as a sense of "having the wind knocked out of one." It may render one breathless or speechless, thus demarking it as an experience of *chi* (Ch./ *ki,* Jp.), the basic life force. It often leaves one on the verge of tears, if not actually crying. There is thus an effluence of deep emotion.

2. There is a state of heightened consciousness that tends toward a generalization about life. One experiences the moment as revealing the ultimate significance of life as either absolutely valuable or utterly pointless. If pointless, then everything is robbed of meaning; if valuable, then the poignant juxtaposition of being alive and the inevitability of change and death brings home to one a keen sense of what is most and least important, what is worth living and dying for.

These two aspects of the experience poise one at a certain existential edge where we face the question *What shall we do?* with what has been experienced. If we disregard it like the passing of most moments of our lives, an opportunity is lost to go deeper, to enter into a deeper level of awareness of self and other; yet to enter into the experience more deeply is daunting. Dōgen, Merton and Jung all used some form of yoga as part of their method for exploring their experiences of emptiness. For Dōgen, it consisted in doing *zazen*, meditation while sitting in the lotus position. Merton and Jung adapted what they knew of yoga to their own methods. Merton described the physical sensations connecting experiences of emptiness as centers of impacted feeling with the release of such feelings during contemplation.[4] Jung used yoga during his "confrontation with the unconscious" in order to keep his emotions in check and calm his mind.[5]

As much as we can, we usually try to manage the anxiety and pain or joy of this question by diversion, avoidance, suppression or denial, often resorting to truisms (e.g., "it's God's will," *"que sera sera"* or "it's my karma") to rationalize our turning away from the experience of emptiness, and the many questions it raises. The maintenance of normal functioning gets top priority, where "normal functioning" means carrying out our consciously determined priorities and goals. In short, we will do almost anything to avoid changing our life, bringing into question our fundamental assumptions about self, other, world, our purpose, our pet prejudices and peeves. As much as possible, we tend to cling to the familiar—emotionally, physically, spiritually, intellectually.[6]

Yet this basic life question of what to do with our experience of emptiness demands a response from us that is perhaps less in words that in a decision about what to do and how to be. Even avoidance and denial constitute, willy-nilly, decisions about how we will respond. They represent the perhaps unconscious selection of an act of omission over an act of commission. In each such decision, we choose how much of ourselves to risk and how much to hold back, how fervently or timidly to commit, how large or small to draw the circle of community with which we will identify, how much reality to face and how much to deny, how much to hope for and how much to be held back by fear.

Introduction

The three great traditions to be considered here agree that the full realization of oneself, which necessarily involves the experience of emptiness, is a psychological and spiritual imperative that has a price:

Buddhism's founder, Shakyamuni, left his family, his wealth, status and power in order to pursue self-realization. Bodhidharma, who is credited with bringing Zen to China, cut off his eyelids so he would not go to sleep in prolonged meditation. His first and primary student, Hui-k'o, stood all night in the snow and cut off his arm to prove his sincere desire to learn the Way. To pursue one's truth requires jumping off a one-hundred-foot flagpole, or as Master Kyogen said,

> It is like a man up a tree, hanging from a branch by his mouth; his hands cannot grasp a branch, his feet won't reach a bough. Suppose there is another man under the tree who asks him, "What is the meaning of Bodhidharma coming from the west?" If he does not respond, he goes against the wish of the questioner. If he answers, he will lose his life. At such a time, how should he respond?[7]

Jesus declares that this realization is so important that one must give up everything. To obtain the pearl of great price, a man goes and sells everything he has (Matthew 13:46). When Jesus calls someone to be a follower, he commands them to drop what they're doing and leave their business (Matthew 4:18–22), not even to stop to bury one's dead father (Matthew 8:21–22), to leave all semblances of security and do the impossible: walk on water (Matthew 14:28–33).

Much of Jung's clinical work, as well as that of the other psychologists, was spent analyzing the vicissitudes of the self's struggle to be and resistance against being. He was one of the first to say that neurosis was a product of the refusal of the demands of the individuation process.[8]

> Individuation means...becoming one's own self....[One] has a strong feeling of what should be and what could be. To depart from this divination means error, aberration, illness.

However risky and terrifying it may be to choose a path of trans-formation, all three traditions warn of an even greater peril if one does not:

From Zen, Mumon issues the warning,

> If you go forward, you will go astray from the essence. If you go back, you oppose the principle. If you neither go forward nor back, you are a dead man breathing. Tell me now, what will you do? Make the utmost effort to attain full realization in this life! Do not abide in misery forever.[9]

Jesus warns in the parable of the talents (Matthew 25:14–20), that the man who refuses to risk what he has loses even what he was given and is cast into outer darkness.

For Jung, failure to pay attention to the psyche has vast conse-quences:

> ...the psyche not only disturbs the natural order but, if it loses its balance, actually destroys its own creation....In the same way that the atom bomb is an unparalleled means of physical mass destruction, so the misguided development of the soul must lead to psychic mass destruction.[10]

This very fact—that we can choose for or against our own realiza-tion—is evidence of our rootedness in a transcendent dimension.[11] It also points to the fact that for all three traditions being studied here, emptiness may be viewed as the key to the paradox of selfhood: We must let go in order to have.

Dōgen says, "To study the self is to forget the self; to forget the self is to be at one with all things."[12]

Jesus says, "Whoever would gain life, must lose it; whoever loses her life for my sake will find it" (Matthew 10:39).

For Jung, each stage of the individuation process has the character of the crucifixion, in which one feels in conflict between two mutually exclusive alternatives; the death of the ego is required for resolution and entry into a deeper level of the Self.

Introduction

Thus all three traditions, either implicitly or explicitly, view the pivotal experience of emptiness not as something painful to be avoided, but as a door, leading to a larger vision and experience of connection to all life, including death, to being and nonbeing and what is beyond both.

At the initial juncture of an experience with emptiness, an individual faces the choice between response or avoidance. One either recognizes and responds to the experience via introspection or overt action, or one continues, albeit at a high price, on the path of avoidance. But far from the common understanding of introspection as self-indulgent navel-gazing, all of the three traditions explored here assert that faithfulness to one's self and faithfulness to being-itself are one, and that the refusal of one is the lack of faith in the other. To refuse the path of transformation will necessarily add to the burden of suffering, on personal, familial, and communal levels—by what was not done as much as by what was done. Whether understood as karma, sin or neurosis, the transgenerational effects of how we respond to the experience of emptiness ripple not only throughout the human community, but the environment.

Yet we remain deeply ambivalent about becoming ourselves. Afraid of the anxiety that attends self-knowledge, afraid of the possible demands of authentic life, we run away, hiding in false selves, or smaller selves, avoiding the challenge of our true self.

Like blind tightrope walkers, we hesitate to move into the unknown. We hold onto whatever is within grasp: a handle, a straw, a house, a marriage, an idea, an identity, a belief, a piece of chocolate.

Sometimes, as if impatient with our hesitation, especially if we seem to have failed to get the first message, life pushes us off the edge, erases all graspables, and we plunge in free fall, wondering whether a wise coach or a vicious, cruel fate has engineered the move.

That we shall all die is certain. Whether we shall have fully lived is less certain and far more problematic, for it is the testimony of many great thinkers, such as those chosen for this study, that the quality of our life is at certain crucial points a question of consciousness and courage, and that being true to oneself is fraught with many difficulties. To flee from the pain of emptiness is to flee from some truth of one's self and of life that is seeking to be seen. The importance of being true to one's self and the meaning of living life fully lies not merely in the individual satisfaction it may or may not bring. Despite the subjective nature of the experience of emptiness, the failure to take upon oneself the task of responding to the experience of emptiness, by becoming oneself, will necessarily result in failures to serve well the human community.

Whether we enter into the initial experience of emptiness by choice, consent or the push of external circumstances, the *entering consciously and deliberately into the experience* constitutes an all-important step into the second stage of emptiness. The first stage is an event, a fact, a thought, a feeling or an experience that confronts us with a basic life question. The second stage constitutes our response as a decision to engage the depth dimension of that question or issue that life has presented to us. By entering into this second stage, we accept responsibility for our lives as subjects, not mere objects. We take upon ourselves the task of knowing, discovering, being aware. We move from a position of innocent victim to being one who "takes the backward step" (Zen tradition), is a "learner in the kingdom of God" (Christian tradition), one who seeks to "make the unconscious conscious" (depth psychology tradition).

What began as an experience of emptiness causing great pain or disorientation now turns into a thread that seems to go on and on infinitely and with infinite branchings; a tree with never-ending roots and shoots which, when followed, may lead into vast realms of dark unknown; it is a diving into the deep waters.

Once the experience has been engaged, like Jacob's refusal to let the stranger go without a blessing,[13] the theme of emptiness continues along the path of transformation in different forms, with different implications, indefinitely. To "enter the Way," to "take up one's cross," or to "make the unconscious conscious" through systematic self-observation, is to adopt transformation not as a one-time event, but as a way of life that consists in ever-expanding awareness, continual letting-go of attachments and increasing freedom and service to all of life, to being-itself. The experience of emptiness may be viewed in this way not only as the personal biographical door to a single transformation, but the recurrent door into the unending stages of transformation where what was once foreboding becomes a feast.

These chapters give an account of the three stages of the experience of emptiness to show how three great explorers of the process of transformation (1) experienced emptiness in their own lives, (2) used that experience to embark on their own path of transformation and (3) returned to offer their particular experience as a method for others to use.

Emptiness is primary to all three men, yet they each view it differently; paradoxically, the self which is let go of, also remains, but transformed. For Dōgen, in emptiness, we let go of everything, including self, including emptiness itself; what remains is no-thing, insubstantiality, which is neither nothing nor something, but it in fact leads us back to the Self[14] which is at once "ten thousand things,"[15] which is everything. For Merton, in letting go of everything, there remains the self that is empty; in this sense, emptiness is poverty, yet a poverty that leads to the fulfillment of the true self as known only in God. For Jung, emptiness is the sacrifice of the ego to Self,[16] which transcends individual consciousness.

Each of these traditions has evolved various ways of identifying the path to self-transformation, to the self's becoming itself that may follow the experience of emptiness. These usually follow a pattern of descent/ascent. For the Zen Buddhist, a descent into Self *via zazen* (sitting Zen), in which one lets go of all attachments, is a prerequisite to Enlightenment, the ascent of the mountain, and is followed by another descent, a return down the other side of the mountain to the marketplace.[17] For the Christian, Christ's death, entombment, descent into hell, resurrection and ascension are the paradigm for all spiritual life. In Jung, the descent is into the unconscious via the *anima* or *animus*[18] and an exploration of the unconscious contents, particularly of the shadow, to reach a deeper integration of the contents of the unconscious into conscious life. In each of these paths, there is a time when what is known and reliable is relinquished (or perhaps torn away), leaving one with a profound experience of emptiness that, if attended to properly, becomes a resolution beyond having and not having, being and not-being.

Every great spiritual tradition seems to have this experience as part of its path, whether it is something that is cultivated over time with discipline, or something that seems to happen suddenly, by surprise. In psychology, every psychotherapist has seen patients unable to move forward because they are holding on to something, and only when they are willing to accept the experience of emptiness and be in that space and explore it, are they able to go to what is next. Thus, in their different ways, for all the writers discussed here, emptiness is the key to the paradox of full selfhood.

Dōgen

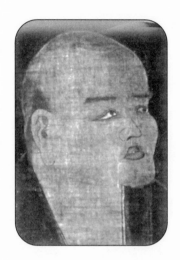

Chapter 1

EMBRACING EMPTINESS IN THE EAST

Buddhism's Beginnings in India and its Entrance into China

The first known appearance in the world of the concept of emptiness as an essential aspect of spiritual awareness was in Buddhism in the sixth century B.C.E. From Buddhism's very beginning, emptiness[1] was an essential, central doctrine, deriving from the basic idea of no-self, or selflessness (*anatman* in Sanskrit). The entire history of Buddhism could be written as an ongoing discussion of emptiness,[2] just as, in the West, the history of philosophy could be written as a history of the understanding of being and nothingness.[3] Further, the history of the West's understanding of the East could be written in terms of the changing understanding (read, usually, *misunderstanding*) of emptiness, that too easily became associated with the nothingness that was the opposite of being. In this parallel discussion of Eastern and Western traditions, the problems, contradictions and paradoxes of all dualisms arise.[4] It is useful, therefore, to consider in a very summary way the major developments and three of the early explorers of the concept of emptiness in

Buddhism before Dōgen, to understand better the context of Dōgen's own work.

From Abandonment to Enlightenment: Shakyamuni Buddha[5]

Shakyamuni Buddha, regarded as the founder of Buddhism, was born in Kapilavastu, India, near present-day Nepal, into a wealthy warrior clan in approximately 563 B.C.E. under the name Siddhartha Gotama or Gautama.[6] Shakyamuni's mother is reported to have died when he was seven days old, as had been foretold. This early death of the mother finds parallels in Dōgen's and Merton's lives, and becomes, from the depth psychological point of view, a foundational experience of emptiness, a deep psychic wound[7] that provides an underlying motivation for a profound, relentless and determined spiritual search. As we shall discuss later, such an extremely early experience of emptiness may become determinative, as it was for Shakyamuni, creating a restlessness and an ache that cannot be satisfied by normal life. Just as adopted children often feel compelled to search for their genetic parents as a way of knowing what is real about their origins,[8] Shakyamuni (and, as we shall see, Dōgen and Merton) were motivated to search for what was even more real than their origins, than their biological parents, that is, absolute reality or God.

Like most of us, however, Shakyamuni tried the normal life. His father, fearing the prophecy that his son would leave his legacy in order to become a monk, tried to protect him from the hardships of life and surrounded him with comfort, pleasure and social position. Shakyamuni married at the age of sixteen and fathered a son. But at one point Shakyamuni insisted on seeing the world beyond the protective gates of the family compound and, once outside, he encountered old age, suffering and death. Shakyamuni was so profoundly moved by this encounter, tradition has it, that he became dissatisfied with his life of ease and plenty and sneaked out of the palace in the middle of the night to embark on his spiritual quest.

From a depth psychological point of view, such a radical life change requires some inner predisposition stemming from an antecedent experience of emptiness. Even Buddhas do not embark on a spiritual path without some breaking up of inner soil.[9] It is this author's interpretation, therefore, that Shakyamuni's encounter with old age, suffering and death struck a profound chord in him, reviving, consciously or unconsciously, the experience of emptiness associated with the loss of his mother. The result of this was that he experienced a gnawing discontent with his own life, which called into question the value and purpose of what he was doing.[10] As with countless others before and since him, the experience of emptiness acquired an inner insistence, demanding conscious attention, robbing ordinary goals and pleasures of their satisfaction. The loss of his mother thus became associated with an all-pervading experience of human suffering: the particular experience of emptiness led to the universal question of life and death. To be hounded[11] by this question is the essence of the spiritual imperative.[12] An initial experience of emptiness, therefore, consciously or unconsciously, tends to "raise the *bodhi* mind," to stimulate the quest for enlightenment.

Thus, at the age of twenty-nine, Shakyamuni literally abandoned all his wealth, sociopolitical status and his entire family in order to pursue his spiritual path. This pattern of "home departure," in which family ties, social position and wealth are abandoned in order to embark on a spiritual path, is the paradigmatic event for all Buddhist monks upon taking monastic vows, and was manifested centuries later in the life of both Dōgen and Thomas Merton. As can be observed from an examination of the desert fathers[13] and medieval Christian ascetics, this practice also evolved in the West.

As was common in his day, Shakyamuni's spiritual path initially consisted of becoming a mendicant and undergoing strenuous exertions and deprivations of the body, including fasting, going without sleep, enduring pain and suffering the vagaries of life with no fixed abode.

After six years of this process, he decided that self-imposed hardship, deprivation and suffering had led him no closer to accepting and learning from his fundamental experience of emptiness. He tried, in other words, the path recommended by the best collective[14] wisdom of his day and found it wanting. It did not reach deep enough to heal his inner wound and resolve the fundamental issues of life and death.

He decided, therefore, to seek his own path, to find his own way. This is one of the hallmarks of the individuation[15] process: Shakyamuni had tried satisfying all human craving and found it wanting. Then he tried ascetic denial, and found that that still did not reach the depth of his experience of emptiness. Both satiation and denial are common collective answers to the experience of emptiness. It is only after all collective understandings have been exhausted that one begins to forge one's own unique path and to discover therein the treasure that is worth bringing back to the world. Undaunted by the failure of collective answers, Shakyamuni persisted in attending to the questions raised by his experience of emptiness.

After restoring his health with food, water and rest, he resolved to sit under the *bodhi*[16] tree until his fundamental quest was resolved.[17] This decision—to sit under the *bodhi* tree reflecting on a problem until it is resolved—is an archetypal and symbolic act, similar to the planting of a flag upon newly discovered or vanquished land. By so doing, one stakes a claim, demarcates a territory as distinct from the rest of the world, thus making it a sacred space, since sacred means set apart. For the Buddha, as for all subsequent practitioners, to "take one's seat" is to demarcate the search for a resolution within the territory of oneself, one's own mind or psyche, rather than outside oneself, and to commit to staying with the issues until they are resolved. Such tenacity requires courage as well as highly developed skills in paying attention. To sit with one's thoughts and feelings, as everyone who has done meditation or been in some form of psychoanalysis or psychotherapy knows, is not easy. One discovers how difficult it is to stay with experiences that are unpleasant and how quickly and subtly the mind moves to other things. Whatever was repressed returns, albeit usually in disguise. Memories, dreams, fantasies abound and compete for attention. The meditating body that looks on the outside to be so serene that many might assume it is at peace contains raging fires, driving torrents and images that are sometimes not only frightful but disgusting. The urge to run away manifests itself in phantasmic flights of imagination. Regardless of one's initial determination, the question always comes up at some point: Why am I putting myself through this difficulty rather than walking on a beach, making love or making money?

The depth of one's despair in the initial experience of emptiness determines the magnitude of faith and determination required to continue: The deeper and more universally encompassing the pain, the more one requires an answer that is beyond the elimination of merely personal pain. The more one allows oneself to be aware of others' suffering, the more one requires an answer that speaks to the entire human condition. And the more one allows oneself to be aware of the suffering and destruction of waters, trees, and mountains, the more one requires an answer that speaks to all beings. Implicit in the steadfast attention to a personal experience of emptiness, therefore, is the need for a vision that is large enough to include everything. This is the process Shakyamuni went through in order to attain enlightenment and this is the scope of the vision that Buddhism offers.

It is said that at the end of his all-night vigil Shakyamuni experienced enlightenment upon seeing the evening star, and announced,

> "Isn't it incredible! All sentient beings have the Buddha nature. At the very same moment, I and all sentient beings enter the Way."[18]

It is often forgotten that, whether this was the result of one all-night vigil or three days or forty-nine,[19] the experience had been prepared for by the years of ascetic practices and studies under other teachers. Shakyamuni was not the first Buddha and was not the first to experience enlightenment. Tradition has it that he was preceded by six other Buddhas: Vipashyin, Shikin, Vishvabhu, Krakuchchanda, Konagamana and Kashyapa.[20] *Buddha* means "Enlightened One" or "One who is awake," thus declaring Buddhism's supreme valuing of human consciousness as a total experience, unassimilable by reason or logic alone, to be inherent in its very foundation.

Shakyamuni Buddha was thirty-five when he experienced *anuttara-samyaksambodhi* (Sn.), supreme enlightenment. Knowing that his experience could not be conveyed in words, he retreated into silence until, implored by the friends who had earlier abandoned him and now saw the radiant effect of his transformation, he began teaching. Thus, for almost half a century, until he died at the age of eighty, Shakyamuni Buddha returned to offer his particular experience as a method for others to use. He had many disciples, one of whom, Ananda, remembered everything Shakyamuni Buddha said and recited it for others to remember and record. The teachings come down to us mostly in the Pali canon and in numerous sutras in Sanskrit. Shakyamuni Buddha's enlightenment experience is one that every serious Zen practitioner aims to replicate for the sake of the experience of liberation that comes with it.

Thus, in the life of Shakyamuni Buddha, we can see the positive results of a person's taking the experience of emptiness and, rather than finding a way to dismiss it, working with it, making it an object and subject of study, attending to it, learning from it, and bringing what one has learned back to the human community.

At every point along the way, Shakyamuni had alternatives. He could have stayed in his palace and not looked beyond himself. Once seeing others' suffering and life's transience, he could have used his wealth and status simply to do a more effective job of avoiding pain and increasing pleasures. He could have suppressed the experience of emptiness based on the prior ethical claims on him of his wife and child. When his ascetic practices didn't help, he could have gone home again, declaring the futility of the quest. When he achieved his own enlightenment, he could have ignored the pleas of his friends and retreated into solitary self-satisfaction. To have taken any of these detours, as is not only common but—especially in the case of return to the family—considered meritorious, would not only have frustrated his personal psychological and spiritual growth, but would have deprived humankind of Buddhism's contribution to the issues of the human condition.

The contribution of Shakyamuni Buddha to the world, although it comprises hundreds of volumes of lectures and sutras, has been summarized in his Four Noble Truths. In brief, these are: (1) Unenlightened life is suffering. (2) The cause of suffering is desire. (3) We can put an end to suffering. (4) We can end suffering by following the eightfold path of Buddhist practice. Underlying this diagnosis and prescription is an understanding of reality that was in complete opposition to the prevailing Brahmanic religion of Shakyamuni's day. Shakyamuni's declaration of no-self, or selflessness (*anatman*, Sn.) was a deliberate "No!" to the central notion of the fixed self in Brahmanism which served as the linchpin holding together the prevailing class distinctions and privileged hierarchies of the time. Shakyamuni saw in his day the way in which the idea of a fixed nature or essence of self served as the basis for justifying prejudice, discrimination, cruelty and war. Once people draw a boundary—in this case, around the smallest element, the self—they arrange their life, their thoughts, beliefs and institutions, and their actions to defend it. To mix cultural metaphors and heroes, in the understanding of no-self, Shakyamuni discovered the Archimedean point by which to move the world. This was nothing less than revolutionary, as Thich Nhat Hanh notes, and adds,

> "...the notion of not-self is aimed at liberating us from the prison of dogma....the notion of not-self was born in reaction to the Brahmanic notion of the self, and not as a discovery independent of the thought of the time."[21]

The other elements that are essential to Shakyamuni's contribution are related to the concept of no-self. They include: (1) the doctrine of impermanence, according to which everything is constantly changing. Every second, every cell in the body is in process of being replaced, and nothing stays the same. This is true to such an extent that we can say both that there is no such thing as now, because by the time you hear/read it, the now of the speaker/writer has already past; and we can also say that there is only now, because each moment is complete in itself. The doctrine of impermanence was taken up by Dōgen and occupies a very central place in his point of view. (2) The doctrine of cause and effect, according to which everything has a cause and every cause has an effect. This might seem obvious, but in direct personal experience, it is astounding to what degree people are prone to operate out of wish fulfillment or reality-denial, rather than this simple truth. (3) The doctrine of interconnectedness or, to use Nhat Hanh's term, "inter-being." If everything changes and everything has a cause and produces an effect, then everything is interconnected. Again, this may seem too obvious to require stating, but when taken seriously, it is a profound statement about the interrelatedness of the personal and the political, the interrelatedness of thoughts and actions, and the practical truth of both karma and sin. As shall be shown, these ideas were critical to the fuller understanding of the experience of emptiness as they were dealt with by Dōgen.

FROM ENLIGHTENMENT TO EXPANSION:
THE MIDDLE WAY OF NĀGĀRJUNA

Although the understanding of emptiness is inherent in Shakyamuni's original proclamation upon enlightenment, the full, systematized development of the doctrine of emptiness waited four to six centuries for the work of Nāgārjuna, who lived sometime between the first century B.C.E. and the second half of the second century C.E. Though his actual history is surrounded with a great deal of uncertainty, there is consensus that he was born in Southern India, in a town called Vidarbha, to a Brahmin family.

Of particular interest to our understanding of the experience of emptiness as it impacts on Nāgārjuna's path of transformation is the prediction of an astrologer that he would die before he finished his seventh year of life. Hoping to circumvent this, his parents turned him over to a mendicant order of Buddhists. Thus, in Nāgārjuna's case, the experience of emptiness was the direct threat of his own death. More often, awareness of mortality is an inference from the experience of others' deaths. We must imagine the anxiety Nāgārjuna lived with, as felt by his own parents and which he absorbed from them. The deliverance of him by his parents is the same "last resort" move that most people make on their own to a spiritual path, usually later in life.

He wandered from teacher to teacher, until he met his primary teacher, Rahulabhadra, at the monastery Nalanda on the Ganges plain.[22] The mixture of legend and history is inherent in his name, which was given to him because of his association with the great sea dragons, called *nagas*.

> The boy was ordained as the monk Shriman, and soon became a master of the Buddhist teaching, as well as adept at medicine and alchemy. His fame as a teacher spread so widely that he attracted several *nagas*, mythical dragon-like beings from the depths of the ocean, whose magic powers included the ability to assume human form when visiting among humans. When Shriman recognized them, they acknowledged themselves as *nagas* from the ocean kingdom. They then told him of the great treasury of scriptures they had kept there from the Buddha's time, among which were the *100,000 Verse Transcendent Wisdom Scripture*, the *100,000 Verse Garland Scripture*, and the *Jewel Heap Scripture* (known as *Prajnaparamita, Avatamsaka* and *Ratmakuta Sutras*). Shriman accepted the invitation to visit and spent fifty years in the *naga* kingdom, whence he eventually returned, bringing numerous scriptures of the Universal Vehicle, which was all but unknown in India at that time....
>
> From this he became known as "Nāgārjuna," "one who has achieved (his goal) with the help of the dragons"....[23]

Nāgārjuna's descent into the ocean realms of the *nagas* is the mythological expression of the delving into the unconscious that is of the essence of depth psychology, echoed in the West in the stories of descent that appear in the myth of Orpheus, Homer's *Odyssey*, Virgil's *Aeneid*, and Dante's *Divine Comedy*, among others. It is also an essential feature in the Christian understanding of Jesus that between the crucifixion and the resurrection, "he descended into hell."[24] One goes into the depths to reach for a truth about the essence of life that includes, but goes beyond, not only the personal, but the limits of the local collective. Thus, there is always entry into an area of darkness, of the unknown, the strange and foreign that reflects the decision to go into, rather than away from, the initial experience of emptiness. It is a journey into the depths.

His descent into the realm of the nagas was a revolutionary event in Buddhism, very much parallel to Freud's and Jung's descent into the unconscious by means of dream interpretation. What is dark, unknown and dreaded becomes, upon descent and observation of the unconscious, meaningful in a way that, upon return, enlightens one's conscious reality. The discovery of such a depth dimension of life gives a fullness, context and purpose both to ordinary life and to events that we would otherwise tend to discount as irrelevant, however painful. By going into the "foreign" territory where "strange" creatures called *nagas* live, Nāgārjuna was able to forge an understanding of Buddhism that was ready to engage other foreign lands and cultures. In sum, Nāgārjuna, with his development of the Mādhyamika philosophy, the School of the Middle Way (also called Centrism[25]), made Buddhism even more portable.

The Mādhyamika philosophy became known as the *Mahāyāna* ("Great Vehicle") tradition in contrast to the Hīnayāna ("Lesser Vehicle") tradition. Based on the words used, it should not be surprising that a judgment is implied in these terms, a judgment in which the *Mahāyāna* is assumed to be "better than" as well as "different from" the Hīna*yāna* tradition. Though this distinction was intentional in the early history of Buddhism as groups sought to distinguish themselves from one another, the differences cannot be identified with particular teachers or groups.

> Traces of Mahāyāna teachings appear already in the oldest Buddhist scriptures....it is clear that Mahāyāna developed in organic connection with the whole of Buddhism...followers of both vehicles lived peacefully for a long time side by side in the same monasteries, observing the same Vinaya discipline.[26]

What was different enough and important enough to warrant a new and distinguishing appellation was a clarification of consciousness that required (1) an increased cohesion of thought (systematized into philosophical concepts), (2) a clarification about not only the nature of the goal of enlightenment, but, (3) a clarification about the relation between the phenomenal and noumenal realms (relative and absolute), and therefore, (4) a clarification about the nature of Buddhist practice, including the relation between monastics and lay practitioners.

Nāgārjuna accomplished these in his compilation of the *Mahāpra-jñāparamita*, the *Mādhyamika*, and *Dvadāsanikaya Sutras*. Just as Shakyamuni fought the notion of self with that of no-self, Nāgārjuna dealt with the resultant tendency of people either to reify the notion of no-self into another concept, or to disguise the idea of a permanent self in some qualification such as a moment in time. As Nhat Hanh reports,

> The fear of nothingness brought about by misunderstandings of the doctrine of not-self, gave rise to the need to confirm the existence of things....In the Sarvastivada School, for example, it is taught that from the standpoint of the noumena, things exist in the past, present and future, but from the standpoint of phenomena, they exist only in the present moment.[27]

As one of the early explorers of the conceptual frontier of emptiness, what Nāgārjuna had to deal with, therefore, was every way in which people tend to divide reality into concepts that separate subject and object in order to keep at least some piece of reality as permanent and unchanging, safe from their only known alternative, which is often "nothingness." This tendency to understand "no-self" as equivalent to "nothingness" was repeated in the history of the West's early attempt to understand Buddhism.[28] This misunderstanding by the West of the Eastern view of śūnyatā as "nothingness" rather than "emptiness" was based on the Western philosophical frame of reference in which "nothingness" is the opposite of being.

In the East, Nāgārjuna was working from Shakyamuni's proposal of "no-self" (*anatman*) to the Brahmic concept of "self" (*atman*); and anatman was applied to all things to mean śūnyatā, or "emptiness." But in the West, the "no-self" was understood as not-existing, and śūnyatā was understood as "nothingness" or *nihil*, as opposed to "being." Thus, Buddhism was understood in the West as being nihilistic. This gross mis-understanding could only be corrected by a fuller understanding of śūnyatā as emptiness, not by the simple substitution of one word for another. While this distinction may appear, on its face, to be the prod-uct of hair-splitting semantics, the difference in ramifications for the

Western reading of śūnyatā as a negative realm of "nothingness" as opposed to Nāgārjuna's construction of śūnyatā as a positive and productive realm of "emptiness" was enormous. The dynamic concept of emptiness propounded by Nāgārjuna, far from being nihilistic, aimed at releasing human consciousness from its basic dualism-creating propensity. This is the liberation from suffering that is promised in the Third Noble Truth.

Nāgārjuna observed a tremendous fear at the heart of our initial view of emptiness. While it was clear that experiences of emptiness on the psychological and everyday level were often triggers to the motivation for persistent engaging of a spiritual path, initial experiences of emptiness were, by definition, experiences of transience and loss that raised fundamental questions concerning the nature of life and death. Thus, lurking in the heart of the experience of emptiness was the terror of the possibility of our own not-being. This terror is preverbal, psychological and existential. This terror could be so great, that, as Nāgārjuna discovered, one might subconsciously try to hold out something permanent in some conceptual form whenever faced with the threat of emptiness that would effectively facilitate a sidestep of the experience of emptiness.

It is to tear away methodically all such hiding places that Nāgārjuna developed his dialectic of the "eight negations." The fundamental problem is the human tendency to confuse concepts with reality in order to achieve stability, but to do so in any form necessarily entails developing a dualism. This process is not merely the typical Hegelian thesis-antithesis-synthesis. In Nāgārjuna, negation is a continuing process that is engaged in order to

> break...down concepts to the point where the practitioner comes
> to rid himself of all discrimination and penetrates undiscriminated
> reality.[29]

"Undiscriminated reality," however, turns out to be ordinary, conventional reality, now understood as insubstantial, without essence, but nonetheless itself.[30]

> Whatever is dependently co-arisen
> That is explained to be emptiness.
> That, being a dependent designation,
> Is itself the middle way.[31]

A distinction must be made, according to Nāgārjuna, between two truths of reality:

> The Buddha's teaching of the Dharma
> Is based on two truths:
> A truth of worldly convention
> And an ultimate truth.[32]

On the level of ultimacy, or the absolute, there is nothing, all is voidness. This is the emptiness of emptiness on the absolute level. On the level of the relative, the level of ordinary life, since we have sense organs we have phenomena, and having phenomena, we use words to describe what our senses experience. These words are verbal conventions, not descriptions of something that has an absolute existence independent of our sensing experience of phenomena.

> Emptiness and the phenomenal world are not two distinct things. They are, rather, two characterizations of the same thing....To view emptiness in this way is to see it neither as an entity nor as unreal—it is to see it as conventionally real.[33]

Nāgārjuna did not substitute one form of thinking for another, therefore, but offered a method by which the entire human propensity toward reification via conceptualization could be short-circuited in order to enable a direct experience of emptiness. This method was a breakthrough in terms of finding an effective means of avoiding the human inclination to shortchange, sidestep or misunderstand our experiences of emptiness.

Nāgārjuna's contribution to our understanding of the experience of emptiness and his achievement in making that experience more accessible, via a rejection of the limits of our normal, conscious view of reality, was enormous. In its achievement, Nāgārjuna brought Buddhism a giant step forward in terms of answering the question of the universality of its message.

Similar to the revolution in the West's understanding of consciousness triggered by the development of depth psychology, Nāgārjuna's method of Mādhyamika not only opened up the realms of emptiness in ordinary life and consciousness (the realm of the relative) to the realm of the absolute, but introduced a way of reintegrating them so that the absolute and the relative were understood as inseparably and dynamically related. In short, Nāgārjuna's Middle Way, by recognizing the complete interdependence of all things, facilitated a fuller understanding of the experience of emptiness. This advance was similar to the way in which Freud's recognition of the interconnectedness of our conscious and unconscious could facilitate a fuller understanding of our psyches.

Although his prophesied death at age seven never occurred, Nāgārjuna's early experience of emptiness, which was triggered by the anticipation of that prophecy, was productive. As can be seen from this cursory treatment of his life, rather than ignoring or rejecting his initial experience of emptiness, he worked with it, exploring the depths, and then returned to the world to offer, through his teachings, the fruits of his experience of emptiness.

Just as was shown in the case of Shakyamuni, Nāgārjuna had many points along the way at which he could have sidestepped his experience of emptiness. For example, on his eighth birthday, when the prophecy of his death at age seven was not fulfilled, he could have had a party and left the monastery forever. Similarly, after his breakthrough in the depths with the *nagas*, he could have remained where he was to bask in his self-understanding and not returned to share what he had learned with the world. However, faced with the extremely difficult task of psychologically reconciling his early traumatic experience of mortality, any detour of his experience of emptiness would have frustrated his personal growth and progress toward individuation. Additionally, such a detour would have deprived the world of what he was able to offer it, once he learned what he had to learn. This is illustrative of the twin requirements in Buddhism of wisdom and compassion; either without the other is seen as insufficient. Only if wisdom leads to active compassion can it bear fruit; only if compassion is guided by wisdom can it be effective.

FROM INDIA TO CHINA: BODHIDHARMA

Although legend vies with historicity in all the stories of Buddhism's teachers, in the figure of Bodhidharma, colorfulness and exaggeration ride boldly roughshod over any concern for such paltry questions as literal truth to produce a dashing, memorable character as the founder of Zen (Jp. *Chan*, Ch.) in China. Whether such a person actually existed at all is questioned. Assuming he existed, whether he came from southern India or western India, or even perhaps Persia, is debated. He is credited with founding the Shaolin temple in China, but it existed years before he is supposed to have arrived there. He is credited with bringing Zen Buddhism to China and one of the most famous Zen koans assumes this as fact when a student is asked "Why did Bodhidharma come from the West?" But by the time he purportedly came to China, Buddhism was already quite widespread,[34] having been introduced at least as early as 148 C.E.[35] He nonetheless occupies the place in Zen lineage charts as the twenty-eighth Indian patriarch and the first Chinese patriarch.

Amid such uncertainty, the story persists that Bodhidharma was born a Brahman in southern India about 440 A.D. It is said that his original name was Bodhitara, and that he was the third son of a rajah, or king, who was very devoted to Buddhism.[36] The king's teacher in Buddhism was Prajnatara,[37] who also instructed the sons. Bodhitara proved to be an exceptionally astute pupil, grasping quickly the fundamental truths of Buddhism.

> ...when the king died and everyone was mourning, Bodhitara sat alone in front of the casket and went into a trance. He came out of the trance seven days later, then went to Prajnatara to request ordination as a Buddhist monk.

> Prajnatara knew the time had come, so he ordained the prince and invested him with the precepts...and...gave him thorough instructions in the subtle principles of meditation....Then Prajnatara said to him, "You have already attained full comprehension of all principles. Dharma has the meaning of greatness of comprehension, so you should be called Dharma." Thus he changed his name to Bodhidharma.
>
> [Further, Prajnatara told him,] "Though you have realized the truth, you should stay in southern India for a while; sixty-seven years after my death, you should go to China and teach those of great potential."[38]

Here again we find the death of a parent precipitating the experience of emptiness that serves as the fundamental spur to pursuing a spiritual path. Amid so much that is story already, it is remarkable that nothing is said about Bodhidharma's mother. Since Bodhidharma responded to his father's death by becoming a monk, one wonders whether her death had preceded the father's, because the tie with the mother is usually stronger for a man than the tie to the father. Had she been living, one would expect some record of her encouraging his ordination, or discouraging it, along with his response. All of this, of course, is mere speculation.

Some sixty years after his teacher died, the story goes, Bodhidharma set out for China. Because the overland route was blocked by Huns, he traveled by ship around the Malay Peninsula, arriving in southern China about 475.[39] The story is told that his first encounter was with Emperor Wu of the Liang Dynasty in Chienkang.

> The emperor asked, "Since ascending to the throne, I have had temples built, sutras transcribed and monks ordained. What merit have I gained?"
>
> The master answered: "No merit at all."
>
> The emperor replied: "Why no merit at all?"
>
> The master said: "All these are but impure motives for merit; they are the faulty fruit of rebirth as a human being or a deva [a god]. They are like shadows that follow the form, having no reality of their own."
>
> The emperor then asked: "Then of what kind of true merit?"

> He answered: "It is pure knowing, wonderful and perfect. Its essence is
> emptiness. One cannot gain such merit by worldly means."
> Thereupon the emperor asked: "What is the sacred truth's first principle?"
> The master replied: "Vast emptiness, nothing sacred."
> The emperor said: "Who is this who faces me?"
> The master replied: "I don't know."[40]

It is at that point that Bodhidharma is said to have left and traveled north to the kingdom of Wei to establish the Shaolin temple, where he studied by facing a wall for nine years.

The important part of the story about the encounter with Emperor Wu is the central emphasis on emptiness in Bodhidharma's teaching, and, in his move to Shaolin, the practice of facing the wall as the primary mode of meditation practice, so that the emptiness of mind itself could be seen. His comment about no merit in anything the emperor was doing applied directly to the methods of studying scripture and building stupas, methods of practice common to Hinayana Buddhism.

"Direct pointing of the human mind," awareness without reliance on "words and letters," assumed a radical new emphasis in Chinese Zen. This became a resounding theme in all Zen: the emphasis on experience that is not only beyond any written scriptures, but beyond speech itself; the experience of emptiness as not only ineffable, but beyond linear, sequential logic. While inherent in Shakyamuni's original enlightenment experience, the emphasis in Zen was manifested in an even greater attention to the practice of meditation as a way of embracing emptiness in order to reach enlightenment.

The enormity of commitment required for reaching enlightenment in Zen practice is also a fundamental point in the Bodhidharma stories: In order to meditate without falling asleep, he is said to have cut off his eyelids. Thus, all pictures of him show large, bulging eyes, lidless. They also show him as missing his front teeth as a result of stones thrown at him by jealous teachers. Bodhidharma demanded such persistence amid adversity from his pupils as well as himself. The first one, and the one who received his transmission, was Hui-k'o, who beseeched Bodhidharma to teach him. After his request was refused time after time, Hui-k'o is said to have sat outside in the freezing snow and, asked for one final sign of his resolve, to have cut off his arm at the elbow and offered it to Bodhidharma, who then accepted him as a student.

These stories are held up as exemplary in Zen practice.[41] The requirement for enlightenment is total and absolute: Nothing can be held back. Bodhidharma is reported to have lived a rather lengthy life, surviving numerous attempts to poison him. Finally Bodhidharma placed the poison intended for him on a boulder and the boulder split. This he took as a sign that his mission was over, so he sat up in regular meditation posture and died, presumably about 543 C.E. Even the grave was not the end for his stories, however, because he had been told to return to India and someone reported seeing him with one sandal, traveling west. Upon opening his grave, his body was not found and only one sandal was left. Thus, pictures of him often show him walking with one sandal at the end of his walking stick, an Eastern parallel to the resurrected Christ.

There are also several important parallels between Bodhidharma's life and teachings and the work of depth psychology, especially in that of Carl Jung. First and foremost, the nature of mind (in depth psychology, the psyche) was all-pervasive for Bodhidharma, extending everywhere, and could not avoid being manifested in every detail of a person's life. As he put it:

> Language and behavior, perception and conception are all functions of the moving mind. All motion is the mind's motion. Motion is its function. Apart from motion there's no mind, and apart from the mind there's no motion. But motion isn't the mind. And the mind isn't motion. Motion is basically mindless. And the mind is basically motionless. But motion doesn't exist without the mind. And the mind doesn't exist without motion....Even so, the mind neither moves nor functions, because the essence of its functioning is emptiness and emptiness is essentially motionless.[42]

But Bodhidharma also underscored this point in another way in the statement that justified his claim to be the founder of Zen in China,

> Buddha is Sanskrit for what you call *aware, miraculously aware.*
> Responding, perceiving, arching your brows, blinking your eyes
> moving your hands and feet, it's all your miraculously aware nature.
> And this nature is the mind and the mind is the buddha. And the bud-
> dha is the path. And the path is zen.[43]

While this was not the first use of the word *zen* in Buddhism, it was the word Bodhidharma chose to translate the Sanskrit word *dhyana*, which means "meditation." Thus, he delivered one of the first instances of Zen's characteristic paradoxes.[44]

As stated above, Bodhidharma is renowned for his emphasis on "fac-ing-the-wall" meditation as the key to enlightenment, and in this central, crucial statement, he declared that true meditation was in every move-ment of the body, in everything one does, whether lying down, walking, sitting or sleeping. Through this view, Bodhidharma rescued Zen practice from an isolated practice of meditation alone and pointed to the manifes-tation of Buddha mind in everything.

> Not thinking about anything is zen. Once you know this, walking,
> standing, sitting, or lying down, everything you do is zen.[45]

Depth psychology makes a similar claim in its position that there is no way of avoiding expressing oneself or manifesting one's mixture of con-sciousness and unconsciousness. The unconscious will always be mani-fested, most of all, of course, when we are trying to suppress it. Thus, Freud found meaning in slips of the tongue, in the foundations of humor, in things forgotten and in selective perception, as well as dreams. The mind/psyche is manifested in every moment of our waking and sleeping, and there is no Archimedean point outside oneself from which one can view oneself.

Beyond his broad view of the mind, Bodhidharma also maintained that persistence in pursuing the meaning of one's own experience of emptiness ultimately results in going beyond oneself to the larger human family. Regardless of whether Bodhidharma's "I don't know" to Emperor Wu was the "I don't know" of someone stupefied by a question he couldn't answer, or was the calculated response of a master who realized the student was not ready to hear what he had to teach, the net result was that Bodhidharma went off for a longer look at himself, a deepening of his own understanding of emptiness by proverbially "facing the wall" for nine years. He was, in any case, manifesting by his life the truth of his own teaching, "Someone who seeks the Way doesn't look beyond himself."[46] As a result of looking inside oneself, one discovers one's essential identity with others:

> According to the world there's male and female, rich and poor. According to the Way there's no male or female, no rich or poor. When the goddess realized the Way, she didn't change her sex. When the stable boy awakened to the truth, he didn't change his status. Free of sex and status, they shared the same basic appearance.[47]

One is reminded of the parallel statement in Paul's letter to the Galatians:

> There is no such thing as Jew and Greek, slave and freeman, male and female; for you are all one person in Christ Jesus.[48]

This movement, in which the way "in" to oneself becomes the very place where one discovers others, is paralleled in every successful experience of psychotherapy. Thus, for Carl Jung, going into the unconscious became not merely a movement beyond egocentrism, but a gateway into the unconscious life of entirely different cultures, races and religions. More than any other depth psychologist, Carl Jung showed the already existing dynamic of the unconscious around the world on every continent. He did this by going "in," into his own dreams and into the dreams and symbols of other cultures. He traveled to India, Africa and the western United States to study other cultures directly. He studied Yoga, Hinduism, Buddhism (especially Tibetan). He made a comprehensive study of alchemy in the West and shamans in many cultures, including Native Americans and Africans.

In terms of how Bodhidharma arrived at his insights, one can identify his initial experience of emptiness at the death of his father, and probably his mother, and his choice to go into that experience of emptiness in depth by becoming a Buddhist monk. As is even more pronounced in his story than that of Shakyamuni and Nāgārjuna, Bodhidharma was confronted repeatedly with diverting possibilities: he could have stayed in India and enjoyed the fame he had acquired instead of traveling for three years around the southeast tip of Asia. He could have fudged on his answer to Emperor Wu and commended the building of stupas and developing of monasteries, thereby assuring himself of a sinecure, rather than insisting on the central importance of the experience of emptiness. He could have been satisfied with a lower level of his understanding of the experience of emptiness and begun more public teaching, instead of facing the wall in *zazen* for another nine years. But he persisted in his practice in spite of having his teeth knocked out, his eyelids cut off and numerous attempts to poison him. His unstopability in his pursuit of the meaning of the experience of emptiness set the standard for all who followed, and the example of such tenacity is at least as important a bequest as any of his writings to those who came after him.

Beyond this powerful demonstration of tenacity, Bodhidharma's nine years facing the wall, and his great reluctance to shift his attention away from himself, even to teach, underscores another aspect of the experience of emptiness: Once one has learned something, one is not finished; constant attention to the experience of emptiness is imperative not only to continue one's own learning and development, but to keep what one has fresh and vital. The path one begins by attending to the experience of emptiness has no end, and one's personal transformation is never finished. Thus, Zen masters and depth psychologists alike continue their self-exploration in their own practices for their entire lives.

From a brief look at these three landmark explorers of the experience of emptiness, Shakyamuni Buddha, Nāgārjuna and Bodhidharma, one can glimpse some of the ground on which Dōgen based his own exploration of the experience of emptiness. Shakyamuni Buddha was the first to underscore the imperative to pay unswerving attention to the experience of emptiness, and to resist the inclination to run from it. Nāgārjuna expounded and elaborated on Shakyamuni Buddha's teachings in a way that made such experiences of emptiness more accessible to others. Bodhidharma, then, began the work of extending the understanding of emptiness into China, and establishing the unique features of Zen in China.

A complete sketch of Zen in China would include stories and writings of many more of the Zen patriarchs for the six hundred or so years between Bodhidharma and Dōgen. Most importantly, attention would be paid to Hui-neng, the sixth patriarch and author of the Platform Sutra, to Hong-zhi, the master of "silent illumination," to the issues at stake in the division between northern and southern schools of Zen in China and the unique aspects of Chinese Zen. Instead of treating them separately, however, they will be introduced directly out of the issues raised by the writings of Dōgen himself, in his grappling with them for the formulation of his own understanding of the experience of emptiness.

From China to Japan: Zen Master Dōgen

EARLY LIFE AND EXPERIENCES OF EMPTINESS

Dōgen[49] was born January 2, 1200 C.E. in Kyoto, the Imperial capital of premodern Japan. He was born of aristocratic and politically influential parents, though they were not married and their identities are difficult to ascertain with certainty. The only birth record available states: "Buddhist Dōgen: family name, Minamoto; of Kyoto; and an heir of the gentry."[50]

Most authorities reconstruct evidence supporting the claim that Dōgen's real father was Koga Michichika of the Minamoto family, descendants of the Emperor Murakami. According to Kim, at the time of Dōgen's birth, Michichika was

34

Lord Keeper of the Privy Seal, [and] the family was at the height of its power and prosperity and controlled both the dominating power of the Fujiwara family and the pro-shogun force within the courtly circle in Kyoto. In addition, Michichika stood unparalleled in the literary circle....[51]

Michichika died suddenly on October 21, 1202, perhaps by assassination, when Dōgen was only two.[52]

Dōgen's mother is usually assumed to have been Ishi, the daughter of Fujiwara Motofusa, once a regent at court. According to Gudo Nishijima, she was not married to Michichika, but "became his mistress when her first husband (presumably Kiso Yoshinaka[53]) was exiled."[54] Her younger brother, Fujiwara Moroie, wanted to adopt Dōgen in the hope of training him as an heir and thus consolidating the link between the two families. This ambition was resisted by his mother, and Dōgen was evidently brought up by his elder brother, Minamoto Asho, whom Dōgen himself refers to as his stepfather.[55]

Such intrigues—intentional marrying of children into families for political purposes, assassination and exile, and the use of religious institutions for political considerations—were common in medieval Japan (as, for that matter, in medieval Europe). Nevertheless, on the personal level, it is significant that there is no record of Dōgen's given name before he became a monk. It is almost as if he had no name and thus no identity *until* he became a monk—a point which he asserts is true to Buddha nature, but he surely must have felt this as a certain lack or tenuousness to his own natural identity. To live among powerful, aristocratic families, each vying for recognition and power, and not to know clearly to whom one belongs would tend to leave one with a core uncertainty, perhaps even shame. A similar conflict was experienced by Moses, born an Israelite but raised in the house of the Pharaoh.[56] The experience of an uncertain identity as the main form of emptiness in Buddhism will be drawn out in greater detail below in this study's treatment of Thomas Merton.

Additionally, to have one's father assassinated and know that one's mother's husband was exiled, and then to be expected to become part of the drama must have underscored the impermanence of all things, which became central to Dōgen's formulation of the experience of emptiness.[57, 58]

In 1207, when Dōgen was seven, his mother died and "left an earnest request for him to seek the truth of Buddhism by becoming a monastic and to strive to relieve the tragic sufferings of humanity."[59]

As he was watching the smoke rise from the incense at his mother's funeral, profoundly struck by the all-pervasiveness of impermanence, Dōgen resolved to follow the Way.[60]

In fact, in the opening words to his autobiographical *Hokyō-ki* Dōgen declared (in the third person), "Dōgen developed the mind for enlightenment (*bodai-shin*, Jp.) in his childhood."[61] He made the connection directly by quoting Nāgārjuna,

> Many people call the mind for enlightenment one mind. Nāgārjuna said, The mind that simply observes the impermanence of birth and death in the world is called the mind for enlightenment. [62]

Although the death of his mother may be viewed as the circumstance that triggered his own aspiration for enlightenment by following the Buddha Way, this pivotal event must also be viewed in the broader context of his earlier experiences of emptiness. Clearly, the intensity and profundity of the impact of his mother's death was magnified by the loss of his father by assassination, the loss of his mother's husband by exile, the continuing intrigues and maneuvers for power within the family and the ongoing uncertainty as to his own identity.

The death of a parent at any age, even into mature adulthood, has a powerful impact on a person: the severity of loss, the meaning of the parent to the son or daughter, the question of who one is without that living reference point and the question of what to do with one's life are all part of the tumult stirred by a parent's death. When one parent dies, a tie to the surviving parent, especially in childhood, becomes singularly focused. The surviving parent then is one's "world," in the sense of being the central point around which life's vicissitudes are overridden by cohesion. Thus, if the second parent dies, there is not only the loss of this final connection to the source of one's being, but the loss of "world" as a sense of cohesion to the disparate parts of experience. The external world becomes a series of isolated events without a center, without a direction or purpose, and above all, without continuity or reliability. Without such a world that is continuous, one's own sense of self is fragmented and tenuous. Faced with such trauma, Dōgen found in Buddhism, with its declaration of the impermanence of all things and the nonsubstantiality of the self, a perfect mirror for his own lived experience, and therein, perhaps, found his own salvation.

Nishijima makes the connection with profound sensitivity between Dōgen's mother's death and his setting out upon the spiritual path:

> The early death of his mother was a shock, but I feel that the more important effect of her absence was that it filled him with longing: a longing for something most of us find in the touch of our mother's skin, but which, in Master Dōgen, became a longing for Truth.[63]

In this single sentence, Nishijima connects for us the bundle of issues in this study: the relation between the personal/psychological and the religious/spiritual, the relation between an experience of early childhood and spiritual motivation, the way in which emptiness is the only resolution to emptiness. Dōgen moved from his experience of emptiness as his deep yearning for his mother's skin to the experience of emptiness in the hard, often lonely practice of *zazen*, to the experience of emptiness of all things, in which one is no longer a separate, isolated person but part of the entire phenomenal universe.

This connection to one's earliest years, much less earliest months, of life, is not readily understood by many people. Unless one has undertaken an intensive experience of psychotherapy, psychoanalysis or a prolonged practice of meditation, one may find it hard to believe that the earliest experiences of infancy and childhood continue to be formative in personal history, even when they cannot be recalled, even those that happened before we learned words. Yet, as clinical psychiatrist Daniel Stern has demonstrated in his empirical studies of infants:

> Infants begin to experience a sense of an emergent self from birth. They
> are predesigned to be aware of self-organizing processes. They never
> experience a period of total self/other undifferentiation. There is no con-
> fusion between self and other in the beginning or at any point during
> infancy. They are also predesigned to be selectively responsive to exter-
> nal social events and never experience an autistic-like phase.
> ....once formed, each sense of self remains fully functioning and
> active throughout life. All continue to grow and coexist.[64]

The Buddhist understanding of cause and effect and the Judaic
understanding of children suffering for the sins of the fathers[65] find confirmation in empirical psychological studies. Nothing is lost, and no
experience fails to have an effect on an infant, no matter how young.[66]

Though it was another five years before Dōgen officially entered a Zen
monastery, his conscious spiritual search can be confirmed by the report
that he read the Vasubandhu's *Abhidharmakosa*, a basic Buddhist text, at
the age of nine, thus demonstrating his personal initiative and interest in
seeking for a spiritual resolution to the experiences of emptiness triggered
by the deaths of his father and mother. With a mix of motivations (both to
escape the dangers of secular power for which his stepfather had been
preparing him and to pursue the meaning of impermanence, which was so
much a part of his life from its inception), Dōgen "escaped during the
night"—before the ceremony that would have made him an heir—in the
spring of his twelfth year, to enter the monastery of his uncle, Ryōkan
Hōgen, at the bottom of Mt. Hiei. According to Kodera, "It was common-
place for aristocrats who had misfortune in those days to renounce the
world and become monks."[67]

Nonetheless, as was pointed out in the stories above of Dōgen's
Buddhist predecessors, a person makes a decision either to pursue the
spiritual path in its ongoing evolution as a way of engaging the self in
depth, or one returns to what is considered normal life. Dōgen decided
to become a monk and stayed with the gnawing questions triggered
by his experience of emptiness. Without, perhaps, the overt religious
interest, people today commonly enter into psychotherapy in a similar
fashion, spurred by their particular experience of emptiness.

DEVELOPMENT OF THE GREAT DOUBT

Dōgen's uncle, Ryōkan, sent Dōgen to study with Jien on Mt. Hiei. Before the year was out, Jien died and was succeeded by Koen, from whom Dōgen received the precepts and his monk's name.

As Nishijima pointed out, Dōgen's personal experience of emptiness moved into the questions of spiritual truth. Instructed in the Japanese Tendai sect of Buddhism on Mt. Hiei, Dōgen became preoccupied with an inner contradiction in the Tendai point of view, a contradiction that expressed the conflict in his own experience of emptiness.

Amid an atmosphere of "lifeless formalism"[68] on Mt. Hiei, in which many monks were engaged in copying sutras and others were actually monk-soldiers, Dōgen questioned the discrepancy between the promise of enlightenment and the practices on Mt. Hiei. Like Shakyamuni's questioning of the practices of fasting and self-denial, and like Bodhidharma's questioning of the building of stupas and temples (and, indeed, prefiguring Thomas Merton's questioning of a monastic lifestyle that included drinking beer and watching football on television), Dōgen questioned the value of the sort of monastic life he encountered on Mt. Hiei.

Although many people were apparently satisfied with the monastic practice as it existed on Mt. Hiei, Dōgen found fault with it because it lacked the focus, power and clarity he needed to resolve his inner turmoil. As was shown above, the complex of experiences of emptiness that culminated in his mother's death led to a high degree of inner ferment within Dōgen. Dōgen had already abandoned what most people of his time would have considered a great opportunity, the assumption of political and social power, because he knew it could not resolve his inner turmoil. When he got to Mt. Hiei, he found a similar paucity of shared concerns among other monastics. The place that promised healing and restoration and true self-life was not reaching deeply enough into its own raison d'être to accomplish its stated purpose. Thus, for him, the problem on Mt. Hiei was not merely a problem of the gap between ideal and real practice, but a problem he had in actually experiencing within himself the truth of Buddhism's claim that all sentient beings originally possess the Buddha-nature. His experiences of emptiness left a gap between his own experience and Buddhism's promise, and the laxity among the monks at Mt. Hiei did not help him to bridge that gap.

> Out of such an atmosphere was generated an intense doubt in Dōgen's mind. The doubt concerned the passage on the Buddha-nature in the *Mahaparinirvana Sutra* that was customarily read as "Sakyamuni Buddha said: 'All sentient beings everywhere possess the Buddha-nature; the Tathagatha exists eternally and is without change.'" If all sentient beings originally possess the Buddha-nature, Dōgen wondered, why do we still develop the mind for enlightenment and engage in ascetic practices in pursuit of it?[69]

The experience of emptiness, on the personal and psychological level, introduces one to the consciousness of what one is not, of the great, gaping hole inside oneself, the pain of isolation, the yearning for a wholeness of self and relatedness with others, and the gap between one's own possibilities and one's actual reality. So the religious quest is a search for wholeness, for the manifestation of one's true self, and, at the same time, for a rootedness in that which transcends the personal self.

An experience of emptiness can be so unsettling that the usual assumptions and tasks of life lose their meaning and their power to draw a person into socially recognized, or conventionally acceptable pursuits. Perhaps the deeper one's experience of emptiness, the fewer things one can find satisfying, so that one is pressed into what Zen Buddhism has called the Great Doubt.[70]

The doubt rises out of, and is an expression of, an inner division within the person, a splitting in the personality, perhaps to a clinically significant degree. In such a case, the pain of the experience of emptiness has been so great that, in order to continue functioning, the psyche divides itself into different pieces, some good and some bad. In such cases, from the spiritual point of view as well as the psychological, the inner self is experienced as separated from its original union. Thus, the search required by Great Doubt can be a search for healing aimed at reuniting the pieces of self that have fragmented. Rarely can any merely verbal answer resolve such an intense inner division.

Great Doubt can take any number of forms and be manifested in a variety of questions. That search can lead one in many possible directions, into art or music, literature, medicine, law or religion. What is doubted is the adequacy of any known possibilities to relieve one's inner turmoil. It is called the Great Doubt because the doubt reaches to the broadest possible extent, the nature of being itself, the meaning of life and death.

The Great Doubt has within it, however, in addition to the aspect of pain and division, another aspect, which is some semblance of hope, or as Kapleau puts it, Faith.[71] To be driven by Doubt is to be on a quest. Without some inkling that the quest can be fulfilled, there is nothing but despair.

As one goes further into the depths of one's experience of emptiness, the questions manifested by the Great Doubt frequently accelerate from the general or abstract to the specific and back again. Dōgen's focus was on why practice is necessary if everyone inherently has Buddha-nature. Augustine's focus was on the destructive consequences of Manichaeism. Martin Luther's focus was on the nature of conscience and human authority in Christian discipleship. For Jung and Freud, their focus was the nature of the psyche, especially the unconscious.

It is a great gift to find a language or a field in which to wrestle with the questions generated by Great Doubt. Whatever that language or field may be, it provides a framework within which the inchoate inner strivings, precipitated by the experience of emptiness, may find expression and structure and thus rise to consciousness in a way that can be worked with. Religion, psychology and philosophy have traditionally offered the broadest scope to the questions generated by Great Doubt. But not everyone finds those languages or fields helpful. Einstein worked mostly within physics. For Bach, Beethoven and Mahler, music was the metier. Michelangelo used painting, sculpture and poetry, coming close to the "Triple Treasures" in the Chinese tradition of poetry, painting and calligraphy.

Whatever the language or field one uses, it is the ability to express the inner experience in that language or field that enables a person to take his/her very personal experience of emptiness and work with it. The language or field gives to one a means of having conversation with others who have had similar experiences, and comparing one's experience with theirs. Out of such a conversation can evolve clarification and insight, which can then be conveyed, within that language or field, back to the larger experience of humankind. The language or field enables one, therefore, to wrest out of an experience that otherwise would appear only idiosyncratic and personal, a contribution that is of value to the larger human community.

The initial experiences of emptiness are triggered by a kind of crisis for a person, in which one decides either to enter into the experiences more fully to glean meaning from them, or one tries to avoid them and minimize their impact on one's life. If one undertakes to pursue the meaning of one's experience of emptiness, one thereby enters into some form of spiritual or psychological path (certainly not necessarily one of the three traditions we are considering here). As one pursues that path, the form the quest takes is in the form of a spiritual, theological, psychological or existential question or doubt, as mentioned above. That question, which has the force of an imperative, a driving demand for resolution, is synonymous with the Great Doubt in Zen.

One might say that "little doubt," that is, one's supposedly personal and private pains and troubles, becomes "Great Doubt" when, in the process of exploring them, one begins to see the connections between one's personal issues and the larger issues of life. Why isn't my marriage working? becomes What does it mean to be alive? Who am I? becomes Why is there suffering in the world? What should I do with the second half of my life? becomes How can I save all sentient beings? Questions of personal peace or happiness become questions about the suffering and liberation not only of all people everywhere, but of the trees, rivers, oceans and air.

Although the form of the questions may change, the path of transformation requires a continuing focus on the experience of emptiness because in order to continue down the path, one learns that one must die. At some point along the path, one comes face to face with one's own death, in two ways. The first way one confronts one's death is literally in comprehending the fact that one will inevitably die. While everyone knows this intellectually, its significance is largely ignored by most people as much as possible. A person on a path of transformation travels with this fact as a mantra, a koan or a mystery, using that fact as a foundational reference point to judge and evaluate all decisions, issues and events. The second way in which one confronts one's death is in the death of the ego, as described in the next section.

Dōgen's particular driving question that forced him to pursue the meaning of his experience of emptiness was the basic question of consciousness: Why do I have to be conscious? Why do I have to work at being conscious, rather than just being "spontaneous"? All three traditions being studied here recognize that increased consciousness requires effort and intentionality. Dōgen's question about why practice is necessary for enlightenment if all beings are originally endowed with Buddha-nature parallels the Christian issue of grace as prevenient. If God in Christ has already forgiven us our sins, why do we have to do anything else? Why can't we roam freely in the fields with animals and simply eat of the fruit of the garden? Or, even more closely resembling Dōgen's question, if I am made in the image of God (Genesis 1:26), why is anything more necessary?

There is a parallel to Dōgen's question in the question many people ask who are considering psychotherapy. Though they may have tried everything else they can imagine and though nothing has yet worked, many people resent and resist the requirement to examine their lives at the cost of time, energy and money. Why do I have to go through this? is the implied question. There seems to be a prevalent human propensity to insist on self-sufficiency—or, more poignantly, the sufficiency of one's current level of consciousness—to solve one's problems, in the face of every obvious failure to do so. To be driven by Great Doubt on a religious quest, as well as to be driven to face oneself in psychotherapy, require a certain humility, an acknowledgment that one does not know how to resolve one's problems, in addition to Great Faith and Great Determination.[72]

Such driving doubt underlies all the great spiritual questions in whatever form they appear for the individual. Triggered by the experience of emptiness, the question may come in the form of Who am I? or Why is there evil and suffering in the world? or What is the meaning and purpose of life? In whatever form, the question takes on the force and direction of an inner necessity, demanding an answer, and requiring that the person orient his/her entire life toward its resolution.

SEARCH FOR AN AUTHENTIC TEACHER: EARLY YEARS IN JAPAN AND QUEST IN CHINA

Driven by his question and the search for an "authentic teacher" who could resolve this "Great Doubt,"[73] Dōgen left Mt. Hiei and went to Onjōji to study with Kōin. Unable to satisfy Dōgen's doubt, Kōin recommended that Dōgen go to Yōsai[74] at Kennin-ji, which he probably did in 1214.[75] Yōsai died the following year (1215), and Dōgen returned to Kōin at Onjōji. Kōin died the following year (1216), and Dōgen went back to Kenninji to become a disciple of Myōzen, Yōsai's successor. Toward the end of that year, Ryōkan, his uncle to whom he had first gone to enter monastic life, died.

Thus, by the time he was sixteen, both of Dōgen's parents and the first four of his teachers were dead. Unsatisfied with what they offered in any case, his experiences of emptiness continued, one on top of the other, both driving home to him the fact of impermanence and driving him further in his quest to understand those experiences of emptiness.

Myōzen became a respected teacher for Dōgen, but perhaps more as one who shared Dōgen's doubt than one who resolved it. On perhaps a simply human level, Dōgen may have found in Myōzen a companion of the heart, since Myōzen's monastic life was also triggered by his experience of both his parents' deaths, although Dōgen certainly would not have stayed for that reason alone.

Indeed, Dōgen never justified any action on the basis of loyalty to any other person or value over the Dharma. It was Dōgen who tipped the scale of Myōzen's mind about leaving for China. In addition to other difficulties in arranging for the trip, Myōzen's own teacher, Myōyū Ajari of Mt. Hiei, became gravely ill and asked Myōzen to postpone the trip until after he died. Myōzen was undecided and consulted his own disciples, all of whom recommended that he wait. Dōgen, however, sounded another perspective: "If you think your realization of the Buddha Dharma is satisfactory as it is now, you should stay."

Myōzen decided to follow Dōgen's advice and go on to China, arguing that his master's death would neither be deferred nor alleviated by Myōzen's staying, whereas Myōzen's own life was as unpredictable as any man's. Dōgen had pointed out to Myōzen that the imperative to follow the Way would bring benefits to everyone, including his master, whereas to forestall it might hinder Myōzen's own enlightenment as well as bring negative karma on Myōyū.

Dōgen was in this case his own teacher's teacher. Anyone who has had this experience at an early age knows the ambivalence of both pride at having something to offer and sadness that so few people seem able to see any farther than themselves.

Driven to press his quest back to China to study Zen at the source, on February 27, 1223, Dōgen set out for China, accompanying Myōzen, exemplifying further his determination to pursue the meaning of the experience of emptiness. After a six-week trip across the China Sea aboard a merchant vessel, he arrived in China in early April of 1223.

Dōgen states (speaking of himself, as above, in the third person):

> In his home country, he pursued the Way under various teachers and acquired some understanding of the origin of cause and effect. However, he had not yet realized the true goal of the Buddha, of the Dharma and of the Samgha.[76] He stagnated aimlessly within the realm of names and forms. Later he went into the monastery of Master Yōsai and heard the teaching of the Rinzai School. Then, accompanying Master Myōzen, he went to Sung China. Sailing many miles, entrusting his ephemeral existence to the roaring waves, he finally reached the Great Sung.[77]

Journeys into Emptiness

While Dōgen's biographers consistently make his entry into China the beginning of a new stage of his life and writings, this distinction reflects an attention more to geography than to Dōgen's actual experience and self-understanding. Whether we date Dōgen's conscious embarkation on a spiritual path from the age of seven, when his mother died, or from the time he left home to go to his uncle Ryōkan at the monastery, Dōgen's period of searching for an authentic teacher did not end with his crossing of the China Sea, but continued in a steady line for another two years.

After all the effort that went into arranging for Dōgen's trip to China, once he arrived off the coast of Ch'ing-yuan Prefecture in Ming-chou, Dōgen was forced to stay on the ship for three months. The reason is not clear, but the issue most writers point to is the fact that although Dōgen had received the Bodhisattva Precepts of Mahayana Buddhism, he needed to receive the "Complete Precepts of Theravada, which may have been required to legitimize entry into China as a monk-student."[78]

Myōzen went ahead, Kodera argues, "...perhaps because he had received the Complete Precepts at Todai-ji in Nara before the trip to China."[79]

Such an argument is questionable, however, since at no point is there any mention of Dōgen receiving the Complete Precepts of Theravada in order to be allowed off the ship. Kim simply says the question of why he had to stay on the ship for three months cannot be answered.[80] Whatever the reason, both the fact that Dōgen was forced to stay aboard ship and the fact that Myōzen left him and went on by himself are striking. Questions arise for which we have no evidence to answer: Why was Dōgen not allowed off ship? What happened that eventually allowed him to disembark? With what degree of sensitivity did Myōzen forge ahead, leaving behind the man, his student, without whom he would have remained in Japan? How did Dōgen handle the situation and how did it affect his own capacity to trust in Myōzen or, by extension, any other teacher? Remaining aboard ship had to be, in any case, another experience of emptiness for Dōgen.

Apart from two memorable meetings with the chief cook from Ayuwang Mountain, Dōgen, once allowed to leave ship, spent the next two years wandering around from temple to temple, learning what he could but never really feeling satisfied. The meetings with the chief cook from Ayuwang Mountain are referred to several times in Dōgen's writings, preeminently in the "Instructions for the Zen Cook" (Tenzō kyōkun). Though Dōgen did not understand the cook's teachings when he first heard them, clearly they stayed with him as holding a mystery that true practice would reveal to him. They served, therefore, not only as a key to the resolution of his Great Doubt, but as a force that triggered the very Faith motivating his voyage to China in the first place, reassuring him that resolution was possible.

Similarly, as Dōgen traveled to various monasteries, he observed other principles at work in Zen practice, such as the centrality of the documents of transmission, in which a teacher attests to a student's understanding—that they are of one mind, which is one with the Buddha mind. He also was taught the basic ways to practice, from how to arrange the physical space of a *zendō* to the precise method of sitting meditation, which he would come to call *shikantaza* (Jp.).[81] Thus, while following the central thread of an experience of emptiness, there is much learning going on, the value of which may not be clear until later.

After two years of going from one teacher to another, Dōgen decided to return to T'ien-t'ung Mountain to resume studies with Wu-chi, as well as to be with Myōzen. On the way, however, he was given the news that yet another teacher, the one to whom he was returning to try again, Wu-chi, had died.

Dōgen strongly considered returning to Japan at that point, when two things happened: he met an "old monk" who told him that the man replacing Wu-chi was the best teacher in all of China, Ju-ching, and that if Dōgen was serious about his quest, he must study with this man.

The use of the phrase "old monk" was also applied to the chief cook from A-yu-Wang Mountain, whom Dōgen met while he was waiting on board ship at his arrival. The term *lǎo* in Chinese means "old," and is used in an honorific sense for someone who is in a position of authority or who has special knowledge or expertise, most especially teachers (as in *lǎo shī*). Throughout the *Shōbōgenzō*,[82] Dōgen refers to "my old teacher" and to various people of whom he approves as "the old Buddha." Thus when Dōgen uses *lăo,* it always conveys a certain sense of numinosity, signaling that we are in the presence of Buddha activity, in which what is going on has meanings and implications beyond the immediate. The numinosity is also suggested by the fact that, contrary to most of Dōgen's encounters, no actual name is given for either the old monk from A-yu-Wang Mountain or the one he met at the juncture of his despair, thus signaling the encounter of an impersonal, larger-than-personal dynamic. The significance of the encounter is acknowledged in Dōgen tradition by the effort of one biographer, Menzan, to claim that the old monk was a reincarnation of an arhat.[83] One might even call such an encounter an epiphany (to borrow from Christian language) whenever Dōgen uses this term. Certainly, in these instances of Dōgen's meeting of these two "old monk[s]," they function as emissaries from the transcendent realm, guides from the depths, paralleling Nāgārjuna's encounters with the *nagas.* In Jungian terms, we may be alerted to the activity of an archetype, the archetype of the wise old man.

The second thing that happened is that Dōgen had a dream in which the patriarch of Ta-mei Mountain appeared to Dōgen with a branch of plum blossoms.[84]

Plum blossoms are a major symbol throughout Chinese and Japanese arts and literature. They are a primary subject of painting, symbolizing the Tao (then, later, of course, Buddha-nature), inherent in all of life. In Zen, plum blossoms symbolize the activity of Buddha-nature, of the Dharma, an understanding of which constitutes enlightenment. Thus, Dōgen understood his dream to foretell his own participation in the document of succession,[85] which gave him encouragement to continue. Later, he devoted a major fascicle, or chapter, of the *Shōbōgenzō,* to the study of plum blossoms and named the chapter "Plum Blossoms" (*Baika*). Significantly, Dōgen wasted no time or words analyzing these two events. Their meaning to him was self-evident, and thus he set off immediately for T'ien-t'ung Mountain.

Dōgen first met Ju-ching on May 1, 1225. The significance of this encounter merits a close look at Dōgen's description of the event in the opening paragraphs of the *Hokyo-ki*. In keeping with the custom, as a traveling monk, Dōgen introduced himself with his reason for being there. As mentioned above, he writes in the third person about himself:

> He [Dōgen] was granted enrollment in the [monastery of] Monk [Ju-ching]. This was the blessing merited in a previous incarnation. The Monk [Ju-ching] was greatly compassionate and sympathetic. Even if he was untimely and not properly dressed, what this lowly man from a far-away foreign country wanted most was to visit the Abbot's quarters frequently and ask questions, however audacious they might be.
>
> [Ju-ching said,] "The impermanent world passes away swiftly, birth and death are vital matters. Time awaits no man. If you depart from the sacred, you will surely regret it." The authentic teacher, the Abbot, the Great Monk and the Great Master [Ju-ching], was greatly compassionate and sympathetic. He pitied Dōgen and allowed him to be heard as he sought the Way and the Dharma. As [Dōgen] bowed down and supplicated, [Ju-ching's] compassion radiated [toward him]. Disciple Dōgen prostrated himself 100 times.
>
> "Dōgen, you must seek instruction from now on, whether during the day or the night, whether clad in a formal monk's robe or not. Come to the Abbot's quarters without reservation to inquire the Way. I will always forgive your lack of propriety, as would a father."[86]

There are several extremely poignant things to notice in this short report by Dōgen himself on his initial encounter with Ju-ching.

Dōgen was granted enrollment in the monastery. He had traveled to several other monasteries and met with other teachers, but nowhere does he mention being granted enrollment. In Zen monasteries, down to and including many today, one cannot simply walk in and become an active member of the monastery, not even if one is a monk from another Zen monastery. A distinction was made between the resident monks and everyone else, a distinction that gives resident monks access to the teacher and full participation in the liturgy and meditation sessions that outsiders are not granted. In Dōgen's own *Eiheiji* that he founded in Japan and that is still an active monastery today, visitors are allowed to sit *zazen* only in a special section, separated from the primary *zendō* where resident monks practice. To be granted enrollment, therefore, was a great privilege and apparently was bestowed immediately when Dōgen introduced himself. Additionally, the privilege of having a teaching relationship with the Abbot, most especially being welcomed to come with his questions at any time to the Abbot's own quarters, was not granted even to all of the residential monks. Thus, with one fell swoop Dōgen leaped over two major barriers by the teacher's own invitation to have full, open access to Ju-ching.

This must be seen as more than an acknowledgment of Dōgen's precocity. The quickness with which Ju-ching gave Dōgen such intimate and immediate access to himself can only be understood as signifying the profound resonance and identification that both Ju-ching and Dōgen experienced at their first meeting. In the best student-teacher relationships, there is a mutual identification: The student identifies with the teacher and aspires to what he sees in the teacher, and the teacher identifies with the student in the student's sincere yearning for knowledge and understanding. This reciprocal process was reflected in a dream that Ju-ching had the night before Dōgen appeared. In Ju-ching's dream,

> Tung-shan Wu-pen, the first patriarch of the Ts'ao-tung School of Ch'an, appeared in his reincarnation, (thus making the encounter between Ju-ching and Dōgen parallel to the encounters of Shakyamuni and Mahakasyapa, Bodhidharma and Hui-k'o, and Hung-jen and Hui-neng). Whatever the circumstances of the encounter between Ju-ching and Dōgen might have been, its decisiveness, in terms of both Ju-ching's and Dōgen's initial impressions and also of Dōgen's eventual enlightenment experience, cannot be overemphasized.
> Thus, Dōgen finally found the "authentic teacher" [shoshi]. To him, the encounter with the "authentic teacher" and the final resolution of his "Great Doubt" were one and the same.[87]

Several things are remarkable about this meeting. First of all, dreams figured prominently in the expectations each man brought to the encounter, demarcating an episode of what Carl Jung called synchronicity.[88] For Jung, sometimes things turned out in retrospect to be meaningfully connected, that is, they happened without any connecting causation, spontaneously, but nonetheless meaningfully. This phenomenon has important parallels with the Buddhist concept of codependent origination.

Further, the power and singular significance of this meeting for Dōgen is marked by the fact that nowhere else in any of his writings does Dōgen describe himself with such self-deprecation as here:

> Even if I was *untimely* and was *not properly dressed,* what this *lowly man* from a *far-away foreign* country wanted...was to...ask questions, *however audacious* they might be....[Dōgen] *bowed down and supplicated....Disciple* Dōgen *prostrated himself 100 times* [italics added for emphasis].

However much both the Chinese and Japanese cultures did and do take on a formal submissive posture as a gesture of courtesy, this kind of humbling of himself is not repeated by Dōgen anywhere else in his writings.

Similarly, paralleling Dōgen's own humility is his depiction of Ju-ching's compassionate response:

> ...the Great Master [Ju-ching] was *greatly compassionate and sympathetic.* He *pitied* Dōgen....you must seek instruction...*whether clad in a formal monk's robe or not....I will always forgive your lack of propriety, as would a father* [italics added for emphasis].

This is not simply Oriental courtesy at work. This is an extremely profound encounter between an ardent student pouring his heart out in his strongest expression of desire for healing truth, his acknowledgment of the emptiness of his own capacity to attain it without help, being met by an equally empathic teacher whose own heart is stirred by the vulnerability and yearning displayed before him. It is also the meeting of two people who have both been humbled by the earnestness of their own quests, and recognize in each other a shared dedication of their lives to the Way. Thus, in this humbling of himself, Dōgen does not suffer humiliation but is in fact restored to authenticity.

Ju-ching's comparison of their relationship to that between a father and son needs to be appreciated in its inner meaning for Dōgen (as well, perhaps, for anyone else whose mentor steps into that position). On the literal level, Dōgen lost his father when he was two years old. On a social level, Dōgen had a number of other people step into the would-be father slot, including Minamoto Ashō as well as Myōzen, and surely these people helped Dōgen manage his world. On the profoundest level, however, Dōgen remained emotionally and psychologically fatherless. That is to say, he had never had a father who knew him intimately, who cared for him directly and invited him into his house (i.e., his private space), who also knew more than Dōgen did about the inner life and could serve as a guide to the unknown. Here, one's search for one's true father and one's search for an authentic teacher are the same. They are also, as will be discussed in chapter 3, the same as the search for the true self.

There is, in Ju-ching's invitation, the most profound invitation to intimacy. There is no holding back, no reserve of closed off space or time. In this openness is the greatest acceptance of the other that is possible. Dōgen's foreignness—the vicissitudes of which were never mentioned ever before—is wiped away. All barriers between an "I" and a "Thou," to borrow from Martin Buber, are removed. The teacher takes in the student without reservation, and the student takes in the teacher by the full giving of himself, also holding nothing back. Such intimacy is as rare as it is precious. Implicit in it is the teacher's complete and unconditional acceptance of the student as he or she is.

This is the profound dynamic underlying every genuine experience of transformation. And in order to receive it, in order to let it do its work, one must be, as Dōgen presented himself to Ju-ching, completely empty. The discovery of one's authentic teacher, which is to say, someone who speaks to and for one's own authentic self, is another form of the experience of emptiness that one can only have by being empty oneself, empty of judgment, empty of knowing, empty of ability to make it or heal oneself on one's own. Dōgen commented that "This was the blessing merited in a previous incarnation." Whether or not due to a previous incarnation, Dōgen found his authentic teacher, as each of us does, because he went through what he had to go through to get there. The search for the true teacher and the search for the true self are the same process, and neither is found in the Yellow Pages. An active, ardent, exhausting search is required.

Dōgen found Ju-ching. Ju-ching found Dōgen. In finding each other, both are fulfilled. It is a mutual process. Just as it is said that "When the student is ready, the teacher appears," so it may be said that "When the teacher is ready, the student appears." Not only so, but the teacher is not really a teacher until the student comes. Only then is the teacher manifested as the teacher. The ability of the student draws out the ability of the teacher, just as much as the ability of the teacher draws out the ability of the student. This is an example of the Buddhist understanding of codependent causation. Rather than the linear, sequential logic in which A causes B which causes C, codependent causation recognizes that not only is B caused by A, but A is caused by B, so that causation is not one-directional but circular, or coarising.

This process works the same way in psychotherapy. A psychotherapist can only be as good as her patients are. And neither party, therapist nor patient, student nor teacher, can engage this process of codependent causation without entering into his/her own emptiness. If either student or teacher, patient or therapist, stays in a preconceived role, true learning, true intimacy, and thereby true transformation, cannot occur. It can only happen when both parties empty themselves of their roles, of all that protects, defends and limits them, in order to be open to the reality of the moment.

Dōgen's period of wandering and searching should not be reduced to a question of dogma and practice. As we shall see, Dōgen learned from his various teachers, and it is questionable whether the one who he finally found to be authentic and who led him to great enlightenment, Ju-ching, did so because of his superior realization or simply because he provided the empathic support, parallel determination and devotion to purity of practice that allowed Dōgen to realize it himself (which, finally, may be all anyone can do).

Without subtracting in the slightest from the centrality of the religious concern inherent in Dōgen's Doubt, we can recognize that he was undergoing an important period of being unsettled, without roots either in the past or into the future, a period in which his personal growth needs (not a term he would have used!) were not being met on the deepest level by any existing institution or person. He was, in contemporary parlance, a man in search of himself. And since one finds oneself to a large degree by being seen by another, his search for an authentic teacher was to a large degree a search for a mirror of his own interior depths, someone who could also be a guide into the process that entering those depths to which his experience of emptiness had brought him would induce.

His search for an authentic teacher may just as well be said to have been a search for a certain kind of person, a person who is credible because he is able to see into one and find one more credible than one does oneself. The late teens and early twenties are notoriously tumultuous for people in every culture and era. Dōgen's turmoil had a focus and a form, but the question of the personhood of the teacher was every bit as essential to him as it is for most adolescents en route to adulthood. The authentic teacher is the one in whose presence one feels understood on a level that confirms inner strivings too amorphous for words. Other people may know facts and be correct, but an authentic teacher, by empathy, by knowing the inner path and therefore one's inner needs, and by a personal integrity in which the quest is supreme, wins devotion. The connection, though felt, happens on an unconscious level and is a "deep calling to deep,"[89] that is a quintessential intimacy. The student and the teacher are one in heart and mind. This can be signaled by the subtlest of gestures or tone of voice, as well as by extended speaking or writing. Invariably, the teacher (or analyst—it is the same process) steps into some of the empty space of mother or father, the better to carry on an unfinished process of psychic growth. Intimacy, identification and idealization work together, and, as we have seen with Myōzen, at times the roles of teacher/student reverse; at times they disappear.

The conclusion of this close look at Dōgen's initial meeting with Ju-ching is to underscore the deeply human and personal nature of their relationship. This is in no way to reduce it to any kind of psychological type but rather to bring attention to a dimension of the Zen teacher/student relationship that is rarely seen or articulated in the Western world. The fact that Dōgen had not heard of Ju-ching until he met the old monk makes it clear that Dōgen's immediate response to Ju-ching was not based on Ju-ching's long, drawn-out articulation of the Dharma as understood in the Ts'ao-tung School to which he belonged. No such intellectual precondition was in Dōgen's mind, because in fact he had studied with people of the Lin-chi School and found them inadequate, but was headed back to try again with Wu-chi of that school when he heard Wu-chi had died.

> ...the authenticity of Ju-ching as a teacher derived from Ju-ching as a person, and not from his sectarian affiliation....
>
> Therefore, Dōgen's encounter with the "authentic teacher" in the Ts'ao-tung School must not be interpreted as proof of the supremacy of the Ts'ao-tung School over the Lin-chi School. Ju-ching and Dōgen repeatedly warned against sectarian concerns not only within Ch'an in particular, but also within Buddhism as a whole.
>
> For this reason, it can be asserted that...*personhood* (*hito*, Jp.) [is] the sole medium in which the Buddha-nature can be embodied and through which the authentic Dharma can be transmitted [italics added for emphasis].[90]

In Dōgen's search for an authentic teacher, he was simultaneously searching for his own authentic self, a self that had become fragmented by his experiences of emptiness. In meeting Ju-ching, Dōgen experienced a powerful mirror of his own true self in the dynamic, unconditional acceptance into an intimate, personal relationship that laid the basic trust necessary for him to continue exploring the meaning of his experience of emptiness.

THE EXPERIENCE OF GREAT ENLIGHTENMENT

Compared to the time usually spent with a teacher before experiencing enlightenment, Dōgen's time with Ju-ching was extremely short before his enlightenment experience. Having met Ju-ching in May, Dōgen experienced his Great Enlightenment during the summer Ango[91] training period of 1225, after, therefore, only two to four months from the time they met. This is testimony to the years of intense study Dōgen had done both in

Journeys into Emptiness

Japan as well as with other teachers in China and to the extraordinary trust that he immediately experienced with Ju-ching. Such trust is a precondition for the utter abandonment and letting-go that is required for enlightenment. If, as was mentioned in the introduction, Zen practice—just like Christian discipleship and psychotherapy—requires a leap off a hundred-foot flagpole, such risk taking and abandonment of concern for personal safety can hardly be done without complete trust in one's teacher. Only trust in the teacher-student relationship makes such a leap a movement of wisdom rather than foolishness (though it still may feel like foolishness!).

The pivotal experience for Dōgen occurred while sitting in deep meditation. It is reported that

> Ju-ching shouted at a disciple, "When you study under a master, you must drop the body and mind; what is the use of single-minded intense sleeping?" Sitting right beside this monk, Dōgen suddenly attained Great Enlightenment. Immediately, he went up to the abbot's quarters and burned incense. Ju-ching inquired, "What is the burning of the incense for?" Dōgen replied, "The body and mind have been dropped; that is why I have come!" "The body and mind have been dropped; you dropped the body and mind!" said Ju-ching approvingly. In humility, Dōgen said, "It might have been a momentary delusion; please do not give me the Seal (of approval) indiscriminately." Ju-ching assured him, "I do not grant you the Seal indiscriminately." Dōgen pursued the point, "How can you say that you do not grant the Seal indiscriminately?" Ju-ching replied, "You indeed have dropped the body and mind." When Dōgen made obeisance to Ju-ching, the attendant Kuang-p'ing from Fu-chow, who was sitting beside Dōgen, exclaimed, "This man from a foreign country attained the Great Matter. This is indeed not a trifling matter at all." Thereupon, Dōgen left humbly.

Zen history is replete with stories such as this that, to the general reader who has not experienced Zen practice directly, are enigmatic, implying a meaning and significance that is unfathomable from the point of view of common, everyday reasoning and experience. Koans, of course, are the famous form of Zen enigmas.

In this case, however, we have to do with an actual experience of Dōgen. According to Kodera, this event is not necessarily reliable in the details, because it is not told in Dōgen's own writings. It is mentioned in two biographies, *Kenzei-ki* and *Eihei-ji sanso gyōgōki*.[92] However, there is absolutely no doubt that the phrase attributed to Ju-ching as "dropping off body and mind" was the trigger in Dōgen's own mind to his experience of enlightenment and served as the central teaching for the rest of his life. It is repeated throughout his writings. It also continues to serve as a primary phrase of teaching and encouragement in both Sōtō and Rinzai Zen traditions down to the present day in America. The phrase must therefore be acknowledged for its central role not only in Dōgen's personal experience of enlightenment, but in everything else he wrote and taught subsequently. It becomes important, therefore, to consider how this phrase served to resolve Dōgen's Great Doubt and thus why it continues to have transformative power to Zen practitioners today. The answer to this question will also reveal what is particularly distinctive and unique in Dōgen's Zen. In order to arrive at an answer, it will be helpful both to step back and recall some points made previously and to anticipate others that will be elaborated more fully in chapter 3.

As one explores the experience of emptiness, whether in meditation or psychotherapy, one begins to recognize that there is an inherent inner propensity to organize one's life in such a way as to reduce or avoid pain and to maximize pleasure, and that this effort is often done by paying a price in consciousness, that is, by a selective tuning out of things one does not want to hear, see, feel or know, and that such reduction of consciousness has resulted in delusion (Zen Buddhist perspective), sin (Christian perspective) and neurosis (depth psychological perspective). The dynamic of this systematic self-deception is the ego.[93] Its primary function is to defend the self as it defines itself (most often as this individual person bounded by flesh), which includes everything that substantiates the self's claim to be itself by itself, and to give it whatever it wants, to the point of its being the center of the universe (egocentrism).

This ego is identical with the atman that is the bête noire of Buddhism. This is the part of the psyche that tries to reify itself into invincibility. Depth psychology and Buddhism agree on this dynamic tendency in each person to build up defenses against the experience of emptiness by putting painful associations into things that are seen as "not-I" and putting pleasure-associated things into a collection of characteristics and beliefs with which one identifies ("I"). The earlier and more severe the development of this ego (which is only one part of the personality, so that the self is divided within itself), the more a person will tend to divide his/her experience into two aspects, good/bad, self/other and so forth. Buddhism asserts that this is a basic human tendency common to all people.

Under conditions of early trauma, more severe than is common, or genetic vulnerability, such a division within the ego is known in depth psychology as *splitting*,[94] and is an unconscious process that is usually set in motion very early in life. Under conditions of a split in the ego, projections become especially strong as the rejected part of the self is put into the outer world. While *splitting* is a technical term in depth psychology for a pathological condition of the ego that not everyone shares, the same psychodynamic tendency to divide consciousness into pleasant and painful is common to all humanity and is the source of what Buddhism calls dualism. Thus psychological splitting and Buddhist dualism share the same tendency, the tendency to divide all experience into two in order to maintain the illusion of a separate self.

In Christianity, this division within the self was accounted for mythologically in the story of the Garden of Eden, in which self-consciousness was first experienced as a knowing of the difference between good and evil.[95] At its best, the ability to distinguish between good and evil is crucial for a person to survive and flourish. At its worst, the inner world can be so divided that one is ruled by paranoia.

Thus, there are important parallels, as well as distinctions, among Buddhist dualism, psychological splitting and the ability to make distinctions between good and bad. Each process has a positive function and a negative possibility, both sides of which need careful articulation.

Experiences of emptiness, especially the earlier they are and the more severe they are, are so painful and threatening that they often result in this splitting process within the self. Once that division is made within the self, all experience becomes bifurcated, analyzed in terms of its being pro or contra the defensive ego with which one becomes increasingly identified.

The questions that drive one to a spiritual path are always questions that reflect this division within the self, that come from the pain and anxiety of an inner split, and are often expressed as and experienced as an outer split, which Buddhism recognized as dualism. The campaign against dualism that was launched so forcefully by Nāgārjuna and remains the focus of subsequent Mahayana thought is rooted in the urge to heal this split within the self that is seen as the source of a false consciousness and the source of all evil in the world.

Dōgen's driving question of Great Doubt—why practice is necessary if all beings inherently have Buddha-nature—is itself a reflection of Dōgen's own divided consciousness, a division we may understand as precipitated by the multiple traumas of his initial experiences of emptiness. All philosophies and theologies—indeed, all human expression, verbal or not—necessarily reflect and convey the state of consciousness of those who construct them. Ideas and constructions of meanings, therefore, carry different levels of consciousness and are therefore worthy of evaluation.

To say here that divisions within the self are the origin of dualistic thinking is not to reduce epistemology or philosophy to psychology. The drive to resolve a spiritual, theological or philosophical problem requires resolution on its own terms. Any resolution of the problem of the divided self will also, insofar as the resolution is efficacious, entail a transformation within the self of the explorer, so that there is inner healing as well as a healing idea in the language (philosophy, religion, psychology) of the original problem.

In Dōgen's case, the resolution of his Great Doubt occurred upon hearing Ju-ching shout "Drop off body and mind!" In essence, to drop off body and mind is to let go of all that separates one from everything else, all thought or concern about a separate body, all thought, image, feeling or idea of an "I" separate from other things. Implicit in Dōgen's question of Great Doubt, Why is practice necessary if all beings inherently have Buddha-nature?, is a division between an idea and an actual situation. That all beings inherently have Buddha-nature is an idea, a cognitive expression unrelated to anything actual in the moment, because practice is seen as something separate from being, from talking or writing or breathing. The question of Great Doubt, therefore, is rife with the divisions within Dōgen's own self and could not help but be an expression of that division until he experienced an inner cohesion.

That inner cohesion could only happen by the "dropping off of body and mind," the letting go of all semblance of separation between self and other. To "drop off body and mind," therefore, is to kill the ego, to let go of the dominant tendency within the self to see itself as autonomous. The central control that works so hard and ingeniously at preserving the self must face and accept death as its own inevitable reality.

Furthermore, and, as Dōgen came to underscore, this realization itself would be unattainable apart from actually doing the practice that is only an idea in the original question of Great Doubt. Practice, as was mentioned above, is, centrally for Dōgen, the action of *shikantaza*, Dōgen's way of doing *zazen*. The only way of answering why practice is necessary is to practice, that is, no longer to separate oneself from the idea, but to actualize it by doing it.

There were, therefore, three aspects to Dōgen's experience of Great Enlightenment: a healing of his divided self, as mentioned above; a fundamental shift in his understanding of the Dharma; and a change of consciousness experienced in large part due to the practice of *shikantaza*.

The shift in his understanding of the Dharma is examined carefully by Kodera by comparing the original problem Dōgen felt regarding practice and inherent Buddha-nature with his rendering of the issue in the *Busshō* fascicle of the Shōbōgenzō.

Kodera begins by noting that Dōgen's statement of Great Doubt was based on a Chinese translation of the "Mahaparinirvana sutra," which is usually read as "Shakyamuni Buddha said, 'All sentient beings exhaustively possess the Buddha nature; the Tathagata exists eternally and is without change.'"

The problem with this rendering is its implication that there is an immutable substance to Buddha-nature (or the Tathagata), and, Dōgen queried, if it is immutable, why is it necessary to do anything to achieve it?

After undergoing the decisive enlightenment under Ju-ching, Dōgen in the *Bussho* chapter of the *Shōbōgenzō*, gave a new reading to the same passage. Its ramification is of paramount importance in considering the meaning of the solution of his "Great Doubt." Dōgen read it as: "Shakyamuni Buddha said: *'All are sentient beings, all things are the Buddha-nature; the Tathagata exists eternally and is nonexistent and yet existent, and changing.'"*...Dōgen rejected the interpretation that there is an eternal element of the Buddha-nature in all sentient beings, who are subject to constant change. Rather, he proposes that all things that are sentient are the Buddha-nature. Thus, according to Dōgen, the Buddha-nature is not some kind of changeless entity, but is none other than the eternally rising and perishing reality of the world. This is the *Mahayana* affirmation, especially that of *prajnaparamita*, that *nirvana* is *samsara* and *samsara* is *nirvana*....

All that is said of the Buddha-nature applies to "all things." That which constitutes "all things" has nothing outside of itself to be compared to or contrasted with. "All things" exhausts the whole world; nothing whatsoever is excluded from it. *The realization of "all things" or the Buddha-nature, is the dropping of the body and mind. When one realizes "all things," the body and mind are dropped. When the body and mind are dropped, "all things" is realized. They are one and the same.*[96]

There is not, in sum, an immutable Buddha-nature separate from the world of change. It is not that there is an absolute Buddha-nature that somehow undergoes change, but rather, the world of change is itself Buddha-nature. This was the idea that resolved the fundamental question of Dōgen's Great Doubt.

Interestingly, according to Kodera, this most famous phrase of Dōgen," dropping off of body and mind," does not appear traceable to any of Ju-ching's sayings. It does not appear in the *Ju-ching ho-shang yü -lu*, the primary record of Ju-ching. The phrase Ju-ching is known to have used and that *does* appear in his record of writings is "dropping the dust from the mind." The *pronunciation* of that phrase in Japanese is the same as Dōgen's phrase, but is importantly different in Chinese, reflecting the difference in Chinese characters.

The Chinese phrase found in Ju-ching's record, *Ju-ching ho-shang yü -lu* is *xīn chén tōlō*, in Japanese, *shinjin datsuraku*, which means, "dropping dust from the mind." The Chinese characters for Dōgen's "dropping body and mind" are *shēn xīn tōlō*, which is pronounced in almost the same way as *xīn chén tōlō*. Recall that Dōgen was Japanese, though fluent in Chinese. Ju-ching was Chinese, speaking in Chinese. Is it possible, therefore, that Dōgen heard *xīn chén tōlō* from Ju-ching, but in an unconscious movement of creativity, heard it as *shēn xīn tōlō*? Was, in other words, Dōgen's most original formulation of the key to enlightenment actually learned from his teacher, or was it completely original with Dōgen himself?

The difference between these two is enormous, paralleling the famous contrasting verses of Hui-neng and Shen-hsiu. When asked to compose a verse demonstrating their understanding of Zen by the master, Hung-jen, the head monk Shen-hsiu wrote,

> The mind is the Bodhi tree,
> The body is the mirror stand.
> The mirror is originally clean and pure;
> Where can it be stained by dust?

In reply, Hui-neng wrote,

> Bodhi originally has no tree,
> The mirror has no stand.
> Buddha-nature is always clean and pure;
> Where is there room for dust?[97]

Hui-neng's answer was deemed superior and he was secretly (for political reasons) made the Sixth Patriarch of China.

> While Ju-ching's expression aims at the restoration of the original state of the mind by removing defilement from it, Dōgen's expression assumes nothing to which an original state of purity needs to be restored.[98]

Similarly, if Kodera is correct, Ju-ching's actual teaching fell short of Dōgen's own realization, a fact that would have made Dōgen's own story of his encounter with Ju-ching upon enlightenment impossible. The only way such a misunderstanding could have slipped by is if they conversed in Japanese, where the sounds are the same in both phrases. But the common language at the time was Chinese, and therefore the mistake could not have passed by unnoticed. One is left to conclude that the phrase, "Dropping off body and mind," is original with Dōgen. What is possible is that Dōgen heard Ju-ching use Ju-ching's phrase, but Dōgen subconsciously translated it into his native Japanese, which triggered the association to the superior perspective. It was perhaps only subsequently that Dōgen attributed the phrase to Ju-ching, in order to consolidate a sense of continuity and honor his teacher, whom he certainly held in great esteem.

The implication of the difference in these two phrases for understanding the experience of emptiness is fundamental. In general, whether people tend to assume continuity (when things are going well), wish for it or feel that they have a right to it, there is a tendency to assume substantiality, that a thing is more the same from moment to moment than not. Faced with a major experience of emptiness, the discontinuity is seen as intrusive, as abnormal, a disruption of ordinary ongoingness. From this point of view, a "healthy" outlook might be to "wipe the dust from the mind," in other words, "get over it." But Dōgen's phrase, dropping body and mind, challenges the original assumption of continuity of a substantial mind to begin with. *All* is change. Change is the very nature of the phenomenal universe. It's just that we don't usually see it.

The change in consciousness was made possible by Dōgen's intense practice of *shikantaza* (Jp., single-minded sitting). Since this is the method of Zen meditation most commonly associated with Dōgen, it is a central part of anyone's path who aims to follow Dōgen's practice. Although meditation in the lotus position[99] is a practice common to all forms of Buddhism in differing degrees, for Dōgen sitting (*zazen*) in meditation is of the essence of Zen practice and realization.

The primary mode of *zazen* for Dōgen is what is commonly called "just sitting" or *shikantaza*. Taken largely from the "Silent Illumination" of Hongzhi[100] (1091–1157 C.E.), Dōgen's *shikantaza* emphasizes the elimination of all effort to achieve any result or to control the mind's process.

Journeys into Emptiness

There is no focus, but rather a defocusing. Thoughts or images arise, and one lets them pass. One attends to the breath, deepening breathing into the *hara* (Jp.)/*dantian* (Ch.), which is one of the central energy points in the body about two inches below the navel. In the course of extended sitting, increasingly intense images, thoughts and feelings arise, including suppressed conflicts and memories, and seemingly bizarre confluences.

As one sits and watches the flow of thoughts and feelings somewhat like watching a movie, one also notices the constant tendency to shift attention, to hold onto particular thoughts or ideas, to avoid going into deeper layers of feeling and awareness. This tendency to avoid by diversionary thoughts or images is known in depth psychology as resistance, and is related to fear of the emergence of unpleasant memories and feelings. In *shikantaza*, as, indeed, in all Zen meditation, the resistance is seen as the struggle of the ego to maintain its hegemony. Continuous practice requires a deepening of the awareness of one's thoughts and feelings, and therefore a constant delving into ever deeper layers of things one has unconsciously worked very hard to keep hidden.

This process continues indefinitely as an ongoing process of self-emptying. *Shikantaza*, therefore, is an ever-deepening process of the experience of emptiness, a continual emptying of thoughts and feelings. Somewhere during this process, the body experiences pain and one has a strong urge to move, just as the mind resists being forgotten in the developing of *samadhi*. Continuing to sit still at such points enables one to break through to new levels of memory and feeling.

Shikantaza has several virtues that make it especially suitable to spiritual and psychological healing. The instruction is simply to sit, attend and let go. This not only deepens thoughts and feelings as they arise and leave, but it keeps one without any expectations about what is supposed to happen, except in this most general way. In this process, one essentially confronts and manifests the experience of sheer being, without having to do anything, without having to react or direct. One experiences the power of *being* rather than *doing*.

To this extent, *shikantaza* resembles contemplation, as will be discussed in the next chapter. Purposelessness gives a freedom that gives tremendous support to one's true self, and, in fact, the process of *shikantaza* usually works to bring into heightened awareness the degree to which one has been reactive, acting in response to external stimuli or expectations or actions. As different pieces of feelings and thoughts emerge, one's psychological depths are tapped. In places where one has resisted particular feelings, thoughts or images from the unconscious, the process of allowing them to rise and letting them go brings a release that is not only calming but energizing.[101]

In *shikantaza*, one faces oneself, including everything that one previously avoided. One rejects nothing, clings to nothing, and thus the entire universe opens up.

If, as Buddhism claims, the basic source of suffering in the world is a divided consciousness that is compelled to sort reality into dualisms, then the only cure is a unifying consciousness that leaves nothing out, that panoramically opens to everything. In order to be healed, one must go back and face whatever was run from, reclaim whatever was thrown away, denied, split-off. For Dōgen in particular, one may well imagine that, with the strong connection felt to Ju-ching, Dōgen was able finally to reach back into the deepest parts of his earliest experiences of emptiness, the deaths of his father and mother, and to face what he had not been able to face before, including his own ultimate death.

Dōgen's fame in urging the practice of *shikantaza* has led some people to believe that he and his Sōtō School followers reject the use of koans (Jp.)/*kung-an* (Ch.). That is hardly the case, as is demonstrated by his collection of three hundred koans in Chinese,[102] as well as the appearance of most of them in the various fascicles of the standard ninety-three fascicle edition of *Shōbōgenzō*. The difference in the use of koans in Dōgen's Soto School and their use in, for example, the Rinzai School, is far too complex a topic in itself to be answered here. Suffice it to say for now that in Dōgen Zen, everything is intended to serve the purpose of the realization of one's true self, which is none other than one's original Buddha-nature.

These three aspects of Dōgen's Great Enlightenment, the new insight into his understanding of Buddha-nature, his formulation of a method of pursuing the experience of emptiness, and his experience of inner healing, were simultaneously accomplished in his experience of the dropping of body and mind.

Thus, for Dōgen, to drop off body and mind is to experience the Great Death[103] of Zen Buddhism. This is the entrance (not, to be sure, the final destination) into the experience of emptiness, śūnyatā (Sk.), kōng (Ch.) and kū (Jp). This is the "dying to self" that Jesus calls people to, Christ's own kenosis, which his followers must imitate. This is the ego that depth psychology acknowledges must be sacrificed in order for deeper aspects of the self to emerge.

The death of the ego becomes the goal of everyone on a path of transformation because it becomes apparent that the ego holds one back. The ego must die if one is to move from an initial, personal experience of emptiness as negative to an experience of the emptiness of all things, from an experience that seems to separate one from others, to an experience that unites one with all other beings.

Having experienced the Great Enlightenment, Dōgen resolved his Great Doubt and achieved what he wanted to by traveling to China. On September 18, 1225, Dōgen received official transmission from Ju-ching and thus became the first monk from Japan to be included in the document of succession in the history of Chinese Buddhism.[104] He nevertheless stayed for another two years, refining his understanding with Ju-ching and manifesting his own gifts for conveying the Dharma to others. Records indicate that Dōgen was popular with laypeople because of his concern and involvement with them and that he was also very much respected by high officials, who relied on Dōgen for family rituals, such as funerals. In a somewhat thorny compliment, Ju-ching expressed his desire that Dōgen stay on as his attendant, saying, "Although a foreigner, you are a man of potential."[105] Dōgen however, was sensitive to how it would be perceived among the other monks for a foreigner to continue to hold such a high position, and decided to return to Japan. Upon announcing his intention clearly to Ju-ching, he also received Ju-ching's Dharma robe and the full document of succession and returned to Japan in 1227.

Not having visited too many Ch'an monasteries but having only
studied under the Late Master Ju-ching and plainly realizing that the
eyes are horizontal and the nose vertical, without being deceived
by any one, I came home empty-handed. Therefore, I returned without a trace of the Buddha Dharma and depending upon destiny, I
let the time take its own course. Morning after morning, the sun rises
in the east; night after night, the moon sinks in the west. The clouds
disappear, and the mountains are manifest; the rains pass, and the
Four Mountains are low.[106]

Dōgen returned, in other words, simply as himself, nothing extra, which
is of the essence of the transmission of the Buddha Dharma. Dōgen's experience of emptiness led to the experience of emptiness as enlightenment,
which led to the experience of his true self as continuingly empty. His
enlightenment was the fruit of his labor with the experience of emptiness.
The experience of emptiness thus becomes an ongoing process of transformation.

TRANSMISSION OF THE LIGHT:
DŌGEN'S RETURN TO JAPAN AND BEYOND

Dōgen returned to Kenninji in Kyoto, Japan, the monastery where he
first began his study of Zen, and declared what was to be the primary
basis of his teaching in "Broad Recommendation of *Zazen*." In it, following his teacher Ju-ching, he set out the practice of *zazen*, particularly the method of *shikantaza*, to be the single and sufficient practice
necessary to attain enlightenment. In contrast, surrounding Tendai
monasteries advocated a practice that included the chanting of sutras,
reciting the Buddha's name and observing rites of repentance, and
were so intent on their point of view that they actually destroyed the
tomb of Hōnen, a teacher in the Pure Land school, in the same year as
Dōgen's return. Dōgen's proclamation, therefore, amounted to a knocking of the chip off his neighbors' shoulders, and, under their threat, he
moved out of Kyoto to Fukakusa in 1230.

Within three years, he began a small practice center there named Kannondōri Temple, after the Bodhisattva of compassion (*Kannon*, Jp./*Guan Yin*, Ch.).[107] The next year, 1234, Dōgen's successor-to-be and amanuensis par excellent, Ejō, arrived to be Dōgen's student. Within a year, a formal monks' hall was built at Kannondori and Ejō was appointed head cook. Another addition was made to the hall in 1239. Within two years, five other monks who had been friends of Ejō came to join Dōgen's rapidly developing community. With his increased popularity, among laity as well as monks, came increased criticism and threats from the Tendai group on Mt. Hiei. The threat became severe enough that Dōgen accepted the offer of one of his lay students, Lord Hitano, to build a new temple on land to the northwest, in Echizen Province on the Sea of Japan. At first called Daibutsu, Dōgen renamed it Eiheiji in 1246. That temple still stands today as the primary temple with which Dōgen is associated and the historical center of Sōtō Zen practice.

In 1253, Dōgen became ill and went to Kyoto to seek a cure. Perhaps anticipating his death, before he left, he made Ejō abbot of Eiheiji and gave him a robe that Dōgen had made with his own hands. On August 28, Dōgen died in the city of his birth, Kyoto.

Dōgen's writings lay in obscurity in Sōtō libraries for about five hundred years due to the fact that they were written in a vernacular difficult to understand, rather than the Chinese of respectably educated men, and also because of state control over popular access to liberative teachings. In 1770, in an effort to gain more respectability for Dōgen, Fuzan translated the *Shōbōgenzō* into Chinese. This is ironic, since Dōgen's original writing was among the first in Japanese Zen to be written in Japanese in a colloquial style more accessible to the common people, rather than in the socially "correct" Chinese. Until the first publication of the *Shōbōgenzō* in Japanese in 1816, his position as founder of the Sōtō School left him open to whatever interpretation the school needed at the time, even among the monks. It is only with the gradually increased publication of Dōgen's writings that he has begun to be appreciated as a philosopher, poet and Zen master with something to say to the entire human community.

In modern times, it was the well-known Japanese philosopher, Watsuji Tetsurō, who brought Dōgen to people's attention when he wrote several essays (1920-23) on the profundity and uniqueness of Dōgen and stripped away the myths that the Sōtō School had attributed to him for their own purposes. This brought Dōgen out of the confines of the Sōtō School. The first English translation of any of Dōgen's writings appeared in 1958, in Reihō Masunaga's *Sōtō Approach to Zen.*

In the United States, knowledge of Dōgen has usually sprung from Zen practice centers, first in San Francisco, led by Shunryu Suzuki in the 1960s, and later in Los Angeles under the direction of the late Hakuyu Taizan Maezumi Roshi. In the past twenty years, particularly since the full English translation of the *Shōbōgenzō* by Kōsen Nishiyama and John Stevens in 1983, Dōgen has begun to be known and highly regarded among Western philosophers and poets, as well as practicing Zen Buddhists.

Although Dōgen did not suffer, so far as we know, the kind of physical assaults that Bodhidharma is reputed to have undergone, he certainly exemplifies a similar tenacity in his pursuit of the meaning of the experience of emptiness. He could have remained in the family after the death of his mother to "get on with his life," as is so often said today to justify a refusal of reflection and an unconscious resumption of the pursuit of collectively valued goals, usually including status, power and money. Instead he went to a monastery. Discouraged by the shallowness of the practice at so many monasteries, he continued to visit others. Whereas most people are stopped by the death of only one person close to them, Dōgen suffered the deaths of several teachers and both of his parents, yet continued his search for an authentic teacher, ultimately crossing the hazardous (for that time, especially) China Sea. Presumably, in the face of being detained aboard ship for three months, he could have given up, taken such a problem as a sign he had gone in the wrong direction and returned to Japan. He persisted in China, going from one teacher to another, from one monastery to another, when he could have simply told himself that things were no different here than in Japan, so why bother? Finally, he was ready to give one teacher another chance only to find out he also had died.

Additionally, once he had found Ju-ching and had had his Great Enlightenment, after staying for a couple of years to refine his understanding, he could have stayed in China and enjoyed the fruits of his long search.

Instead, he took up the challenge of bringing his learning about the experience of emptiness back to Japan. There, he met with further obstacles in the form of actual physical threats from people who disagreed with him. Dōgen was not unaffected by the years of threats from the Tendai School. His forced retreat, first to Fukakusa and Kannondori, then to Daibutsu, which became Eiheiji, led him to focus on the purity of practice and the stringent requirements for it. In contrast to his earlier openness to and optimism regarding lay practice and the participation of women, Dōgen increasingly felt that full understanding and integration of the Dharma, true Enlightenment, was only possible by complete "home departure," the taking of monk's vows and living in a monastery entirely devoted to following the Way. He could have acquiesced or watered down his teaching, but, instead, he moved as needed to find a place for the thing that counted most for him, true practice in which the experience of emptiness is thoroughly understood.

DŌGEN'S LEGACY

What Dōgen brought back to Japan and the rest of the world from his exploration of his experience of emptiness in the process of self transformation may be divided into three major contributions. The first, and the one for which he was most known, is his organizational founding of the Sōtō School of Zen Buddhism. The second is the method he refined and advocated for exploring the experience of emptiness, *zazen*. The third gift to the world is his writings, which remain utterly unique not only in Japanese literature, but in the entire world.

Founder of the Sōtō School of Zen Buddhism

It is ironic that, apart from those who have begun direct study of his writings, Dōgen is primarily known as the founder of the Sōtō School of Zen because Dōgen, following the view of his teacher, Ju-ching, repeatedly argued against being associated with any sect, including a "Zen" sect. From Dōgen's own era of the thirteenth century, the Rinzai School was much more influential among the ruling class in Japan than the Sōtō School and was behind the particular evolution of "Zen" culture, including painting, landscaping, *noh* drama, *ikebana* (flower arranging) and the tea ceremony. Today, however, the Sōtō School is one of the largest Buddhist groups in Japan, with fourteen thousand temples, fifteen thousand priests and over five million members.[108]

Understandably, during the period in which Dōgen's writings themselves were not well known even within the Sōtō School, the School underwent changes that lost some of the rigor and focus for which Dōgen so ardently strove. He would not have appreciated this development, all the more since he did not intend to found another school in the first place, but simply to develop an organization that would protect and advocate a rigorous form of true Zen practice. The recovery and translation of his writings has made possible the restoration of Dōgen's true practice.

Teacher of Zazen as the Fundamental Practice for Realization of the Self

The whole point of *zazen* is to liberate the self from the constrictions it imposes on itself. These constrictions are directly related to the nature of consciousness and the use of thought and language, not just to *express* experience, but, as often as not, to *control and delimit* experience. As was noted above, the problem of dualism, which Buddhism considers the fundamental problem of human life, is often rooted in and grows out of divisions in the psyche that are prompted by the initial experiences of emptiness. These divisions in the psyche "set the program," in contemporary computer parlance, for people to filter all their experiences, inner and outer, and to put them into categories based on their potential to help or hinder the defensive ego.

Thus the fundamental problem of the human tendency to limit, restrict and control consciousness based on fear is met in *zazen* with a countermove, to be open to what is, to be aware of all that comes into consciousness of thoughts, images or feelings and to notice it without reacting to it or running from it or trying to change it.

This process parallels the process of psychoanalysis and psychotherapy, in which patients are instructed to say whatever comes to mind, to free associate without the imposition of a previously determined agenda or goal. In both analysis and *zazen* the mind excludes nothing. One is committed to awareness of what is, and in that commitment is a vital, fundamental spiritual as well as psychological attitude that is of the essence of faith in being itself.

This is an enactment of the repeated affirmation process in Genesis 1, wherein each thing that is created Yahweh calls "good." But here—as, we would claim, in the deeper meaning of Genesis—"good" is not good in contrast to bad (which would make it one half of the dualism), but good in the sense of trustworthy, in the same sense that Job declared, "Though he slay me, yet will I trust him." Whatever comes up can be faced. This is the antidote to repression and a divided consciousness. This is faith in the fundamental reliability of reality, without requiring that it obey one's narcissistic demands. This is the faith and the commitment that one makes when one sits in *zazen*. One empties oneself of one's own demands, expectations and judgments, and allows what is to be. This is the emptying of the cup, without which one cannot receive. It is also the emptying of a small "ego" identity that moves toward a felt identification with all things.

According to Dōgen, *zazen* is the process by which the experience of emptiness transforms the self by the self's study of the self. The process is put very simply in this verse from "Geniōkōan," the fascicle Dōgen put first in his initial collection of the *Shōbōgenzō:*

To study the buddha way is to study the self. To study the self is to forget the self. To forget the self is to be actualized by myriad things. When actualized by myriad things, your body and mind as well as the bodies and minds of others drop away. No trace of realization remains, and this no-trace continues endlessly.[109]

In these few words, the entire process of zazen and its effect is outlined. There is first the identification of following the Buddha Way with the study of the self. This is a fundamental principal of Dōgen Zen. The truth that is sought, the resolution yearned for, is within. One reaches it by going within the self, looking at one's own consciousness, in deep meditation (samadhi). In this state of concentration, one forgets oneself. Without shutting out the outside world, one reaches a point of concentration in which distinctions between self and other, inside and outside and so on disappear. When that happens, one experiences oneself as authenticated by "myriad things." What is forgotten, what is dropped away, is, of course, the ego with all its defensive maneuvers to keep it separate from everything else.

Francis Cook describes the inner movement this way:

> ...the inauthentic self is obsessed with fear for its own security and endurance, and authentic selfhood is the self which has been liberated from clinging to life and fearing death....authentic selfhood...called "enlightenment"—consists of ceasing to fear and hate the life-death process and searching for authenticity apart from it....[110]

> ...the authentic self is actional and dynamic in a way impossible or at best difficult for the inauthentic self, for in contrast to the inauthentic self which merely observes and interprets, the authentic self as concrete immediate experience is profoundly immersed in experience, which is to say, the world. In other words, the life of the authentic self is none other than the life of everything....for Dōgen, authentic selfhood is an authentic selfhood for others—that is, its proper function is that of eliminating suffering and struggle in the world.[111]

What is termed in Zen practice as "the backward step," in which one stops one's ordinary pursuits to look at oneself, becomes, when engaged in *zazen,* a transforming process in which initial experiences of emptiness are followed through to the point of letting go of everything that is nonessential to a core experience of reality that is understood to be itself empty of all inherent substance and identity. From this experience of the emptiness of all things, one discovers a unity with all that is, so that one no longer goes through life trying to separate oneself from it. One is freed to be *for* others, for the world, as needed. Thus, the experience of emptiness, which initially tends to lead one in a constrictive and self-protective direction, becomes, through the practice of *zazen,* an expansive awareness and a readiness to be *for* all things.

It should be noted that Dōgen is particularly concerned that anthropocentrism as well as egocentrism be overcome. In Zen realization, human beings are not privileged over and above, or in any way apart from, the rest of the phenomenal universe. To understand the emptiness of all things is to know the intrinsic interrelatedness and oneness of all things:

> It is not only that there is water in the world, but there is a world in water. It is not just in water. There is a world of sentient beings in clouds. There is a world of sentient beings in the air. There is a world of sentient beings in fire. There is a world of sentient beings on earth. There is a world of sentient beings in the phenomenal world. There is a world of sentient beings in a blade of grass....Wherever there is a world of sentient beings, there is a world of buddha ancestors. You should thoroughly examine the meaning of this.[112]

Dōgen takes us from emptiness as loss to the emptiness of "all things," including the self, so that, in effect, we go from an experience of not-having to having (without owning or holding onto, but, essentially, receiving) the entire universe as oneself.

In a small part of the "Mountains and Waters Sutra," Dōgen not only underscores this identification with all things, but offers what may actually have been the key to resolving his own initial experiences of emptiness in the deaths of his father and mother:

Priest Daokai of Mt. Furong said to the assembly, "The green mountains are always walking; a stone woman gives birth to a child at night." ..."A stone woman gives birth to a child at night" means that the moment when a barren woman gives birth to a child is called "night."

There are male stones, female stones, and nonmale nonfemale stones. They are placed in the sky and in the earth and are called heavenly stones and earthly stones. These are explained in the ordinary world, but not many people actually know about it.

You should understand the meaning of giving birth to a child. At the moment of giving birth to a child, is the mother separate from the child? You should study not only that you become a mother when your child is born, but also that you become a child. This is the actualization of giving birth in practice-realization. You should study and investigate this thoroughly.

So we move from loss to gain, from emptiness to a fullness that is beyond fullness, because the distinction between self and other has been left behind.

Writer and Thinker

It would be impossible, of course, to have Dōgen's writings without the method he used to explore his own experiences of emptiness. Yet the profound character of Dōgen's thought and his unique use of language deserve mention in addition to his method of realization. In a tradition whose hallmark is the "mind to mind transmission without reliance on words and letters," Dōgen used words in a special way to go beyond words. Just as Nāgārjuna carried negation dialectically beyond negation, Dōgen took words beyond both words and no-words.

Whereas most Zen stories focus on the obfuscating aspect of words, Dōgen sees words as having the ability to themselves *create* a reality that is experienced and to liberate thought from its distancing tendency:

How pitiable are they who are unaware that discriminating thought *is* words and phrases, and that words and phrases *liberate* discriminating thought![113]

Kim underscores the possibility Dōgen opens up for language:

> In spite of inherent frailties in their make-up, words are the bearers of ultimate truth. In this respect, words are not different from things, events or beings—all are "alive" in Dōgen's thought....even [words'] natural weaknesses can be soteriologically appropriated without violating the principle of absolute nonduality/absolute emptiness. [114]

Words for Dōgen are simply another activity of the body/mind, and the way in which all tendencies toward dualism are overcome is by the principle of total exertion (*ippo-gujin*, Jp.). Dōgen applies the same principle which is the essence of *zazen* to the use of words and to all activity. It is the principle of "the total exertion of a single thing."

This is brought out most directly in Dōgen's fascicle, Gabyō, "Painting of a Rice-Cake."

> Do not use the measure of oneness or difference as the criterion of your study. Thus it is said, "To penetrate one thing is to penetrate myriad things...."
>
> An ancient buddha said, "A painting of a rice-cake does not satisfy hunger."....This statement...has become the mere chatter of seekers in grass-roofed huts and under trees....To think this statement means that expedient teachings are useless is a great mistake....
>
> Know that a painted rice-cake is your face after your parents were born, your face before your parents were born. Thus, a painted rice-cake, made of rice flour, is neither born nor unborn. Since this is so, it is the moment of realization of the way. This cannot be understood by the limited view that a painted rice-cake comes and goes.
>
> The paints for painting rice-cakes are the same as those used for painting mountains and waters. For painting mountains and waters, blue and red paints are used; for painting rice-cakes, rice flour is used. Thus they are painted in the same way, and they are examined in the same way.

True to Zen's emphasis on direct experience of reality, teachers traditionally pointed out the fact that a painting of something to eat, such as a rice-cake, cannot satisfy hunger in the sense that one cannot eat the painting, or even if one could, it would not satisfy hunger, which requires nourishment.

But Dōgen sees in this view a false dichotomizing of experience in which, looking at a painting, one simultaneously thinks of the fact that it is not edible and imagines a "real" rice-cake that would satisfy hunger. For Dōgen, this act of imagining something that is not there is a moving away from what is directly experienced, which is the painting, and away from the kind of "hunger" that seeing and paying attention can be. For Dōgen, each thing has its own function and must be appreciated for that function rather than dismissed because it does not fulfill another function.

Furthermore, and essential in Dōgen, the person doing the seeing needs to stay with what is being experienced at the moment and validate the activity happening right then and there. Thus, a painting satisfies a certain kind of hunger appropriate to a painting, fulfilling its proper function as a painting.

This is an example of Dōgen's radical subjectivity, in which each experience must be appreciated and understood ("penetrated") within the context of itself, not judged by some other thought, image or idea. Repeatedly throughout his fascicles, Dōgen admonishes everyone to "thoroughly study" or to "penetrate fully" whatever item he has been discussing. This always means, for Dōgen, the single-minded attention to what is directly experienced.

> "The total experience of a single thing" does not deprive a thing of its own unique particularity. It places a thing neither against others nor against none. To place a thing against none is another form of dualistic obstruction. When total experience is realized unobstructedly (tsū o shite tsū no ge nakara-shimuruni), the total experience of a single thing is the same as the total experience of all things. A single total experience is a single thing in its totality. The total experience of a single thing is one with that of all things.[115]

The Japanese word tsū deserves attention in this passage. Tsū means "to penetrate," to experience directly without conceptual or discriminating thought. Thoroughly to understand something, for Dōgen, is thoroughly to experience it without separating oneself from it by conceptual thought. The "total experience of a single thing" is, for Dōgen enlightenment activity itself in which the true self is manifested. In this principle lies the secret for overcoming every kind of dualistic propensity; it is the central attitude of Dōgen Zen. Whereas the human tendency is to distance oneself from direct experience of everything, not only by cognitive, discriminating thought or by words and ideas, but by a withholding of personal investment of energy, Dōgen's Zen is designed to expose every manifestation of such distancing-by-withholding and to overcome it by the total exertion of one's self. *Zazen* is the place and activity in which one learns how to do this, how to completely focus all one's body/mind energy in a single direction.

This was Dōgen's answer to his own question regarding the necessity of practice. Practice is necessary for enlightenment because not to practice is, *eo ipso,* to withhold oneself from engagement with whatever is in front of one at the moment. Enlightenment is precisely the total exertion of the body/mind self. Practice is the *total exertion* of the body/mind self. Practice and enlightenment are one and the same activity. Enlightenment is not some abstract mental state achieved in isolation from the rest of the world. Enlightenment is activity, the total exertion of the body/mind without hindrance. To be a buddha is to completely exert every microbe of one's body/mind in what is needed now, whether it be attention in *zazen,* in the washing of a dish or in the pushing of a child out of the path of an oncoming car. *Zazen* as sitting sets one free for the *zazen* of living in which each moment is the manifestation of all time and all things.

> The time-being of all beings throughout the world in water and on land is just the actualization of your complete effort right now. All beings of all kinds in the visible and invisible realms are the time-being actualized by your complete effort, flowing due to your complete effort.
>
> Closely examine this flowing; without your complete effort right now, nothing would be actualized, nothing would flow.[116]

Thus, the resolution to the experience of emptiness is total exertion, the complete giving of one's body/mind to the moment, to what is, right now. Where the tendency upon an initial experience of emptiness is to withdraw, to draw a circle of concern narrowly, or to hide in caves of self-concern and abstraction, Dōgen urges one to throw oneself's whole body/mind into what is in front of one. Zazen as a single-minded activity of sitting becomes the zazen of everyday life.

This parallels the action of the Good Samaritan in Jesus' story.[117] The priest and the Levite are people so caught up in their own thought, their own preoccupations and preset intentions, that they are not free to respond to the need of the moment, the need of the man who was beaten, robbed and abandoned at the side of the road. The Samaritan—who certainly has his own life to lead, as exhibited by the fact that after he sees to the victim's needs, goes on about his affairs—is free to respond as appropriate to the need at hand. Such action is, for Jesus, the actualizing of one's essential human nature, one's true self, and is thereby reflective of and a manifestation of the complete giving of God's self on behalf of humankind in the Incarnation, just as for Dōgen, "the time-being of all beings...is actualized by your complete effort right now."

Similarly, Jesus' urging that someone who has two coats should give one to him who has none[118] bespeaks the freedom to act in response to the need of what is, rather than to get trapped in speculations or withhold energy or things based on a projection of a future need.

In depth psychology, such close attention to what one is experiencing in the moment is of the essence of Freud's evenly-hovering attention and Kohut's empathy.

Dōgen's legacy, therefore, includes not only a major world religious organization, and a method for people to pursue their own experiences of emptiness on their path of transformation, but a collection of unique writings consisting not only of profound philosophy and poetry, but writings that in themselves holographically embody and enact the very process of the actualization of reality in a single moment during one's process of reading them.

All buddha tathagathas, who directly transmit inconceivable dharma and supreme, perfect enlightenment, have a wondrous way unsurpassed and unconditioned. Only buddhas transmit it to buddhas without veering off; self-fulfilling samadhi is its standard. Sitting upright, practicing Zen, is the authentic gate to the unconfined realm of this samadhi.

Although this inconceivable dharma is abundant in each person, it is not actualized without practice, and it is not experienced without realization. When you release it, it fills your hand—how could it be limited to one or many? When you speak it, it fills your mouth—it is not bounded by length or width.

...Passing through the barrier and dropping off limitations, how could you be hindered by (joints) in bamboo or knots in wood?[119]

Thomas Merton

Chapter 2

EMPTINESS AS HOMELESSNESS[1] AND THE SEARCH FOR THE TRUE SELF

…when I lay awake at night in the huge dark dormitory and listened to the snoring of the little animals all around me, and heard through the darkness and the emptiness of the night the far screaming of the trains, or the mad iron cry of a bugle in a distant *caserne* of Senegalese troops, I knew for the first time in my life the pangs of desolation and **emptiness**[2] and abandonment.[3] [written about his experience at a French lycée, 1926]

Teach us the way to perfect simplicity and **emptiness** of all created solicitudes, of all things that are not Yourself. (3/10/47)

Meanwhile I will do everything I can to remain **empty**. (3/17/47)

For I know I will possess all things if I am **empty** of all things, and only You can at once **empty** me of all things and fill me with Yourself, the Life of all that lives and the Being in Whom everything exists. (3/18/47)[4]

...there is no puzzle, no problem, and really no "mystery." All problems are resolved and everything is clear, simply because what matters is clear. The rock, all matter, all life, is charged with *dharmakaya*...everything is **emptiness** and everything is compassion....I know and have seen what I was obscurely looking for. I don't know what else remains but I have now seen and have pierced through the surface and have got beyond the shadow and the disguise. (December, 1968 at Polonnaruwa, Ceylon)[5]

Part I

In these brief excerpts from the writings of Thomas Merton, he speaks vividly of his lifelong, conscious wrestling with his experiences of emptiness. Emptiness runs like a multicolored thread through the life of Thomas Merton, from his birth in Prades, France, through his years at Columbia University and Gethsemani Monastery in the United States, through his death in Bangkok, Thailand, to the many Mertons that people continue to find in his writings today. Such an Ariadnean thread,[6] woven of the strands of different kinds of emptiness, lead one both down into and up out of the dark labyrinth of the self's journey. The many experiences of emptiness found in Thomas Merton's life and writings provide a paradigm for the transforming possibilities of the experience of emptiness in everyone's life. Seen in their various manifestations, Merton's experiences of emptiness confronted him with a conscious experience of loneliness and abandonment in childhood, a kenotic[7] goal for monastic commitment, an unconscious dynamic in the reworking of depth psychological issues from infancy and a key to the recovery of his true self. Finally, throughout his monastic years, he recognized the power of the experience of emptiness to open new vistas in spiritual experience, leading to union with God and all things.

Such a paradigm, arising out of the West in the Christian tradition, may be clearer and more accessible to contemporary readers than were the Buddhist teachers of chapter 1. In addition, Merton's accessibility is aided by the fact that he was such a prolific and self-revealing writer.

Thomas Merton was born in the early part of the twentieth century, moved around from place to place throughout his youth, and, by the time he was twenty-eight, every member of his immediate family had died. In the midst of these turbulent beginnings, he ended up at Columbia College as a student of English literature, with a growing interest in religious experience. This latter interest culminated in his decision to become a Trappist monk and his entrance into the Abbey of Gethsemani in 1941 at the age of twenty-six. Over the course of his life at Gethsemani, which covered twenty-seven years to the day between his entrance into the monastery and his death in Thailand, Merton wrote what amounted to about fifty books, hundreds of articles and poems, about four thousand letters and what will constitute, when published, seven volumes of personal journals, much of which chronicle in detail the author's experience of emptiness. These experiences of emptiness ranged from the earliest circumstances of his formative years to his final direct experience of Buddhism in Southeast Asia, while still a devout Catholic. But the seeds for identity confusion were planted early for Merton, in the very circumstances surrounding his birth, which would lead, eventually, to his earliest experience of emptiness.

INFANCY AND EARLY CHILDHOOD

The complex question of Thomas Merton's identity began with his birth in a country (to which neither of his parents belonged) that was in the initial throes of the First World War. He was born in Prades, France, on January 31, 1915, at approximately 9:30 P.M., in the midst of a snowstorm.[8] His mother, Ruth, was American. His father, Owen, was a New Zealander. Both of them traced their families back to Wales. Ruth was raised as an Episcopalian, but when she returned to New York after living in France, went to meeting at the Society of Friends. Owen was Church of England. He and Ruth had met in Paris four years before Tom's birth, where both were studying painting with Tudor-Hart.[9] They were married in London on April 7, 1914, slightly more than nine months before Merton was born, and, after a summer of tenting, settled into an apartment in Prades to paint.

Merton was therefore legally and officially French, since, according to French law, anyone born in the country is a citizen. Yet his parents came from different countries at opposite ends of the globe from his birthplace. Was infant Tom therefore a Frenchman, an American or a New Zealander?

Weighing about two kilos, or about four pounds, Tom Merton knew a tenuous beginning for an infant in 1915. Though it is not clear whether he was premature or in some other way sickly, nonetheless, according to his mother's records, he gained weight rapidly and soon reached a par for his age.

His mother, Ruth, "was determined the boy would be called Tom."[10] One wonders why, since it goes against English as well as American custom to use the informal name as the official one.[11] Whatever the name Tom meant to Ruth, as her first child, it is surely a marker from birth of Merton's preoccupation with the question of identity. Why did he object to this name so strongly, and what did it mean to him to have it, changing it to Thomas for his first published book? Why, further, did he use his family name rather than his monk's name in publishing? Did the name carry expectations or associations for his mother that he resisted and felt constricted by? Was Tom too informal for the world of private schools and thus a stigma of his parents' poverty? Whatever the answers, Merton's identity crisis, both in the question of a name and in the question of character and expectations, was with him literally from day one.

That this was an issue for Tom was apparent not only as part of his deep and central concern with identity,[12] but in a literal constant playing with alternative names, of which Michael Mott lists sixty-one, over the course of his life.[13] Merton played with his name possibilities as he played with his citizenship possibilities. Born in France and therefore legally a Frenchman, he traveled most of his life on a British passport (obtained when he began school at Oakham), but became a U.S. citizen in 1951, after he entered the monastery. He nonetheless continued to refer to other places as his true home: New Zealand, Wales, the Catalan mountains, all of the Americas. Merton became adept at using the complexity of his identity as a way of identifying with people and countries all over the world. He creatively turned a problem into an advantage. Though not arbitrarily mercurial, he seemed able to shift from one identity or standpoint to another with no felt need to reconcile conflicting points of view. Thus, in Merton's own self-understanding, he had a fluid identity, and although he often joked about his many names and playfully exchanged letters with his Columbia friends with various nicknames, once he began writing from Gethsemani, he undertook the question of his identity as a central spiritual task. His identity was no longer a question of his self-defined aspirations or of choosing among his multiple citizenship possibilities, but of searching inside himself for a unity beneath his multiple possibilities, a unity known only in God. The deep-seated uncertainty about who he was derived from the death of both of his parents and from the perpetual dislocation he experienced throughout his childhood. Because he experienced his own identity as a problem—rather than something unquestioned–Merton was pushed to press the question of identity into spiritual significance.

From Tom's birth, his mother, Ruth, wrote down extended notes in a journal on his growth and development, called "Tom's Book."[14] For the first year, she recorded his weight gain on a monthly basis, and his feeding schedule as it changed. She noted his attention span as it developed from the first few weeks. She counted and dated the development of his vocabulary. She recorded the comment of one local peasant who declared, "Qu'il a l'air éveillé!"[15] She marked down when he took his first few steps and when each new tooth came in.

While the "book" (only nineteen pages) presents, on one level, simply the record of a mother excited by everything her first-born child does, it is remarkable not only for what it says about the young Tom, but what it says about the observer mother who wrote it. Tom remembered her watching over him, writing about him. One wonders what that was like for him. Michael Mott interprets Ruth's recording of young Tom's development as a mirroring,[16] but was it the mirroring of the nurturing mother whose eyes gleam and mouth smiles in delight, emotionally feeding the child? Or was it the mirroring of an observing, narcissistic mother who was carefully attending her child's every move, as if it were a performance whose credit would reflect back to herself?

In view of Merton's later struggle with questions of identity, of true versus false self, with self-consciousness as an impediment to spiritual selflessness, and his perpetual restlessness and urge to go elsewhere, the question of his earliest experiences of being held and given attention are fundamental. The issue of the degree and kind of parenting Merton received in the first few months of his life is important for what it reveals of the vicissitudes of his own narcissistic development and needs, which comprise the foundation for his later life struggles.

The hypothesis of this study is that Thomas Merton's lifelong concern with emptiness began preverbally in the first few months of his life. In other words, Merton began his life with an experience of emptiness occurring too soon for words, but which began to be talked about in later experiences and to be pursued subconsciously. This hypothesis is inferred, like most adult diagnoses, from the evidence of adolescent and adult behavior, more than from direct knowledge of mother/infant interaction. When we look at reports either of Merton himself or his mother's record, we are only looking to see whether evidence supports the possibility, not proves as fact, that Merton's earliest experience of emptiness may be located in infancy. With that caveat in mind, several points merit notice in the evidence available.

In the sixth month, July 1915, Ruth wrote: "He held out his arms to be taken."

In the eighth month, September 1915, she wrote, "He…used to come scurrying across the room to embrace us in a sudden fit of affection."

By the time he was twenty-two months, however, on November 1, 1916, she wrote:

> We have been rather careful not to "teach" him anything, not to tell him to "say" anything nor to make him "show off" what he knew.
>
> But from the time he was a few months old and began to furiously kick and scream whenever he had to be dressed or undressed, I found that he kept quiet if I sang or talked to him. So it seemed to me that it tired him less to listen to words and songs than to resist with all his might; and that is how he began to be interested in words and sounds.
>
> However, he never would be rocked, never wanted to be "held" and has never in his life fallen to sleep unless he was expressly put into his bed for that purpose. He has fought sleep always,[7] and is rarely quiet a single moment while he is awake.

There are some contradictions in the report. When she wrote that he "never wanted to be 'held'" she forgot what she wrote the previous year, in July and September. One wonders what happened in between, whether the repeated exposure to a mother

Merton himself described as "cold," whose intellectuality he continued to resent,[18] induced in him a pseudoindependence and a hyperactivity, having given up on having his own needs met on his own
terms.

Alice Miller describes the possible scenario this way:

> What happens if the mother not only is unable to take over
> the narcissistic functions for the child but...is herself in need
> of narcissistic supplies? Quite unconsciously...the mother
> then tries to assuage her own narcissistic needs through her
> child....This does not rule out strong affection. On the con-
> trary, the mother often loves her child as her self-object, pas-
> sionately, but not in the way he needs to be loved....what is
> missing above all is the framework within which the child
> could experience his feelings and his emotions. Instead, he
> develops something the mother needs, and this certainly
> saves his life...but it nevertheless may prevent him, through-
> out his life, from being himself.[19]

On the one hand, every child wants to be seen, and Tom's
mother's writing made it clear that she was watching him, attending
to his every move and mood. On the other hand, she was not relating to him directly, but writing about him, from a distance—emotionally detached—and this is not what a child needs. It would seem
that this kind of relationship created not only a method for his own
continuing self-reflections (nurture oneself the way mother did), but
a degree of schizoid detachment from personal relatedness, so that
the primary mode of relationship to the outside world and others
was through his writing, as observer and reflector rather than participant. This remained true in spite of the fact that Merton had
many friends throughout his life, maintained a voluminous correspondence and was seen as a jokester with a good sense of humor,
a lover of conversation and a man who enjoyed gossip and interacting with his cohorts.[20] Even in such instances of extroversion,
there remained a part of himself observing himself. This is the seed
to a fundamental problem Merton's writing represented to him on

his spiritual journey: the problem of how to see, observe and write without distancing oneself from the experience. In Zen terms, it is a question of letting go of the witness, the self observing itself.

Robert Daggy, one of Merton's most knowledgeable interpreters and the director of the Thomas Merton Studies Center at Bellarmine College, noted that, in spite of Ruth's protestations against requiring Tom to "show off,"

> What came through to her young son, in her desire to make him his own person, was that she was demanding. She *expected* a great deal from him, more in fact than he later felt he was able to deliver. In his late poem "Cables to the Ace," he asks a mother (*his* mother?): "What do you teach me?...What do you want of me?...What do you seek of me?"[21] (Daggy's italics)

Merton wrote of his mother in *Seven Storey Mountain:*

> My mother was an American. I have seen a picture of her as a rather slight, thin, sober little person with a serious and somewhat anxious and very sensitive face. And this corresponds with my memory of her—worried, precise, quick, critical of me, her son....
>
> It seems to me now, that Mother must have been a person full of insatiable dreams and of great ambition after perfection: perfection in art, in interior decoration, in dancing, in housekeeping, in raising children. Maybe that is why I remember her mostly as worried; since the imperfection of myself, her first son, had been a great deception. If this book does nothing else, it will certainly show that I was nobody's dream-child.[22]

We see in these reflections the conflicts of a child who never experienced his own spontaneous true self as good enough to satisfy his mother, internalizing (unconsciously) that observing, watchful, perfectionistic and critical parent, requiring an adaptation of his own performance in the form of a false self dedicated to trying to live up to that parent's expectations.

Journeys into Emptiness

While at Bradford Academy in Haverhill, Massachusetts, Ruth had been "a talented girl who used to dance to entertain her classmates, acted in plays, and wrote well for the college journal—articles, poems, and stories."[23] While she did not entirely abandon painting after Tom was born, one may well ask what it was like for this multitalented person who had already established her own capacity to be on stage and in the spotlight now to have her own aspirations deferred and all her time and energy channeled into the care of an infant. It is easy to understand how her "insatiable dreams" may have emerged in the form of perfectionistic demands for Tom, perhaps to fulfill her own unfulfilled dreams.

In addition, behind the question of the quality of Ruth's care of Tom is the fact of his parents' deeply troubled marriage. As struggling painters, Ruth and Owen were constantly having difficulties with money. Though Ruth's parents had money, she and Owen agreed not to ask for help, and she mainly kept to the bargain, except when Tom's health demanded medical attention. The tension and worry over money often erupted into shouting arguments, and Tom remembers his mother as "worried and drawn."[24] As an adult looking back on the relation between his parents and his mother's family, Merton wrote,

> Our family had been one of those curious modern households in which everybody was continually arguing and fighting, and in which there had been for years an obscure and complicated network of contentions and suppressed jealousies.[25]

How much of the "arguing and fighting" was between him and his younger brother, John Paul, Merton does not make clear. Certainly, in any case, that conflict involved not just money, but also the fact that Owen was away so much. Daggy continues,

> ...it is clear that Owen was gone from his family, pursuing his art, a great deal of the time. There are strong hints that the

marriage may have been headed for divorce when Ruth was diagnosed with terminal cancer. Even then, Owen was away much of the time. He was in England through much of her illness. As late as July 1921 (three months before her death) he was teaching art classes outside London.[26]

As every child knows, parental strife not only robs children of spontaneous attention and affection, it often leads one or both parents to paying an overly compensatory attention to the child (or dog, or cat) that is not at all in the service of the child's true needs. Insofar as one gets attention, it is not for one's true self, one's original feelings or desires, but for some vague, unidentifiable something, to guess which, a child develops a false self, a self that is perceived as wanted by the parent. Here, perhaps, in the writing of "Tom's Book," is the origin of Thomas Merton's experience of emptiness and the beginning of his lifelong search for a true self. His earliest memory of his mother was not of her attending to him or holding him, but of her writing down a record of what he did and said. This proved to be both a blessing and a curse for him: a blessing, in that, by his own writing, he could "mother" himself as he experienced his mother's presence in infancy; a curse, in that such an act requires a self-consciousness that proved a limitation to Merton's spiritual and psychological growth.

As we have only begun to discover with the work of Margaret Mahler and John Bowlby,[27] not mere holding, but the way a parent holds a child is of vital importance, conveying trustworthiness and support appropriate to the child's needs or conveying the mother's own anxiety, restlessness and/or irritability. Was Tom's shift from the wanting to be held at eight months to a restless resistance to being held at twenty-two months a reaction to his mother's failure to know how to hold him appropriately and a resistance to receiving the tension of *her* body? The feeding schedule was—par for the time—based on a clock, not on an attention to the infant's own expression of needs. Additionally, as has been documented by several of Merton's biographers, Ruth spent a great deal of time *reading* about how to be a mother, how to raise the infant child. While this was a constructive thing for her to do as a young mother in a foreign country with her own mother unavailable to consult, one may wonder about the lack of inherent, spontaneous mothering impulse. To what extent was Ruth *uncomfortable* being a mother? To what extent did she tend to turn her own mothering tasks into a performance for which she sought instruction from books? Did she not have an inner sense, derived from her own experience of being mothered, of how to mother her child?

Further, there is the question of "soothing" of an infant's physical, mental and emotional strivings. Ruth discovered that Tom could be quieted if he were either sung to or spoken to. She discovered the use of her voice as an instrument of soothing. This is a wonderful discovery for an infant—that physical and emotional tensions can be eased by certain sounds—music, the human voice. But to what extent was Tom's "kicking and screaming" the result of a failure of empathic holding, to which his mother's voice was an antidote. This question cannot be answered with certainty, but there is abundant evidence in Merton's adult life that he was very uneasy around women,[28] that his relationship with his own body was problematical[29] and that the pattern of Tom's restlessness which his mother observed at the age of twenty-two months continued throughout his life.[30]

Heinz Kohut, M.D., the psychoanalyst and founder of what developed into the school of depth psychology called self psychology, says of patients with narcissistic deficits,

> [They] will describe subtly experienced, yet pervasive feelings
> of emptiness and depression which...are alleviated as soon as
> the narcissistic transference has been established.[31]

Otto Kernberg, M.D., head of Cornell Westchester Psychiatric Hospital, while differing from Kohut in his understanding of the role of aggression in narcissistic disorders, nonetheless echoes Kohut's description:

> When, for various reasons, the normal relation between the
> self and the internal world of objects…is threatened, and
> what might be called an internal abandonment of the self on
> the part of internal objects or a loss of them occurs, patho-
> logical subjective experiences of a painful and disturbing
> nature develop. Among these experiences predominate a
> sense of emptiness and the futility of life, chronic restlessness
> and boredom, and a loss of the normal capacity for experi-
> encing and overcoming loneliness.[32]

When, therefore, Merton wrote, as quoted in the beginning of this
chapter, that he had his first experience of emptiness when he was
eleven, we know he should at least have included his mother's death
at the age of six, and we wonder whether, underneath his conscious
awareness, is a much larger, deeper dynamic going on that was set
in motion in the earliest weeks of his life. Psychological development
is sometimes compared to a stack of coins: To the degree that the
lower coins are skewed, higher ones are increasingly tenuous, and
have to compensate by a counter-skewing. No single coin being
somewhat off-center creates a problem, but the more off-center each
one is, a kind of "weakness" is built into the structure, for which subsequent ones have to compensate. Similarly, in psychological development, the earliest infant/mother interactions may not be
manifested as a significant problem if later things go well. But in
Merton's case, whatever degree of ambivalence was in place by his
twenty-second month, was compounded by his parents' marital
problems, his brother's birth when he was four, his mother's death
when he was six and then his father's death when he was sixteen.
The coins kept getting skewed.

Whatever quality of attention Ruth offered to Tom became
divided when his brother was born in 1918, a bit before Tom's
fourth birthday. Mott considers John Paul's birth significant:

> For three and a half years Ruth had found everything Tom
> did important enough to write down. Now, she was writing
> about John Paul. This baby took his rests. This baby had no

> temper tantrums. Tom now had temper tantrums enough for
> any number of children, yet these did not draw his parents'
> attention to him for long, and they went into no notes.[33]

As Mott concludes,

> His mother's discipline grew harsher....Love, with both encour-
> agement and correction, had been replaced by cold, intellectual
> criticism, making the three-year-old afraid.[34]

Merton's memory of the time contrasts himself and his brother.

> He [John Paul] was a child with a serener nature than mine,
> with not so many obscure drives and impulses. I remember
> that everyone was impressed by his constant and unruffled
> happiness. In the long evenings, when he was put to bed
> before the sun went down, instead of protesting and fighting,
> as I did when I had to go to bed, he would lie upstairs in his
> crib, and we would hear him singing a little tune.[35]

Although this report is from the "confessional" *Seven Storey
Mountain*, later writings convey the same flavor in Merton's perception of his brother, largely as John Paul's being more the kind of son
his mother wanted than Tom was. John Paul's significance, therefore,
was first and primarily in terms of confirming Tom's feeling that he
did not live up to his mother's expectations. Only later was Tom able
to appreciate his brother in his own right. Even then, at their last
meeting at Gethsemani Monastery before his brother was killed in
World War II,[36] he could not really tell him all that he felt.

Further, while one or two episodes of environmental failure do
not make a pathology, the repeated experience of parental expectations overriding one's inner experience may make for a lasting
wound and division within oneself. That repeated experience
becomes a pattern that we often remember as a single episode. Tom
never forgot his experience of being forced to follow what his mother
considered the most progressive educational principles. The only

thing that came of it was his being sent to his room because he did not spell *which* with an *h*.

> I remember brooding about this as an injustice. "What do they think I am, anyway?" After all, I was still only five years old.[37]

In October, a few months before Tom's seventh birthday, his mother was taken to the hospital. His portrayal of this episode is worth quoting in its entirety:

> Everything about sickness and death was more or less kept hidden from me, because consideration of these things might make a child morbid. And since I was destined to grow up with a nice, clear, optimistic and well-balanced outlook on life, I was never even taken to the hospital to see Mother, after she went there. And this was entirely her own idea.[38]
>
> How long she had been ill and suffering, still keeping house for us, not without poverty and hardship, without our knowing anything of what it was, I cannot say. But her sickness probably accounts for my memory of her as thin and pale and rather severe.
>
> With a selfishness unusual even in a child, I was glad to move from Flushing to my grandparents' house in Douglaston....I did not miss Mother very much, and did not weep when I was not allowed to go and see her....
>
> Then one day Father gave me a note to read. I was very surprised. It was for me personally, and it was in my mother's handwriting. I don't think she had ever written to me before—there had never been any occasion for it. Then I understood what was happening, although, as I remember, the language of the letter was confusing to me. Nevertheless, one thing was quite evident. My mother was informing me, by mail, that she was about to die, and would never see me again.
>
> I took the note out under the maple tree in the back yard, and worked over it, until I had made it all out, and had gathered what it really meant. And a tremendous weight of sadness and depression settled on me. It was not the grief of a child, with pangs of sorrow and many tears. It had something of the heavy perplexity and gloom of adult grief, and was therefore all

the more of a burden because it was, to that extent, unnatural. I suppose one reason for this was that I had more or less had to arrive at the truth by induction.

...My grandparents did not have a car, but they hired one to go in to the hospital, when the end finally came. I went with them in the car, but was not allowed to enter the hospital. Perhaps it was just as well. What would have been the good of my being plunged into a lot of naked suffering and emotional crisis without any prayer, any Sacrament to stabilize and order it, and make some kind of meaning out of it?...

I sat outside, in the car, with the hired driver....

It seemed like a very long time.

The car was parked in a yard entirely enclosed by black brick buildings, thick with soot. On one side was a long, low shed, and rain dripped from the eaves, as we sat in silence, and listened to the drops falling on the roof of the car. The sky was heavy with mist and smoke, and the sweet sick smell of hospital and gas-house mingled with the stuffy smell of the automobile.

But when Father and Pop and Bonnemaman and my Uncle Harold came out of the hospital door, I did not need to ask any questions. They were all shattered by sorrow.

When we got home to Douglaston, Father went into a room alone, and I followed him and found him weeping, over by the window....

They hired the same car again a day or so later, for another journey, and this time I am definitely glad I stayed in the car.

Mother, for some reason, had always wanted to be cremated. I suppose that fits in with the whole structure of her philosophy of life: a dead body was simply something to be put out of the way as quickly as possible....When life was finished, let the whole thing be finished, definitely, forever.

Once again, the rain fell, the sky was dark. I cannot remember if Cousin Ethel (my mother's cousin, who was a nurse) remained in the car to keep me from getting too gloomy. Nevertheless I was very sad. But I was not nearly so unhappy as I would have been if I had gone up to that mournful and appalling place and stood behind a big pane of glass to watch my mother's coffin glide slowly between the steel doors that led to the furnace.[39]

Like Shakyamuni Buddha and Dōgen, Thomas Merton lost his mother at a very young age. He was still six. She was thirty-four. Jung also, as we shall see, "*lost*" his mother when he was three years old, by her being hospitalized for several months for severe depression. As a description of Merton's first and greatest remembered experience of emptiness in his childhood, written some twenty years later from Gethsemani, it is worth careful reading.

The passage never ceases to convey intense feeling after many readings, largely, of course, because of the great quality of his writing. But it is great because the writer is completely present to his own memory and to conveying both mood and detail.

Reading it after our culture has discovered the importance of paying attention to dying, death and the grieving process, due to the writings of such people as Ernest Becker, Elizabeth Kubler-Ross and Ernest Grollman,[40] we may feel more shock than is warranted by the cultural assumptions of the time of the event. We may feel outraged at the seeming coldness and indifference of the family in their apparent failure to reach out to the boy, as well as concern over young Tom's own evident lack of feeling. But this would perhaps be to impose too much of our current values and awareness on a previous time, and we must guard against that.

Nevertheless, within Merton's own words, a number of points stand out. His facetiousness and anger in the opening lines regarding the way he was supposed to be, "nice, clear, optimistic and well-balanced," contrasts to "morbid." He indicts the entire family, perhaps especially his mother, when he says he was never taken to the hospital to see his mother and that it was "entirely her own idea." This is the clear, however restrained, voice of someone who is angry at being cheated of a once-in-a-lifetime opportunity for connectedness and reparative union with the most important person in his life. His own suppressed rage, unseemly to a monk, is quickly dropped to give way to compassion in his consideration of how long his mother had suffered and hid it from him, and this consideration leads him to excuse his having described his mother in negative terms. We see, in these few lines, the entire movement from outrage and attack to guilt and reparation, leading to his self-indictment, "...with a selfishness unusual even in a child...." But this indictment is made because there was no one around to hear him out, to help him bear the burden of his loss and to put his feelings into perspective. It is, in fact, this lack of mirroring, this failure to help a child understand feelings that he might have trouble putting into words, that leads to his blaming himself, accusing himself before all his readers as if to his confessor, "I did not miss Mother very much, and did not weep...."

Deeply wounding experiences of emptiness, especially at such an early age, are so new, so strange and powerful, that, without the assistance of adults to give verbal construction and meaning to the event, one's thoughts and feelings remain too strong and too inchoate even to acknowledge as real—one does not, in fact, know what one is feeling until given a framework for understanding the experience.

Furthermore, even though conceptually Merton understood his mother was dying, to know what that means at age six is too much to expect; there is no reference point. As has already been established, the emotional connection between mother and first son was already complicated, marked by an emotional distancing in which Merton experienced his mother as cold, critical and perfectionistic. She was already established in his mind, therefore, as someone to approach with a bit of caution, not as someone to whom and with whom he could express himself trustingly, spontaneously. The awareness, in this context, that she was going to die had to have produced mixed feelings in him: sadness, anger and guilt. We must assume, therefore, that part of his silence in this time is not only the wordless trauma of loss, but the mixture of conflicting emotions, none of which had a chance for a hearing.

If Ruth's choice to tell young Tom about her death by a handwritten note—which, parenthetically, already says a great deal about the parents' assumptions of their son's ability to communicate by the written word—strikes us as further evidence of a certain

distancing and coldness, the father's response must be acknowledged as equally complicit in distancing, unavailability and abandonment—and Owen was physically there!

The point here is not that Owen and Ruth were doing anything
terribly different from any other parents of their time—or, perhaps,
for that matter, most parents of our own time—nor that they were
demonstrating a lack of loving intention. Indeed, given the circumstances at the time, Ruth's note to Tom must be acknowledged as an
act of love and concern on her part. (One does wonder who did
what with John Paul, since he was two years old at the time. He
does not even appear in Merton's account of this event.) The point
is that Tom remembers, and that he remembers what he could not
feel. He is like a mute patient pointing to where it hurts, but no one
is paying any attention. And his experience was that, emotionally,
in this first consciously lived experience of emptiness, he was abandoned not only by the severing of the tie with this primary person
of his life, but was left without succor from anyone else.[19]

Merton's description of himself sitting in the car is resonant with
feelings projected onto sound and sights, the sole mirrors of his
experience. When the family comes back through the hospital door,
it is Merton noticing "Father and Pop and Bonnemaman...shattered
by sorrow," not the father or grandparents attending to the feelings
of the boy whom they left alone with a stranger. He is left alone to
deal with the experience in his own way. Then, most tellingly,
"when we got home to Douglaston, Father went into a room alone,
and I followed him and found him weeping, over by the window."

Owen, however meandering he may have been and however
many problems there may have been in the marriage, evidently
experienced Ruth's death as a loss, and was greatly shaken. But he
was too self-absorbed in his own grief to reach out to his son. The
son came to the father to console the father.

This movement, in which Tom initiated a connection that the
father failed to make and in which Tom extended himself in consideration of his father beyond his father's failure to consider him is

a pattern that continued throughout the rest of Merton's life. Owen Merton continued to be idealized by Thomas Merton, most of all, of course, in Tom's youth, in the writing of *Seven Storey Mountain*. But even in the journals, Thomas never really changed his view of his father as wonderful, loving, considerate and a "genius."

Merton's anger at the failure of his family to provide any religious direction in this encounter with death gets expressed in his attitude toward his mother's desire to be cremated. He is writing, of course, from the point of view of his still-new enthusiasm for Catholicism and monastic life, including the fact that at that time, the Catholic Church prohibited cremation, so Merton is in part apologizing for his mother's wish. In any case, he is certainly correct that a child needs, psychologically, emotionally, a framework of belief for understanding the meaning of death (all the more so in the absence of empathic parents!). But even more significantly, in this recognition of the need for something to fill a void may be seen the nascent strivings of Merton's spiritual search for a way of understanding this most profound experience of emptiness at such a young age.

In the preceding accounts of Nāgārjuna, Bodhidharma and Dōgen, there was a preestablished religious understanding to give a context for the meaning of the experience of emptiness in death, which gave an immediate form and direction to their lives. With Shakyamuni and with Merton, that religious understanding remained to be forged by their own inner struggle. For both of them, that took several more years. As we shall see, although Jung grew up within a specific religious context, with his father being a Protestant Christian pastor, that context was so problematic that Jung's entire career could be described as an effort to work his way through to an alternative.[42]

What Merton realized as he recalled the incident twenty years later was that the burden of grief was not normal for a child:

> It had something of the heavy perplexity and gloom of adult grief, and was therefore all the more of a burden because it was, to that extent, unnatural.

One wonders what Merton, or anyone else, thought the loss of one's mother might be like for a child. The experience of the loss of a parent is a once-in-a-lifetime event at any age. But when it happens in childhood, it has an incommensurability, a meaning with implications that one can only sense, awaiting later discovery. Merton contrasted his actual reaction to what he thought a child should have felt: "pangs of sorrow and many tears."

There is only one report from anyone of having seen Merton cry in public, and it comes from a fellow student who said he saw Merton cry when they were in class reading T. S. Eliot. Merton burst into tears at the phrase, "the greatest treason…is to do the right thing for the wrong reason."[43] This is suggestive not only of Merton's difficulty in expressing deep feeling, but of the fact that for people with great sensitivity and inner awareness, only statements that convey the full degree of inner complexity can touch, and thereby evoke, deep feeling.

But Merton's experiences of emptiness were not yet done.

LATER CHILDHOOD AND ADOLESCENCE

In a pattern that was to continue until his death, Owen Merton left Tom and John Paul with their mother's parents, the Jenkinses in Douglaston, Queens, New York, to pursue his painting career. Hardly had Tom adjusted to his father's absence when Owen reappeared to announce that he was taking Tom with him to Provincetown for the summer. In the fall, Tom was returned to the Jenkins's to resume school but, after only a few weeks, Owen returned to take Tom to Bermuda with him. Once in Bermuda, whenever Owen had a painting to sell, he would go back to New York, leaving Tom behind, perhaps with Evelyn Scott, the woman with whom Owen was involved. Between the time of his mother's death in Queens, when Tom was not quite seven, to his beginning at Oakham School in England at the age of fourteen, he moved eleven times and rarely stayed in one school for a full year. Owen was repeatedly leaving him, returning for him to take him somewhere else and then leaving him there while Owen went off for some artistic purpose. Also, throughout most of this period, John Paul remained with the Jenkinses in Queens, while Tom followed his father's travels, further deepening an estranged relationship between the brothers that was never overcome.

The disturbance these movements created for Tom occurred on at least four levels: (1) The constant appearing and disappearing of his father for a young boy who has just lost his mother must have exacerbated Merton's sense of the unreliability of grownups. (2) The continual moving meant there was no geographical place that could safely be called home. (3) In those crucial, tenuous years of early childhood, when the development of peer relationships and especially a special "chum," as Harry Stack Sullivan emphasized, is so important, Tom had no chance of developing such peer relationships, because his stay in any one place was always being truncated. (4) The constant motion contrasted directly to what was happening with his brother, John Paul, who was simply left in Douglaston with the Jenkinses. While it fed Tom's ego to be so chosen by the father, it also fed his feeling of superiority toward his sibling and deprived the two boys of the chance to develop a real relationship. In Merton's own words,

> I realized today after Mass, what a desperate, despairing childhood I had around the ages of seven-nine-ten, when Mother was dead and Father was in France and Algeria. How much it meant when he came and took me to France! It really saved me.[44]

The emotional point at that time was evidently Owen's appearing and claiming Tom at all. Abandoned by his mother's dying,

Merton naturally put even more hope and longing into his relationship with his father and was grateful every time Owen came
for him. This act, each time it happened, in which Owen manifested his desire to have his son with him, may well be seen to
have "saved" Tom from complete despair. Owen clearly loved Tom,
enjoyed his company and introduced him into the world of seeing things with the eye of an artist.

Nevertheless, insofar as one of the kinds of experiences of emptiness is loneliness and its remedy lies only in a closely felt intimate
relationship with someone, the experience of Tom Merton in his
childhood until his arrival at Columbia must be recognized as an
emotional drought created by chronic dislocation. Merton managed
these times, from all the records, with an admirable adaptability and
sociability, due to his great intelligence, natural interest in the world
and outgoingness. These must be seen, however, as Merton himself
saw them, as expressions of a false self that hid an inner emptiness
that no one was able to see, much less penetrate. In his own words,
"When I reveal most, I hide most."[45]

Merton had an extremely adaptable and serviceable social personality, but it revealed nothing of what was going on inside him
on the deeper levels, at least before his conversion, because he
himself barely knew what he was feeling. He was trying too hard
to escape from the impact of so much dislocation and death. That
he was not expressing feelings on a deep level was indicated in a
foreshadowing event in the fall of 1924, when a message was sent
to nine-year-old Tom that his father was gravely ill and had been
taken to a hospital in London. Tom "accepted the news without
response and went out to play."[46] Far from indicating a disinterest
in his father's life or death, Tom's response is that of someone who
has already been too traumatized by death, including the repeated
deaths of his father's leaving him after each time he retrieved him,
to express the magnitude of the implication that his last loving
connection with the world was about to die. That time, that particular interpretation proved false. Owen recovered.

Journeys into Emptiness

In the middle of Tom's second year at Oakham School in England at fifteen, he was unexpectedly given a position on the cricket team, which allowed him to go to Ealing; he was told en route that his father was at his Aunt Maud's. He realized he had been given his position in order to enable him to be near his father, with the implication that his father was sick. Merton said,

> I could not believe that Father was ill. If he were, I supposed that they would have made more fuss about it. During the tea interval, I went over, and passed through the green wooden door in the wall to Aunt Maud's garden and entered the house and went upstairs. Father was in bed. You could not tell from his appearance how ill he was: but I managed to gather it from the way he talked and from his actions. He seemed to move with difficulty and pain, and he did not have much to say. When I asked him what was the matter, he said nobody seemed to know.
>
> I went back to the cricket pavilion a little saddened and unquiet. I told myself that he would probably get better in a week or two.[47]

Owen did seem to get better, until he took Tom with him to Aberdeen, Scotland, in the summer. Before the summer ended, Owen was sent back to a hospital in London. Still no diagnosis having been established, the father asked his son to pray for him. Tom remained in Scotland until one day when he received a telegram from his father, who was still in the London hospital. The telegram said, "Entering New York harbor. All well."

> I hung up the receiver and the bottom dropped out of my stomach. I walked up and down in the silent and empty house.... There was nobody there. There was nobody in the whole huge house.
>
> I sat there in the dark, unhappy room, unable to think, unable to move, with all the innumerable elements of my isolation crowding in upon me from every side: without a home, without a family, without a country, without a father, apparently without any friends, without any interior peace or

confidence or light or understanding of my own—without God, too, without God, without heaven, without grace, without anything. And what was happening to Father, there in London? I was unable to think of it.[48]

Tom's Uncle Ben gave him the news that Owen had a malignant tumor on the brain. When Tom went to London to see him in the hospital, Owen asked him to pray for him again.

In the fall, Tom returned to school at Oakham. Then he went to London to see his father, who by that time could no longer speak and had a swollen lump on his forehead from the tumor.

> ...the sorrow of his great helplessness suddenly fell upon me like a mountain. I was crushed by it. The tears sprang to my eyes. Nobody said anything more.
>
> I hid my face in the blanket and cried. And poor Father wept, too. The others stood by. It was excruciatingly sad. We were completely helpless. There was nothing anyone could do.
>
> When I finally looked up and dried my tears, I noticed that the attendants had put screens all around the bed. I was too miserable to feel ashamed of my un-English demonstration of sorrow and affection....
>
> One day I found his bed covered with little sheets of blue note-paper on which he had been drawing. And the drawings were real drawings. But they were unlike anything he had ever done before—pictures of little, irate Byzantine-looking saints with beards and great halos.
>
> Of us all, Father was the only one who really had any kind of a faith.[49]

Tom went back to school until he was summoned to the headmaster one morning and presented a telegram to the effect that his father was dead. It was January 18, 1931, just a few days before Tom's sixteenth birthday.[50] Owen was forty-two.

> The death of my father left me sad and depressed for a couple of months. But that eventually wore away. And when it did, I found myself completely stripped of everything that

impeded the movement of my own will to do as it pleased. I imagined that I was free. And it would take me five or six years to discover what a frightful captivity I had got myself into. It was in this year, too, that the hard crust of my dry soul finally squeezed out all the last traces of religion that had ever been in it. There was no room for any God in that empty temple full of dust and rubbish which I was now so jealously to guard against all intruders, in order to devote it to the ownership of my own stupid will. And so I became the complete twentieth century man. I now belonged to the world in which I lived. I became a true citizen of my own disgusting century: the century of poison gas and atomic bombs....[51]

As another profound, major experience of emptiness, the death of Merton's father just before his sixteenth birthday was much more obviously complicated than the death of his mother, not only because he was older, psychologically more mature and resourceful, but because of the direct juxtaposition of the experience of death and the experience of life. Merton was just beginning to feel the full strength of adolescent *eros*, and suddenly *thanatos* came in, lest he had forgotten his first lesson, and pulled the ground out from under him. The sadness and depression vied powerfully with his urge toward life and its multiple possibilities. In the passage above, Merton rues the force of his will, which, from the perspective of the monastery, seemed to him a "captivity." What was happening on an internal level was that Merton had lost the last major container (however flawed and unreliable) for his developing sense of self and was now experiencing the full force of adolescent drives without the limit of a parental connection.

If a sense of self has not yet emerged, the onset of strong erotic drives, drives that include sexuality but go far beyond it, are experienced as alien, as "not-me"; one feels driven by them rather than empowered. To manage his life with such opposing tensions, Merton subconsciously set up a division within himself between the feeling-filled self connected to his father and the erotic drives toward resolution in things and people outside himself. This was the "hard crust of my dry soul," which served to wall off not only the pain of his loss but the basic questions of life which that experience of emptiness, along with his first one, raised. This subconscious splitting—which we noted in the stories of Shakyamuni and Dōgen, and which, as we shall see, was predominant in Jung—served a survival purpose but required twenty-odd years before it could be overcome and an integration achieved.

The effect of this experience of emptiness in his father's death, must therefore be seen as extending over the next several years, manifesting itself in a certain hyperactivity, somewhat difficult to distinguish from ordinary adolescence, replete with the confusion between what is really life and what is really death, thus raising fundamental questions about the meaning and purpose of life. Coming as it did in adolescence, the death of Merton's father planted even more seeds for the burning questions of identity and purpose, seeds that took several years to become manifested in his becoming a Catholic and entering a monastery.

There are several parallels, as well as important differences, between Merton's experience of his father's death and of his mother's. One of the most stunning parallels is the fact that the news of Merton's father's death is delivered by written message. It was, of course, tendered by the headmaster, but one is impressed by the arm's-length manner in which Merton was once again left to deal with such an important event by himself. The fact that it was anticipated never really eases the impact of the death of someone so close.

What was new in his father's death was that Merton knew what he felt and was able to express it. It was a huge loss to him in a conscious way that his mother's death was not. Merton was also able to find, in the telling of his father's story, the seeds to his later interest in Catholicism: his father's request that Tom pray for him and the presence of the Byzantine icons were used by the zealous new monk to see in his father a foretaste of his own religious direction.

There was, most importantly, another dynamic at work in Merton's experience of the loss of his father. When his mother died, Merton immediately began idealizing his father and absorbing any attention he could get with a gratitude that ignored the fact that his father was also repeatedly abandoning him. At the death of his mother, young Tom Merton held on to his father as the primary connection to being cared about and having some sense of security in the world. The bond between them was essentially strengthened upon Ruth's death. When his father died, Merton was left not only without external mother and father, but psychologically, with no one to whom he felt strongly connected, and thus no one to serve as a container for the powerful feelings and energies of the teenage orphan. In a way that was always true, but was now literally and strikingly true, Merton was homeless.

As William Shannon, one of the major biographers of Merton and general editor of the five volumes of Merton's letters, avers, "Thomas Merton never really had a home."[52] Shannon intends this on many levels:

> "Home" is a rich symbol with many layers of meaning. It is a paradigm, an exemplary symbol of harmony and wholeness. "Home" gives us our place in the world. It roots us in the earth.…We go back home in order to find our truest self. Our actual experience of home, while it almost always falls short of this ideal, reflects dimly as in a mirror the reality the symbol is intended to express.…
>
> …"Home" easily takes on the nature of a primordial symbol; that is, it can designate the place from which we come (paradise) and the place to which we ultimately return (paradise regained). Understood in this sense, "home" roots us in eternity. It is the symbol of our final integration; we achieve perfect wholeness in God. This is the deepest meaning of "going home."[53]

What Shannon is describing is the fact that psychologically Thomas Merton never had a place that was trustworthy, where he could feel his truest self acknowledged and supported. The central drive of Thomas Merton's religious quest was for the recovery of his true self, which had been sacrificed, first to his mother's perfectionism and then to the need to constantly adapt to the multiple changes of geography and people, and, finally, to the need to survive practically and emotionally on his own after the death of his father. What strikes contemporary readers most in Merton's descriptions of his parents' deaths is the failure of anyone to be present to him in a deeply compassionate and caring way. That it was "un-English" to display emotions (as well, one might say, as "unmanly") does not take away from the premature independence the young Merton was forced to take upon himself.

As D. W. Winnicott points out, in *Home Is Where We Start From*,[54] when the environment does not provide enough support for the inchoate personality, but rather requires the individual to adapt to environmental needs at the expense of its own spontaneous needs, such requirements are experienced as impingements, and, in its extreme form,

> there is not even a resting-place for individual experience, and the result is a failure in the primary narcissistic state to evolve an individual. The "individual" then develops as an extension of the shell rather than that of the core, and as an extension of the impinging environment. What there is left of a core is hidden away and is difficult to find even in the most far-reaching analysis. The individual then exists by not being found. The true self is hidden, and what we have to deal with clinically is the complex false self whose function is to keep this true self hidden. The false self may be conveniently society-syntonic, but the lack of a true self gives an instability which becomes more evident the more society is deceived into thinking that the false self is the true self. The patient's complaint is a sense of futility.[55]

The experience of futility is another, crucial form of emptiness, and Merton began to experience this deeply after his father died and projected it out onto my own disgusting century: the century of poison gas and atomic bombs. [Merton experienced himself as a] man living on the doorsill of the Apocalypse, a man with veins full of poison, living in death. Baudelaire could truly address me, then, reader: *Hypocrite lecteur, mon semblable, mon frère....*[56]

Merton graduated from Oakham and began studies at Clare College, Cambridge when he was eighteen. His godfather and namesake, Tom Bennett, an affluent and reputable physician in London, with whom he had often stayed, had accepted the task of acting *in loco parentis* and was encouraging Merton to prepare for diplomatic service in England. After his first year at Cambridge, Merton spent a summer in Douglaston, Queens, New York, with his grandparents, fully expecting to return to Cambridge the following fall. However, Merton's behavior during the previous term at Cambridge elicited a different response from his godfather.

Merton had fathered a child out of wedlock, spent a good deal of his time carousing with fellow students and had not performed well at Clare College. He had developed a reputation for such carousing that he was in conflict with his landlord over his "having women in his rooms," and Iris Bennett, his godfather's wife, told him during one of his visits, that she did not want him coming in at very late hours, "usually drunk and always noisy."[57] Bennett was fed up. After making some sort of legal agreement with the mother-to-be and agreeing not to tell Merton's grandparents about it, Bennett wrote to Merton in America and suggested that he would do well to stay there and that his hopes for diplomatic service were ended.

In some mixture, perhaps, of relief and pique at the rejection, Merton immediately agreed with the verdict. In Merton's mind, the experiences of his last several years in England had culminated in a sense that

there was some kind of subtle poison in Europe, something that corrupted me, something the very thought and scent of which sickened me, repelled me....What was wrong with this place, with all these people? Why was everything so *empty?*...For those who had nothing but this *emptiness* in the middle of them, no doubt the things they had to do and to suffer during the war filled that emptiness with something stronger and more resilient than their pride....[58]

The cause of this experience of emptiness was not mere grief over his father's death. This was the culmination of a lifetime, to that point, of abandonment, rejection and suffering that reached so deep that ordinary life, the ordinary pleasures of life, had turned sour. To yet another European (born and educated), America seemed to promise a new life.

One wonders about the meaning of Merton's impregnating a woman at this time in his life. His father died January 18, 1931, a few days before Tom's sixteenth birthday. In June of 1934, Tom Bennett wrote his "don't come back" letter to Merton in America, suggesting he stay there. To what extent was Merton being driven by the same primordial instinctual to make new life that moved Gandhi to break his policy of sexual abstinence and have intercourse the night after his father died, another juxtaposition of *eros* and *thanatos?*

The death of any man's father opens up for him the great abyss of inevitable death, on the edge of which he stands without a mediator. The son whose father died is now in an inexorable "next" position and feels, on whatever level of consciousness, his own mortality in his bones. Regardless of age, the son seeks consolation in two directions—from mother, or the mothering presence of a wife or lover—and in having children. However, Merton had neither mother nor wife nor serious girlfriend. In fact, as far as can be known, he was utterly without consolers.

Perhaps the coup de grâce was the death of his Aunt Maud in November of 1933, two years after his father died. This was clearly a time of great inner turmoil and obsession with sex and death for Merton, as indicated in his "Perry Street Journal" by his excesses of lust[59] and the special, one might even say numinous experience at a party in the middle of November of that year, in which it appears Merton acted out the role of Christ in the crucifixion, an incident that left a scar on his hand.[60] The connection is made directly by Merton in a sentence left out of the final edition of *Seven Storey Mountain*:

> It was embarrassing to receive on my cheek the chaste kiss of one of my aunts, my Father's sister, when my mouth still burned with the contrast of the night before.[61]

In a strange way, Merton was more forthcoming regarding his feelings about his Aunt Maud's death than he was about that of either of his parents'. He also projected those feelings, once again, onto her English countryside and culture.

> They committed the thin body of my poor Victorian angel to the clay of Ealing, and buried my childhood with her. In an obscure, half-conscious way, I realized this and was appalled. She it was who had presided in a certain sense over my most innocent days. And now I saw those days buried with her in the ground.
> ...I could no longer believe in the pretty country churches, the quiet villages, the elm-trees along the common where the cricketers wait in white....none of this any longer belonged to me, for I had lost it all. Its fragile web of charmed associations had been broken and blown away and I had fallen through the surface of old England into the hell, the vacuum and the horror that London was nursing in her avaricious heart.[62]

It is, thus, in the context of his father's death and the death of the last of his family (except for his brother and the distant relations in New Zealand) that Merton's carousing and getting someone pregnant must be seen. This is not the mere (if it can ever be called "mere") foolishness of teen adolescence. Adolescence is always marked by a deep search for identity, as Erik Erikson has amply shown,[63] and it always has death as a timpanic basso continuo because one is so physiologically full of life. The death of Merton's father when he was sixteen magnified the usual adolescent struggle exponentially by robbing him of the last vestige of felt-connectedness and stability. It was like pressing the accelerator to the floor, disabling the brakes and letting go of the steering wheel all at the same time. To have a child in this context is to insert a link of continuity into the future, restoring continuity in the forward direction since both connections to the past have been broken.

When, therefore, Merton wrote, as above, "Why was everything so empty?", the emptiness of that experience had a lot in it: much grief (loss of both parents and his aunt), much uncertainty (his academic performance was mediocre to poor, clearly not up to his godfather's standards), much fear (now clearly an orphan, alone) and much guilt (for the dissipation of energy, money and drink, for the child to be born out of wedlock).[64] The emptiness consisted in the lack of any mirroring person to validate Merton's experience and to establish a continuity of self by reflecting back to him his self, that it is he who is going through so much discontinuity. This experience of emptiness often leads one, as was seen in Dōgen's search for an authentic teacher, to embark on a quest. Without a mirroring presence, one experiences so much inner and outer turmoil as turbulence without a center or a container, as in Yeats's "Second Coming,"

> Turning and turning in the widening gyre
> The falcon cannot hear the falconer;
> Things fall apart; the centre cannot hold;
> Mere anarchy is loosed upon the world
> The blood-dimmed tide is loosed, and everywhere
> The ceremony of innocence is drowned
> The best lack all conviction, while the worst
> Are full of passionate intensity.[65]

The loss of a "centre" that unleashes anarchy was, for Merton, simultaneously a personal experience and a sociopolitical one of England on the verge of war. Merton sees in the events of the time a reflection of his own lost innocence, "lack of conviction" and directionless "passionate intensity." Having a child carried the unconscious intent of reestablishing a center and a continuity for the adolescent Tom Merton.

In the England of the time, especially the England of Tom Bennett, getting someone pregnant was a thing to be swept under the rug, most especially when, as is supposed, the woman was from a lower class. It is clear that some legal and monetary settlement was made with the mother-to-be, thus ending the discussion and the issue, as far as Tom Bennett was concerned. Merton did not forget his responsibility entirely, however, and in the will that he had to draw up upon making final solemn vows he designated part of his estate to go to the mother and child, if they could be found. They never were.[66]

If Merton's carousing and philandering increasingly irritated the adults in his life, he was, from the time of his father's death, also developing a capacity for self-reflection and solitude. It had begun while he was still at Oakham: "...when he wanted to be alone, Tom climbed Brooke Hill."[67] He had already formed the habit of writing a journal, recording experiences and reflections on a regular basis, thus doing for himself what his mother had done: holding him through the written word. On his second trip to Rome,[68] in February of 1933, Merton found himself going to many churches, studying the mosaics. He began using a Bible to find the references depicted in the mosaics.

Michael Mott reports succinctly, "Because he was so often in churches, he began to pray."[69] But surely many atheists and agnostics, as well as other non-Christians have spent hours in churches studying the art without making an effort to pray. Clearly, Merton was developing an inner life, a consciousness of something too subtle and important to be named as yet. Paradoxically and tellingly, every effort Merton made to pray increased his self-consciousness. He worried how others perceived him as his lips formed words.[70] At one point Merton focused on the precise way one should behave in the church he entered, and the question

arose whether to buy a candle for his mother or for his father, and
how they might respond if they saw him doing so. The theme of
the inner struggle clarifies:

> Something held him back. His mother might have seen his
> action as a betrayal. He was a little afraid of her, even beyond
> death. What he could remember best was that she could be
> cutting and cold and intellectual, first filling a small boy with
> a sense of his own importance, then showing him how inad-
> equate he was.[71]

Later that night, back in his *pensione*,

> Suddenly it seemed to me that Father, who had now been
> dead more than a year, was there with me. The sense of his
> presence was as vivid and as real and as startling as if he had
> touched my arm or spoken to me. The whole thing passed in
> a flash, but in that flash, instantly, I was overwhelmed with a
> sudden and profound insight into the misery and corruption
> of my own soul, and I was pierced deeply with a light that
> made me realize something of the condition I was in, and I
> was filled with horror at what I saw, and my whole being
> rose up in revolt against what was within me, and my soul
> desired escape and liberation and freedom from all this with
> an intensity and an urgency unlike anything I had ever
> known before. And now I think for the first time in my
> whole life I really began to pray—praying not with my lips
> and with my intellect and imagination, but praying out of the
> very roots of my life and of my being, and praying to the God
> I had never known.
> ...I was talking to [Father] as well as to God.[72]

A few days later, Merton went to visit Tre Fontane, a Trappist
monastery outside San Paolo, a basilica in Rome. "...and the
thought grew on me: 'I should like to become a Trappist monk.'"[73]

Like Shakyamuni, Nāgārjuna, Bodhidharma and Dōgen,
Merton's experience of emptiness triggered by death—for him, in
the death of both of his parents and his aunt—led him to turn

inward and to begin entertaining the pursuit of a spiritual path. The experience of emptiness in the loss of his parents turned into an experience of the emptiness of ordinary life ("...the fragile web of charmed associations had been broken...") and the emptiness of his own life. In a soliloquy reminiscent of Sartre's *La Nausée*, Merton wrote,

> I fell into the middle of a great depression, and within ten or fifteen minutes everything around me and in me turned sour. I could actually almost feel myself go sour, I could feel myself turning to ashes inside....I became convinced that I was an unbearable person, my ideas were impossible, my desires were beastly, that my vanity was an offense and my pride monstrous.[74]

COLUMBIA AND CONVERSION

When the door closed on continuing studies at Cambridge, Merton transferred to Columbia College in New York City, starting in January 1933. During that time, he lived with his grandparents, the Jenkinses in Douglaston, Queens, and commuted to Columbia. He also joined a fraternity, Alpha Delta Phi, on 114th Street.

In spite of Merton's derisive comment about Columbia's motto, to the effect that *In lumine tuo videbimus lumen* should have been changed to the realistic *In lumine Randall videbimus Dewey,*[75] a slur on two of its important philosophers, Columbia was a truly bounteous alma mater for Thomas Merton. From her he received three precious gifts: confirmation of his ability to write, a group of friends that remained vitally important to him for the rest of his life and an intellectual experience that gave scope and validation to his primary interests in art, literature and religion.

The confirmation of his writing ability came from his teacher-become-friend, Mark Van Doren, whose class Merton rather accidentally entered. Van Doren was one of the giants of Columbia's faculty, and Merton developed a lifelong friendship with him that included Van Doren's ongoing assessment of and commentary on Merton's various writings. In addition, Merton was actively involved in most of Columbia's journalistic enterprises: He contributed to the *Columbia Review*. He was on the contributing board of the *Columbia Spectator*. He became editor of Columbia's *Jester*, a magazine devoted to comedy and satire, to which Merton contributed not only writing but cartoons.

A fellow Columbia student in those days, Barry Ulanov, now McIntosh Professor of English Emeritus at Barnard College, Columbia University, was editor of the *Columbia Review* and received Merton's first religious article. He was also associate editor of the *Jester* and remembers Merton as "full of jokes and cartoons. It was surprising that he was capable of the seriousness of monastic life."[76]

In his senior year, Merton was also editor of the school yearbook, *Columbiana*. In 1937, he was voted "best writer" in a campus poll.[77] Perhaps most important of all, the friends Merton made at Columbia were themselves all writers of varying ilk, people who shared Merton's love of and preoccupation with words, so that the group shared their work and their enthusiasms in day-to-day (and night-'til-dawn) conversation.

That group of friends included Robert Lax, Ed Rice, Robert Giroux and Dan Walsh. Lax and Rice would become writers. Giroux would become a writer, editor and publisher (Farrar, Straus and Giroux, Publishers). Walsh was at first a mentor for Merton, introduced him to Thomism and Scholasticism, then guided him in his quest for a monastic order. Columbia and America offered to Merton an enticing, open field in which he could feel free to express himself and to explore ideas with others who took them as seriously as he did. Never before had he experienced such joy among peers, nor did he again, until he established his own coterie of friends from the monastery via correspondence in letters, poems and books to and from many major figures of the world in literature, poetry, philosophy, politics and religion in the late fifties and sixties. Merton's Columbia friendships were the first important, sustained relationships he had. They were based on the importance of ideas, the importance of writing, and, as became increasingly clear, the importance of the spiritual in the artistic and literary worlds. For the first time in his life, something human held—didn't die or discontinue.

> God brought me and half a dozen others together at Columbia, and made us friends, in such a way that our friendship would work powerfully to rescue us from the confusion and the misery in which we had come to find ourselves.[78]

Columbia was preeminently a place of ideas. Merton was exploring territory for which there was precious little guidance in his family and social background. The great cauldron of experiences of emptiness with which he was struggling needed conceptual ideas and vision that reached as deep and as far as his experiences required. Coming from a family that was not particularly religious and was in fact somewhat consciously agnostic and from an English culture whose highest virtue seemed to be "gentlemanliness" and self-containment, there was little in Merton's background to help him deal with the inner experiences of emptiness and his need for dealing with them in a productive and maturing way. Though he felt aperiodic urges to pray and felt the need to be alone from time to time, nothing in his background prepared him for sorting through the inchoate urges he felt inside.

If, as mentioned above, the experience of emptiness in the death of his father left him like a driver of a car with his foot on the accelerator all the way to the floor but with no brakes and no hand on the steering wheel, he needed not only to take hold of the steering wheel, but also a map of the new inner territory he had come upon. The primary avenues available were from his parents' vocations and interests: art and writing. Merton had, therefore, to discover and forge a way into his inner experience. His journal writing helped, but he needed an intellectual framework, a cognitive pipeline down into his inner depths, to enable a sorting through and a structuring of his understanding of himself.

At the suggestion of his friend, Robert Lax, Merton read Aldous Huxley's *Ends and Means*. In Huxley, Merton found a kindred spirit, a man of intellectual stature who was still engaged in a quest for religious and philosophical truth. Then Merton passed by the Doubleday bookstore and was moved to buy a book he saw in the window, Etienne Gilson's *The Spirit of Medieval Philosophy*. When it came time to propose a thesis for his M.A., Merton decided that it would be on William Blake, without having done a lot of investigation as to where this might lead him. A Hindu monk, Bramachari, appeared among Merton's friends, and when Merton asked him what he would suggest for a guide to the spiritual life, he surprised Merton by recommending St. Augustine's *Confessions* and Thomas à Kempis's *Imitation of Christ*. Thus Merton began laying in the intellectual pipeline to the depths of his experience of emptiness.

Lax was also interested in mysticism, but in his own Jewish tradition. Together they played a game they called "Subway Mysticism," in which, as the subway took off they would go into a trance.[79]

It was in writing his master's thesis that Merton began to make the deliberate connection between the life and mind of art, with which he was so familiar from his father and mother, and the life of the spirit. His thesis was titled, *Nature and Art in William Blake: an Essay in Interpretation*. Whatever the merits of the thesis may or may not be,[80] doing the essay served as a bridge between what Merton knew from his own artistic eye and the construction of spiritual meaning. This was further enabled by his discovery of Jacques Maritain's *Art and Scholasticism*. Although the conclusion that Merton came to in the late '30s and early '40s was that art and religion were basically inimical to each other,[81] nonetheless, these studies enabled Merton to make an intellectual transition from what was familiar to him to what was gnawing and numinous within, a nascent experience of emptiness that would carry him from the negative experiences of emptiness through loss, to the positive experience of emptiness that was a reflection of Christian *kenosis*. Prophetically, included in the bibliography of Merton's thesis are two entries that would take Merton several years to view seriously: one was a book on Meister Eckhart, the other a book on Zen Buddhism by D. T. Suzuki.[82] The thesis also contains quotations from Chuang-Tzu, whom he was later to translate in his own words with the help of John Wu.[83]

Merton was clearly tilling intellectual soil in preparation for a major transformation of consciousness. It is worth noting that Merton basically grew up without a *Weltanschauung*, that is to say, without a clearly-laid-out system of understanding the meaning of life and one's role in it. The closest thing to a systematized world-view that he had encountered before Columbia was in the form of what he considered an English gentleman's Christianity, a superficial touting of the civil manners of the British upper class under the guise of Christianity.

> "Buggy's" [the headmaster at Oakham] interpretation of the word "charity" in this passage [I Corinthians 13]...was that it simply stood for "all that we mean when we call a chap a 'gentleman.'" In other words, charity meant good-sportsmanship, cricket, the decent thing, wearing the right kind of clothes, using the proper spoon, not being a cad or a bounder.[84]

However much a spiritual path may emphasize experience "beyond words and letters" (Zen) or in silence (Christian contemplative prayer), there must be a certain kind of cognitive mapping out of the religious terrain—interpreting the import of an experience, the meaning of life, of self, of purpose—in verbal and cognitive ways. Thomas Merton, however steeped he was in European culture, had never had a systematic outlining of the Christian *Weltanschauung*, and therefore had to construct it piecemeal as part of his search. Such a map may be argued over or rejected, but having one at least gives one the basis for an inner conversation.

There were two more events that pushed Merton's struggle to a greater intensity. In November of 1936, his mother's father, Sam

Jenkins, "Pop," died. In August of the next year, Merton's grand-mother, to whom he felt close and called Bonnemaman, died. Shortly after, Merton described an experience, "…as if some center of balance within me had been unexpectedly removed, and as if I were about to plunge into a blind abyss of *emptiness* without end."[85]

Now twenty-one, he had thoughts of suicide and wondered if he were having a nervous breakdown.

> Now my life was dominated by something I had never known before: fear.
>
> Here I was, scarcely four years after I had left Oakham and walked out into the world that I thought I was going to ran-sack and rob of all its pleasures and satisfactions. I had done what I intended and now I found that it was I who was emp-tied and robbed and gutted. What a strange thing! In filling myself, I had emptied myself. In grasping things, I had lost everything….
>
> If my nature had been more stubborn in clinging to the pleasures that disgusted me: if I had refused to admit that I was beaten by this futile search for satisfaction where it could not be found, if my moral and nervous constitution had not caved in under the weight of my own emptiness,[86] who can tell what would have happened to me?[87]

●

> By the time I was ready to begin the actual writing of my thesis, that is, around the beginning of September 1938, the groundwork of conversion was more or less complete.…I began to want to take the necessary means to achieve this union, this peace. I began to desire to dedicate my life to God, to His service.[88]

As a sign of his resolution, Merton cancelled a date with a girl-friend on Long Island and stayed in Manhattan to go to Mass on Sunday—"the first time I had ever really spent a sober Sunday in New York."[89] He reported that his reading became increasingly

Catholic, that he read James Joyce's *Ulysses* [90] two or three times and became absorbed in the poetry of Gerard Manley Hopkins.

At one point, Merton was reading a biography of Hopkins and became focused on an exchange of letters Hopkins had had with Cardinal Newman about becoming a Catholic.

> All of a sudden, something began to stir within me, something began to push me, to prompt me. It was a movement that spoke like a voice.
> "What are you waiting for?" it said. "Why are you sitting here? Why do you still hesitate? You know what you ought to do? Why don't you do it?"[91]

After a bit more argument with himself, one more cigarette and some more pacing, Merton went down to the church where he had recently attended his first Mass, Corpus Christi on 121st Street, and asked to see Father Ford. The priest was not in, and Merton turned to leave. As he walked out, the priest was coming up the walk toward him. Merton approached him and said, "Father, I want to become a Catholic."

As we have already seen, Merton's interest was never in being a mere convert, but in becoming a monk, and to be one at one of the most severely ascetic monasteries in the United States at that time. As with everything in his life, Merton's decision to become a Catholic and a monk was not simple. No sooner did he have one thought than its opposite arose with equal force and conviction. Although he had had the thought of becoming a Trappist when visiting Tre Fontaine in Italy, it took him another two years after his baptism before he entered the gates of Gethsemani to petition for acceptance as a novice. It took those two years for Merton to clarify and consolidate his conviction to enter monastic life. As Brother Patrick Hart, O.C.S.O., Merton's last secretary, put it,

> Merton could not have come here directly from Columbia and Perry Street. He was not ready for it. He needed the time at St. Bonaventure's to prepare himself for this kind of life.[90]

Merton did not at first believe himself capable of being a monk, much less a Trappist. He applied to the Franciscans, but when he fully revealed the things about which he felt most doubt and shame (which included, presumably, his having had a child out of wed-lock[71]), he was roundly shamed and told to withdraw his application. Devastated, he went to a local priest for consolation and the rejection was repeated. Feeling defeated and reconciled to lay life as a writer, Merton joined the Third Order of Franciscans. After a trip to Cuba, from which he received great inspiration, a year finishing his M.A. and a year of teaching at St. Bonaventure's in Olean, New York, still restless and fighting within himself for more piety and less partying, Merton was finally pushed to press his case with the Trappists with the encouragement of his friend, Dan Walsh. In Lax's inimitable way of cutting to the heart of matters, he told Merton, "All that is necessary to be a saint is to want to be one."[72]

The entire period between Merton's father's death and his entrance into Gethsemani must be seen, in retrospect, as a contin-uing process of his working through his feelings of emptiness in their continually accumulating forms in ways that enabled him to take those initially negative experiences and channel them toward positive direction and outcome. During this period, which included the additional deaths of his Aunt Maud and his grandparents, Pop and Bonnemaman, Merton worked assiduously at constructing an intellectual pipeline to his inner self so that he could establish a relationship to it that could nourish him and lead him to his true self. Without his studies with Mark Van Doren, his readings of Huxley, Gilson and Maritain, Merton would not have been able to develop a mind that had a place in it for a real experience of God. The position taken here is that Merton found in the religious lan-guage of emptiness a way of expressing and working with a deep, inner experience that, under depth psychotherapy, might have been confirmed for him and worked with in a less abstract, more directly personal way.

GETHSEMANI: THE MONASTERY AS A CONTAINER

As has been seen with Merton, the experience of emptiness as loss and abandonment can create great strivings, urges and impulses to flee from the inner experience, to focus on external things and people to divert attention from the inner place of trauma. What is required, if an experience of emptiness is to become transformative, is a container within which all those strivings can be experienced and attended to, learned from, rather than run from. Otherwise, energy is lost, direction is whimsical and unfocused, and years go by without purpose.

On the conscious level, one enters a monastery (or convent), whether Buddhist, Christian or otherwise, for a spiritual purpose: For Zen Buddhists (whose aspirations go beyond becoming temple priests), it is to become enlightened; for Christians, it is to become one with God. On a subconscious or unconscious level, attaining one's spiritual goal entails a search for the true self. To be ready to enter a monastery, one has already made a judgment that ordinary life in the "world" is not satisfying or fulfilling and that one's true self is to be found by entering the cloister. In depth psychology, a similar "setting apart" is required. Jung constructed his own "monastery," which he called "the tower," with the explicit purpose of giving himself a place for his true self to thrive. One may say, therefore, that one enters a monastery to discover one's true self.

The meaning of the true self varies within each of the traditions studied here. For Zen Buddhists, the true self is discovered as one forgets oneself and becomes enlightened by the ten thousand things. For Christians, that true self is "hidden with Christ in God"[95] and attained by the same kenotic emptying of self that Christ accomplished in the Incarnation.[96] For Jung, the true self is discovered in the process of individuation.

To make this discovery requires a focus of attention, concern and effort, a certain compression of one's emotional, mental and physical life, a reduction of all demands that are extraneous to the primary purpose. Zen Buddhism continually emphasizes the "whole body/mind" (*shēn xīn*, Ch. *shin-jin*, Jp.), which is required for pursuing the Buddha way. *Solo Deo!*—God alone! is the motto of many Christian monasteries. This compression requires, for most people, a literal space that serves as a container, within which the battle with the ego, on both psychological and spiritual levels, must take place. The monastery serves as such a container, at its best, offering a reparative, holding and "facilitating environment," in D. W. Winnicott's terms, to support the inner process of finding and living from the true self. Within that container, all the warring elements within the personality, all of the pieces of oneself, strengths and weaknesses, are brought into a unified whole to serve the spiritual purpose.

Without such a container, the inner impulses and the external demands and stimuli dissipate energies and focus is blurred or lost. Dōgen, Merton and Jung each required such an external container, a literal space to which they consented to confine themselves, in order to work through their own experiences of emptiness. Indeed, Merton chose the Trappists rather than the Franciscans because of their very stringency and still wondered if he should have become a Carthusian[97] (which would have meant enforced solitude). Given Merton's very powerful impulses, his very strong thirst for more and for everything, he unconsciously knew he had to have a very strong container to hold himself in, to keep the focus on his inner self. Shakyamuni Buddha was one of the rare individuals who was able to take the entire world as his monastery because of his extraordinary powers of concentration, and thus, when pressed to validate his claim to enlightenment, called the earth itself as his witness. In depth psychological work, the container is established in the framework established for the "analytic hour," the times and dates of meeting, the payment of fees and the rules of conduct.

The process is a holistic inner process, which, because the requirement is "all" or "total," necessarily includes psychodynamics as well as spiritual concerns. In this process psyche and spirit find common territory, common elements (the *prima materia* of Jung[98]) and common cause. The wholeness requirement means nothing can be left out, the psyche must be healed, brought into the realm of spirit, if the spirit is to be opened into its transcendent possibilities/dimensions. Complexes, wounds, deficits and defenses must all be brought into the soul's process. Personal history must be revisited for the spiritual journey to proceed.

The spiritual path is, in relation to the psyche, a bit like marriage. One marries in the conscious purpose of being united with this particular person. But before very long, one discovers that, like it or not, psychologically, there are in-laws in bed with one, and other uninvited guests besides, not only from one's spouse but from one's own self! To make the marriage successful, all parties in each partner's psyche must somehow be given their due in order for the two wedded ones to have a relationship.

Similarly, people embarking on a spiritual path necessarily encounter their own individual psyches, full of uninvited people, images and urges that demand to be dealt with if one is to proceed spiritually. Thus in pursuing a spiritual path, the whole self (all that one is and has, including both strengths and limitations) is surrendered in order that the wholeness of the self (the integrity and integration of disparate parts) can be found.

The connection between the search for the true self and the experience of emptiness is that the experience of emptiness defines where hope is and is not to be found. It is out of an experience of emptiness that each of the people studied here despaired of achieving what most people aim for. In its place, by staying with their experience of emptiness to see where it would lead, they felt hope lay in a spiritual path. Thus, one gives up hope in order to find hope. At Zen Mountain Monastery, John Daido Loori tells Zen students, "Give up hope. There is no hope." One is reminded of Dante's dictum, "Abandon all hope, ye who enter here."[77] One has deliberately given up hope on all known modes of living; only out of such "hopelessness" and entering into that hopelessness is hope to be found in the traditions here studied.

Over the course of his life, Merton constantly played with different names for himself—over sixty-one, as his biographer, Michael Mott, lists.

That shift, from one who hated the world and hated himself to one who loved the world and discovered his own treasured true self, was accomplished by a journey from emptiness through emptiness to emptiness, a journey taken on consciously, deliberately and carefully. Instead of going to a monastery, he might well have finished his Ph.D. at Columbia and gotten a job in journalism, as was his original intention. He might well have become an alcoholic, given his behavior up to the time of his conversion, as writers often do, thus exchanging the true work of the spirit for an imbibing of "spirits" that is ultimately self-destructive.[100] In this sense, Merton's entrance into Gethsemani was definitely seen by him as not only a deliberate entering into his experience of emptiness, but as the only real alternative to his self-destructive possibilities.

Had Merton been interviewed by a psychiatrist or psychologist when he first arrived and been given any of the tests often used now for postulants, the psychological profile would not have been encouraging. Such a psychologist might well have wondered whether Merton's arrival in the late hours after everyone had gone to bed was itself a sign of his ambivalence about being there. After taking down Merton's history of his parents' deaths, his perpetual peregrinations, his chronic impulsive drinking, partying and spending, his denial of his aspiration to be a great writer and his lack of any significant, sustained relationship with a girlfriend, the psychologist might well have drawn the following conclusions:

> Thomas Merton is a very bright fellow with several severe psychological issues that will make his adjustment to monastic life difficult to impossible. The loss of his mother left him with deep, narcissistic wounds and deficits, worsened by her cold, critical attitude toward her son even before she died.

Journeys into Emptiness

The death of his father in early adolescence destroyed a much needed masculine ideal that truncated the son's psychosocial development and stability.

These vicissitudes and the utter instability of any place that might have been called home have resulted in an impulsiveness that is symptomatic of narcissistic pathology and borderline personality. His bouts of drinking excessively are beyond the norm, even for college students, and suggest incipient alcoholism and self-destructive tendencies. His failure to have any significant or lasting relationship with a woman, together with his strong bonds to male friends from his Columbia years, suggest a still-unformed sexual development with latent homosexuality and/or a fear of women, issues from which monastic life is seen (falsely) as an escape.

He uses splitting and intellectualization as defenses and may be expected to vacillate rapidly on any issue with no sense of contradicting himself. For example, the grandiosity of his aspirations to be a great writer are currently denied and muted by his newly discovered Catholic faith and are now being transferred to an aspiration to monkhood, probably to an equally grandiose status as a mystic on the level of Eckhart. Such grandiose expectations are compensatory for his deep-seated sense of worthlessness, rooted in his mother's insatiable demand for perfection and achievement.

His abandonment of and indifference toward a woman he impregnated and the child he sired suggest both callousness and irresponsibility; the remorse he claims to feel is another symptom of his narcissism, focused as it is on his own damaged persona rather than reflecting any concern for the mother and child.

In addition, he appears prone to numerous physiological ailments, such as gastritis, that are very likely psychogenic in origin, manifestations of the great degree of repression of issues as mentioned.

Prognosis for long-term residency at Gethsemani: poor. If he stays, he will be a handful for the Abbot in charge. Strong, clear and firm guidelines must be established to counter his impulsiveness and his need for adulation.

A spiritual master might well have concluded similarly: His faith is too new for its zeal to be credible. It may be too fragile to counter this young man's obvious history of excesses of lust, greed, sloth, drunkenness and pride.

Although such reports present only the negative side of Merton, they would not have been amiss. There is nothing untrue reflected in these analytical comments, and they contain even more information than Gregory Zilboorg, M.D., had when he declared Merton full of "megalomania and narcissism."[101]

Like other postulants (until, perhaps, more recently, when a certain level of psychological self-understanding is part of the general culture), Merton entered the monastery to refine and cultivate his surrender to the will of God, not for psychotherapy. But the path to God in contemplative life is an inner process, replete with all the psychological dynamics of a person's life, and the issues mentioned above in the imaginary psychiatric evaluation were in fact issues with which Merton struggled, sometimes directly and consciously, sometimes indirectly. The wholeness of the spiritual sacrifice meets the wholeness for which the psyche strives, and if the spiritual process works well, it will bring healing and wholeness to the psyche as well.

That struggle was sustained by a dogged focus on the experience of emptiness in its various manifestations. The monastery served as a container within which Merton could face himself, face the turbulent dynamics of the psyche mentioned above and refine and understand that experience of emptiness as a spiritual process of transformation.

> The need to find the right structure, one that would give him confidence in himself to live under the rule of God, had become paramount.
>
> His writing and his restlessness went together.... Writing was his way to himself: in time it might prove a way past himself.[102]

Journeys into Emptiness

Thomas Merton entered Gethsemani, in essence, in need of a great deal of healing. Later, as mentioned above, he actually used the image of being in a hospital in a major prose poem, "Hagia Sophia."[103] But the primary purpose, at least on the subconscious level, of choosing a monastery rather than somewhere else, is because it is where the experience of emptiness is intentionally explored, where the focus is on inner healing, a strengthening of the connection to one's true self, which for Merton was known only in God and through union with God. The monastery (when it does its job well) serves as a protection against impingement, in Winnicott's view, and against the dissipation and destructiveness of chronic impulsivity.

One enters a monastery in emptiness, with significant wounds and brokenness. If one enters any other way—in, for example, some burst of enthusiasm for God or some wish simply to do good—one does not last very long. Consider the frequent phenomenon of Americans alienated from their own culture and religion who enter a Zen monastery in hopes that the exotic and esoteric style of medieval Japan will rescue them from the desert of contemporary American culture. After a few years, or even a few months, the projection of the exotic fades and one faces the self again. Only if one has learned to deepen one's experience of emptiness rather than project it out onto a cultural or religious form, may one proceed.

Consider a case such as Merton's. It begins with conversion, in which one experiences in one's deepest vitals God's living presence. It fills one with unimaginable joy and gratitude, and an absolute conviction in the reality and utter sovereignty and grace of God and in one's miraculously being carried into an eternal plenitude. In order to sustain that connection to God, one abandons secular life and makes an overt, total commitment to love God and to live in and for God alone.

After a few years, however, the ecstasy fades and prayers and words seem hollow and one's fellow monks are more sources of irritation than of Christ's presence. The words of God have become separated from the experience of God, have somehow lost their evocative power, and God has become hidden, *deus absconditus.*

It is at the point where one experiences the loss of God that old experiences of emptiness (of abandonment or betrayal) are revisited and reexperienced in contemplative prayer (Merton) or *zazen* (Dōgen). Whether the old experiences of emptiness arise as memory, with specific images of events, or as more amorphous feeling-states, is determined by the same factors that govern other eruptions of material from the unconscious. In both kinds of meditation, a "de-repression" takes place of material from the personal unconscious, as well as an emergence of material from the collective unconscious. The particular method of meditation used, as well as the personal style of one's teacher or mentor, determines, to a large degree, both what emerges and how it is handled.[104]

At such a time of experiencing the loss of God, the pain of the lost connection may lead one to forget the sense of "real" in the experience of emptiness that brought one to the monastery, and one may become focused on administrative or liturgical details. But it is only by attending to one's emptiness that one stays in the place where healing is possible. Every joint and sinew strains to flee, the mind leaps to anywhere but the *here* of the *now.* Following the thread of emptiness takes one deeper into the self, which becomes, increasingly, the place of "all" as "we" rather than "I." Only by staying still in the experience of emptiness and unknowing through contemplative prayer is there healing. This is the "holding" a monastery provides. This is the healing Merton sought at Gethsemani.

> The monastery is a school—a school in which we learn from God how to be happy....What has to be healed in us is our true nature, made in the likeness of God. What we have to learn is love. The healing and the learning are the same thing.[105]

EMPTINESS IN INCARNATION:
BODY, COMMUNITY, AND WORLD

The method Merton used to engage his experiences of emptiness in order to learn from them and be healed by them was really
twofold: Most obviously and primarily, it was contemplative
prayer.[106] In addition, to a degree that is even more true of him than
of Dōgen, Merton used writing, both in his journals and in his
essays and poetry, as an additional "method" of self-exploration and
confrontation of his experiences of emptiness. In contemplative
prayer he focused on his relationship with God; in the writing, especially the journals and poems, he focused on his relationship with
himself—insofar as the two can be separated.

Much has already been said about the importance for Merton
of his writing as a way of maintaining a sense of his mother's presence. While on a basic level, writing as a mode of being had survival value, it also resulted in difficulties in two seemingly
unrelated areas: his relation to other people and his relation to his
body.

It was in his writing that Merton really encountered "others," the
individuals and groups of people he cared about most.

> Isaias, Job, Moses, David, Matthew, Mark, Luke and John are
> all part of my life. They are always about me. They look over
> my shoulder....I feel that they are very concerned about
> me....*They are more a part of my world than most of the people actu-
> ally living in the world. I "see" them sometimes more really than I see the
> monks I live with.*[107]

With few exceptions, other people existed for Merton in his
mind and he related to them largely on the basis of ideas, conversations about what is important in life: faith, art, literature and the
problems of true self-living. His actual relationship with his community of monks at Gethsemani was problematic.

To me contemplation means solitude and the need to be alone and in silence burns me up from day to day. Does that mean that the community life is a cross I am trying to escape? No. I haven't anything against the community life and no difficulty in accepting it as a cross…but it all seems so *inadequate*, so much of a blank to me.[108]

As Master of Scholastics (5/51–8/55) and then Master of Novices (5/55–8/20/65), perhaps the relationships he cared about most at Gethsemani were those that he had with his students. Broadly speaking, Merton's closest, most vital community up until the mid-1960s was found in the books he read. As his own writing began increasingly to address contemporary world issues, however, he established important relationships with people around the world through correspondence. His relationship with Boris Pasternak was typical. Impressed by Pasternak's *Dr. Zhivago*, Merton initiated a correspondence with Pasternak. It consisted of only six letters, yet Merton experienced such a kinship and intimacy—indeed, a communion—that he wrote in his journal, "I am in closer contact with Pasternak than I am with people in Louisville or Bardstown or even in my own monastery—and have more in common with him."[109]

It was certainly a step toward a more personal way of relating to be dealing with living people, but it still remained largely a relationship via the written word. This experience of relating by the written word in adulthood may be seen as an extension of what he learned in childhood: the important formative experience of his mother's writing down what she observed of him; of her writing to him about her death; of his father's writing to him when he was delirious and dying; and of the telegram telling of his father's death. Writing had always been the way people related to Merton. He *lived* in his mind, in reading and writing. The written word was for him the primary mode of presence, of his presence to others and others' presence to him.

This created difficulties—or, one might say, was a result of the difficulties Merton had—in his relation to his body. The Ulanovs remind us, "When the unlived feminine falls into the uncon-scious, it usually takes the body with it."[110] When Tom was taken to France with his father and left with the Privat family for the summer of 1926, when he was eleven, he learned only later that he had tuberculosis and was there for recovery. Shortly after his father's death, when Merton returned to Oakham at the age of six-teen, he developed an infection in his toe that he ignored. A few days later he developed a bad toothache. The pain finally sent him to the school's dentist, who pulled the tooth, which had become infected. But Merton got worse after returning to the dormitory, and on examination, the dentist realized that gangrene had set in and cut a large hole in the gum to fully excise the infected area. Merton continued to feel sick, first physically, then emotionally, to the point where he didn't care whether he lived or died.[111] When the doctor next came and Merton reported his condition and the problem with his toe, gangrene was discovered to be present there as well, and though the toe was saved, the nail and surrounding tissue were removed.

Coming only about eight months after his father's death, when he was sixteen, this episode is significant not only as a likely psycho-somatic reaction to the loss of his father and his own feelings about his life, but as a forerunner of Merton's lifelong history of bodily ail-ments and his perpetual attitudes toward them of denial and neg-lect, another example of a tendency toward self-destruction.

By the time he was eligible for the draft, in 1940, he was rejected because he had lost most of his teeth, and the ones he had were in bad shape. By 1950, at thirty-five, he already had a history of spastic colitis (a problem well known to have emotional origins), scarred lungs (from childhood tuberculosis) and a nose operation that required the removal of three inches of bone and cartilage.[112] By 1965, when Merton was fifty, the list of ailments had grown to include an arthritic hip, chronic dermatitis that required him to wear gloves,[113] sinusitis (present ever since he reached Gethsemani), per-petual diarrhea, loss of hair and most of his teeth, and a degenerating vertebra, for which he would soon have a spinal operation, that caused numbing in his hands and an ache in his shoulders.[114]

Although both of his parents died young, his grandparents' life spans ranged from the sixties through the eighties, so one ought not to ascribe Merton's body problems to inherent genetic vulnerability. One might say Merton had difficulty experiencing himself as an embodied person, or perhaps worse, that he related to his body the way he related to women, as an irritant, an impediment to the spiritual perfection he sought. "The terrible thing about sickness is that you tend to think you are sick. Your thoughts are narrowed down to your own poor little bitch of a body."[115]

On the other hand, with the body, as with feelings, "we do as we have been done by." Merton treated his body the way it had been treated by the adults of his childhood. His mother left him, and his father kept leaving him; he lived sometimes with grandparents, but mostly with strangers and at boarding schools. Who ever told him to pay attention to his body, to brush his teeth, to eat some things but not others, and when he was in pain to inquire about it?

Merton was not alone in viewing his own body's needs as alien. Much of religious life (both Christian and Buddhist![116]) looked upon it that way and confused a healthy regard for the physical dimension of life with pandering to selfishness and self-pity. The vow of celibacy inevitably clashes with the body's natural need to be touched, much more with the instinctive urge for sexual gratification. It is hard to say no to a natural desire without calling that desire bad, or feeling that one is bad for having such a desire. On another level, of course, dedication to the spiritual life, as to any other intense devotion, may be seen to exact a price, a price paid by the body. Ann Ulanov underscores the seriousness of the conflicting demands of spirit and body:

> If we sacrifice everything to the spirit and forget our body life, then "this passion turns spirit into a malignant growth" (Jung, CW 8, pars. 646–47). If the spiritual impulse drags us away from life, in the body and in the world, then almost invariably it

proves a false spirit and can exert lethal effects. This particular danger threatens spiritually gifted people; their bodies may have to pay the price for an unbalanced enthusiasm for the enormous power of spirit.[117]

Thomas Merton, under the power of a distant, critical anima, experienced, for the first forty-one years of his life, human community and human presence as alien and impinging, and preferred, with the exception of intellectual discourse in the medium of words, solitude. With a history of constant moving around in his childhood, words on a page were more consistent "friends" to him than any peers (after all, the most important events of his life had been conveyed by writing). By extension of that overemphasis on writing under the influence of his anima, he neglected his body and considered it a nuisance rather than an essential way of being incarnate in the world.

Perhaps for anyone on a spiritual path, there is an inherent risk that, in the process of pursuing the "absolute" or the "infinite," one may neglect—or sometimes intentionally disregard or abuse—the "relative" or "finite" mode through which one dwells in the world, one's actual body. In each of the traditions being studied here, however, the absolute, the infinite, the realm of the spirit are known and experienced only in and through the form of finitude, the body, the community. In Zen, the "Heart Sutra" maintains not just a balance between the relative and absolute, but an *identity*: "...form is exactly emptiness, emptiness exactly form." In Christianity, God became incarnate in human form; the infinite emptied itself into the finite. In depth psychology, it is only in the experience of one's personal body and one's experience of embodied others that psychological, emotional and spiritual growth can happen. To fail to appreciate one's own embodied needs—the need for the body to be touched, exercised, fed, given rest, the need for the person to be in significant and intimate (which is not to say necessarily sexual) relationship with others in community—is to confuse emptiness as a spiritual goal with emptiness as deprivation under the guise of pride, denial or masochism. Discernment is called for, as well as careful attention to the various kinds of emptiness; usually a teacher or mentor is required. These issues of Merton's body and his relation to the Gethsemani community remained with him throughout his monastic career, reminding him, in spite of himself, of his humanity, his vulnerability and neediness as essential aspects of his experiences of emptiness.

Part II

MERTON'S WEAVING OF THE MANY-COLORED THREADS OF EMPTINESS

In spite of however much Thomas Merton wanted to go elsewhere, with the exception of visits to the hospital in Louisville, he left Gethsemani only four times after his entrance into the monastery on December 10, 1941, until his trip to Asia, where he died on December 10, 1968. His biography, therefore, largely consists of the story of his spiritual, intellectual and personal development as discerned from his writings, both in his journals and in his published books. As he himself declared, "Our real journey in life is interior: it is a matter of growth, deepening, and an ever greater surrender to the creative action of love and grace in our hearts."[118]

It is the position of this study that Merton's "real journey" can largely be plotted by following his experiences of emptiness as they changed over time. In his working through of his understanding of emptiness, all the major themes of his life are expressed: his conflict between being a monk and a poet/writer; his conflict between remaining a Trappist and becoming a Carthusian or starting a monastery elsewhere; his conflict between world negation and world affirmation; his struggle with an inner, critical mother; and his struggle to be free of self-consciousness.

Journeys into Emptiness

While repetition alone is not necessarily a sign of significance, it is worth noting that the number of times Merton used the word *emptiness* increased dramatically over time. Thus, it is found in only seven places in *Seven Storey Mountain*, published in 1948, whereas it is found at least eighteen times in the collected talks entitled *The Inner Experience*, which comprises about 110 pages, written over a period of several years in the early 1960s. In *Contemplative Prayer*, a book of 116 pages, published in 1968 (earlier published by the Cistercian Society), the word is used forty-three times; in addition, often used synonymously, the words *nothingness, nothing, nada* and *void* are found an additional fourteen times. Merton's last book, *The Asian Journal*, uses *emptiness* four times, and the word *sunyata* at least five times, but in a significantly new way. Tracing the way in which he used this word offers a key not only to the development of Merton's thought in his spiritual journey and his psychological maturation, but to our understanding of how he learned and grew from the facing of, or sometimes failing to face, his own experiences of emptiness.

The designation of categories for Merton's different experiences of emptiness, set out below, follow, in broad strokes, a progressive development over time. One could never, for example, really appreciate emptiness as compassion (#9), without having experienced emptiness as loss and loneliness (#1). Yet these categories must not be mistaken for stages in the sense of leaving the earlier behind to go on to the next. None of them is ever entirely left behind, thus the image is of "weaving" different "strands," into an ongoing thread that leads one into the unknown, into the "labyrinth"[119] of the self.

Emptiness as Loss, Loneliness and Impermanence

The first use Merton makes of the word *emptiness* is one that is common to all humanity and refers to a feeling of abandonment, of being left, being alone, perhaps being somewhat in despair at the loneliness. It was 1926; Merton was 11½ years old, and had just been left off by his father at Lycée Ingres at Montauban, France, and was staying in a dormitory. He had suffered numerous beatings and pummelings from his peers, in part because he was so terrified that he forgot every word of French in spite of being quite fluent. As became the case frequently, his inner feeling is projected onto the landscape:

> ...when I lay awake at night in the huge dark dormitory...and heard through the darkness and the emptiness of the night the far screaming of the trains...I knew for the first time in my life the pangs of desolation and emptiness and abandonment.[120]

Although he does not use the word in his "Perry Street Journal," Merton was clearly trying to come to terms with emptiness as loss, and the impermanence of all things loved and valued. On October 1, 1939, at twenty-four, he wrote,

> Thank God, then, for all good smells and good sights and good sounds; but what is the good of being attached to them, and sitting and turning over their memory and dwelling on the recollections they bring up to you, and cherishing a sadness for these things which are gone away. Pop and Bonnemaman are dead, and it will never again be the same as being sixteen and eighteen and living at Douglaston, in vacations. And as to that, what a vanity it would be anyway to moan over the happiness of those times, because, who can say those were very good or happy years for me when I was full of anger and impatience and ingratitude...proud and selfish, and denied God and was full of gluttony and lust....You will never be sixteen again and you will never be in love again for the first time.[121]

However useless it seemed to him to complain, this passage clearly reflected a mourning and a kind of despair about the possibilities of attaching to and loving and caring about anything. This is a significant aspect of emptiness as loss and abandonment: It can render one hopeless about the value of entering any relationship emotionally, for fear of being abandoned again, thus creating further experiences of emptiness as loneliness, and emptiness as rage at having been denied real loving and then left with the effects of that lack. Such unconscious rage, built up from the repeated experiences of the death of his mother, his father, his aunt and his grandparents, was perhaps a source of Merton's own destructiveness between the time of the death of his father and his entrance into Gethsemani, exhibited in his compulsive drinking, getting a woman pregnant and doing unsatisfactory work at Cambridge.

Emptiness as Moral and Spiritual Vacuity

Looking back upon the England from which he had been ejected at the age of sixteen by his godfather, Tom Bennett, for having gotten a woman pregnant and perhaps projecting his feelings about himself onto the country and the era, Merton experienced emptiness as moral and spiritual vacuity.

> What was wrong with this place, with all these people? Why was everything so empty?...it seemed to me that...the whole of England was pretending, with an elaborate and intent and conscious, and perhaps in some cases a courageous effort to act as if it were alive. And it took a lot of acting...because most of the people were already morally dead, asphyxiated by the steam of their own strong yellow tea, or by the smell of their own pubs and breweries, or by the fungus on the walls of Oxford or Cambridge.
>
> For those who had nothing but this emptiness in the middle of them, no doubt the things they had to do and to suffer during the war filled that emptiness with something stronger and more resilient than their pride—either that or it destroyed them utterly.[122]

Merton is making a moral judgment and is sorting through his own experience of a way of life that he, from the vantage point of his entrance to Gethsemani, had consciously rejected. Out of his own experience of emptiness, he has begun to reflect on the place of values in human existence, and to assess them by their capacity to lead people into a richer, deeper sense of their true selves, rather than values that dissipate energy and talent and concern.

This understanding of emptiness continued into its next use in *Seven Storey Mountain*. Merton was near the end of his college days at Columbia and had recently had an attack of vertigo while on the Long Island Railroad and a frightening disorientation in which he feared he was having a nervous breakdown. The doctor he saw said he was fatigued and should cut back his work and that he suffered from gastritis. For Merton, however, the trauma had far more significance:

> I had at last become a true child of the modern world, completely tangled up in petty and useless concerns with myself....I thought I was going to ransack and rob...and now I found that it was I who was emptied and robbed and gutted....In filling myself, I had emptied myself....if my moral and nervous constitution had not caved in under the weight of my own emptiness, who can tell what would eventually have happened to me?[123]

Emptiness as moral and spiritual bankruptcy is reflected in his last use of the word in *Seven Storey*. He had had his conversion experience and was debating still between monastic life and the possibility of working with Baroness Catherine de Hueck at Friendship House in Harlem.[124] Meanwhile, he was teaching at St. Bonaventure's University in upstate New York.

> I read a story in the *New Yorker* about a boy who, instead of becoming a priest, got married, or at least fell in love or something. And the emptiness and futility and nothingness of the world once more invaded me from every side.[125]

This experience of emptiness is one of the major determinants in a person's decision to enter a monastery: Ordinary life is seen as devoid of meaning and value. From the utter depths of the experience of emptiness as loss and abandonment, one cannot imagine ordinary life as having sufficient depth, intensity or power to heal the great wounds of emptiness as loss. Ordinary life seems superficial, morally and spiritually bankrupt. This experience of the emptiness of ordinary life is also the basis for the Zen experience of the Great Doubt.[126] Life without a deeper dimension is experienced as worthless.

Emptiness as Not Having, as Poverty

In the intermediate period between his conversion and his entrance into Gethsemani, Merton began gradually to connect his experiences of emptiness as loss and as the impermanence of all things to his understanding of the spiritual as the only thing that lasts. He began consciously to divest himself of anything to which he could be attached. Emptiness in this sense was an intentional disowning, a deliberate not-having (which is the root meaning of the famous first koan, *mu*, Jp.).

> I know this much: that the knowledge of what is going on only makes it seem desperately important to be voluntarily poor, to get rid of all possessions this instant. I am scared, sometimes, to own anything, even a name, let alone a coin, or shares in the oil, the munitions, the airplane factories. I am scared to take a proprietary interest in anything, for fear that my love of what I own may be killing somebody somewhere.[127]

This was written in June of 1940. In his journals, Merton showed a great consciousness about the developing war in Europe, and especially in England. It is worth keeping in mind that Merton's entire life might fruitfully be understood as a life constantly under the shadow of war. He was born in France in World War I. His decision to enter the monastery was made during the time when he was to be drafted for World War II. His trip to Asia was greatly influenced by the fact of U.S. involvement in Vietnam at the time. His father managed to avoid the draft in World War I, as Merton did in World War II (he didn't have enough teeth!). Merton's choice of a title for *Conjectures of a Guilty Bystander* (written at the height of the Vietnam War for the United States) must be considered, from the psychological point of view, as absolutely sincere and a conscious attempt to work through his experience of survivor's guilt.

Merton's feeling of fear of owning anything and his commitment to poverty as a spiritual discipline must be acknowledged, therefore, as including a certain sense of guilt for not directly suffering at a time when so many others did. In this excerpt from his journal, Merton has already made the connecting link between an emptying of one's self of possessions on the personal level and the dynamics of economics and war, a connection Merton would take another twenty years to develop more fully.

Some form of the vow of poverty is apparent in all monastic traditions. As has been shown, Shakyamuni and Dōgen left behind family wealth and social position. The universality of this requirement, which is so easily taken for granted when applied to monastics, is rarely seen as containing an important truth for human existence as such. The human propensity to possess things is the basis of war and injustice; the spiritual demand to "go and sell all you have and give it to the poor" addresses economic and political cause and effect. Like the inner process of exploring the experience of emptiness, voluntarily adopting outer poverty as a real way of living appears equally daunting and undesirable.

> Choosing external poverty is thus a voluntary self-emptying. What before was passively suffered now becomes actively sought. What was a cause of suffering now, through accepting it and seeking it, becomes an agent of transformation. What was a noun is embraced as a verb.[128]

The connection between spiritual poverty and literal poverty was explored directly in a talk Merton gave to young monks at Gethsemani, entitled "Inner and Outer Poverty,"[129] in the 1960s. In it he spelled out the way in which exterior poverty is the means to explore the inner spirit of poverty. Both inner and outer were seen as necessary in order for one to be detached from possessions. The spirit of all monastic vows of renunciation, Merton said, was to acknowledge and oppose the fundamental human instincts, in this case, the instinct to possess. He connected the having of things with the issues of justice, noting that one cannot have much while others have little without injustice inhering in the system. Further, he noted that in every renunciation one gives up something in order to get something. In this case, one gives up "things" in order to have "union with God and love of neighbor." Merton said there is a "joy in doing without. Being without is more gratifying than having. You renounce self in order to love." This latter issue returned with vehemence and poignancy just a few years after this speech, when he fell in love with a specific woman.

Emptiness as Kenosis along the Spiritual Path

From the time of Merton's entry into Gethsemani in 1941, the dominant meaning of emptiness for him was connected to the external and internal emptying out, the kenotic action in which one's spiritual practice is an active letting go, a detachment from both external things, people and results of action, as well as internal desires, preferences and feelings in response to whatever the situation may be. The goal is to be completely at one with the will of God, with God Himself, and to eliminate anything to which one might be clinging for safety or security. The action of the self is met by the action of God within oneself.

Give up everything for God.[130]

> I see more and more that now I must desire nothing else than to be "poured out as a libation" to live and surrender my being without concern (2/2/65).[131]

> For I know I will possess all things if I am empty of all things, and only You can at once empty me of all things and fill me with Yourself, the Life of all that lives and the Being in Whom everything exists.[132]

Emptiness as *kenosis* was a theme of lifelong importance for Merton. He developed it most fully in the manuscript entitled *The Inner Experience*,[133] which he stipulated should not to be published as a book. The reason he didn't want it published was very likely twofold: It was a work in progress that he never finished. He started working on it in the '50s and was still working on it up to the time of his death. In addition, Merton expressed a point of view in it that was extremely ecumenical and drew more directly than any of his previous writings on his knowledge of Zen Buddhism, a reliance that might have proved difficult to justify to his Catholic censors.

Emptiness as Nothingness and Helplessness

The first four kinds of experiences of emptiness (emptiness as loss, loneliness and impermanence; emptiness as moral and spiritual vacuity; emptiness as poverty; and emptiness as *kenosis* of the self) preoccupied Merton from his earliest writing to his early years at Gethsemani. From his entrance into Gethsemani until the late 1950s, his primary journey was interior and therefore must be related to his self-understanding as it developed in relation to both his inner spiritual search and his assessment of and response to events in the outside world—to which he was witness rather than participant.

> ...now I experience my own nothingness, and long for God! (12/5/41)[134]

Merton had a deep urge actually to *be* nothing, to surrender not only possessions but power in order to attain ultimate union with God, a union accomplished by the "prayer of the heart," consisting of "...interior recollection, the abandonment of distracting thoughts and the humble invocation of the Lord Jesus...."[135]

Journeys into Emptiness

In such prayer and solitude, the emptiness of inauthentic life is confronted by the emptiness that is the fullness of living by grace; emptiness as a negative is confronted by emptiness as positive.

> ...the way of prayer brings us face to face with the sham and indignity of the false self that seeks to live for itself alone....
> In order to be true to God and to ourselves we must break with the familiar, established and secure norms and go off into the unknown...to a freedom based no longer on social approval and relative alienation, but on direct dependence on an invisible and inscrutable God, in pure faith.[136]

It is under the rubric of emptiness as nothingness that Merton's "lost, middle years"[137] as David Cooper calls them, should be located. This was a period, from about 1950 to 1955, when Merton was ages thirty-five through forty, in which his writing nearly stopped.[138] He wrote no poetry. His journals reflect the hiatus: In volume 2,[139] 417 pages are taken up for December 1946 through December 1950; only 40 pages are written between January 1951 and July 1952. The hiatus continued in volume 3,[140] where only 41 pages are written between July 1952 and March 1955; then, with his appointment as Master of Novices in July 1956, his production increased, amounting to 349 pages into May 1960. The primary "lost years," therefore, are between 1951 and 1955. The only books published were *Bread in the Wilderness*,[141] which is a clue to what he was doing during this period, and a book he was commissioned to write by his order on St. Bernard of Clairvaux.[142]

According to Mott, Merton was focusing on the integration of liturgy and the Bible, especially the Psalms. He was, in fact, going inward, to use his own metaphor, into the belly of the whale: the period is broken by the writing of *No Man Is an Island*, and *The Sign of Jonas*, which did not get published until 1956.

During this period, Merton wrestled with the meaning of his calling, most of all with the conflict he experienced between writing and silence, and between staying at Gethsemani rather than going to a more eremetical order, such as the Carthusians. At this point, part of his urge to go to the Carthusian Order may be seen as a desire to flee the demands of his own order to do work that was for its benefit, unconnected to anything that came from deep inside himself. His focused meditation on liturgy and the Psalms was a search and a clarification inside himself, an acknowledgment of an inner division between what felt true and what felt false, a distinction that could only be recognized by facing the experience of emptiness and silence. The book on Bernard and the earlier one on Mother Berchmans, O.C.S.O.[143] were both forced upon Merton by the order. Merton may well have experienced this as equivalent to his mother's insistence on putting an *h* in *which*. He did not enjoy writing what someone else wanted him to write; it required a compliance of his false self. Even *Seven Storey Mountain*, which enjoyed such success, may have felt to Merton by 1950 as reflective of his false self, not because it was ordered, but because it was written from the undigested pietism of his early conversion enthusiasm, when he was still anxious to please. This period may be seen, therefore, as the time of his inner struggle to find his own voice, his true self in relation to God.

This period was also the beginning of Merton's making a distinction between his felt inner need and the needs (expressed as demands) of monastic institutional life. Regardless of the kind of monastery, regardless, in fact, of whatever the institution, the needs of an institution and the needs of an individual rarely run parallel for very long. In the individuation processs it is essential that the individual distinguish her need from the needs of the collective. In religious institutions, there is a tendency to equate the needs of the organization with the transcendent purpose for which it was formed and to equate obedience to the organization with obedience to the transcendent vocation. Even with the best of intentions on both parts, some disparity in the needs of the institution and the individual is inevitable, but, like Winnicott's "good enough mothering," one hopes the disparity is not so great but that it cannot be managed to the benefit of all.

At this point in spiritual life, when neither God nor one's true self is apparent, emptiness as a state of our own inability even to find, much less be, our true selves is expressed as our nothingness before God.

> ....our meditation should begin with the realization of our *nothingness and helplessness* in the presence of God.... "Finding our heart" and recovering this awareness of our inmost identity implies the recognition that our external, everyday self is to a great extent a mask and a fabrication. It is not our true self. And, indeed, our true self is not easy to find. *It is hidden in obscurity and "nothingness"* at the center where we are in direct dependence on God.[144]

Religious understanding has something important to contribute to the use in depth psychology of the term *true self*. Every one of the three major people in this study used the idea of the true self as an important part of their understanding of the self in transformation. Both Christianity and Zen Buddhism point out that we arrive at the true self somewhat as we arrive at God: by negation, by what it is not. Thus, the true self is primarily what is left if we get rid of or get beyond the false self, that is, the conditioned, adapted self. But, unlike the false self, which is known by its content and form, the true self has no inherent content other than a quality of spontaneity, the "real," which is not only mental and emotional, but physical, an experience of tissue aliveness in the body. Therefore we can say that the true self is empty, in precisely the Zen Buddhist sense of the term as having no fixed substance or essence that is universal. It is in this way that the Buddha said there is "no-self," nonatman. The true self is no-self. And yet, as reflected in the Christian view of the self as the place of the incarnation, this "no-self" is "me," a particular body at a particular place and time. Thus, Christianity and Buddhism both affirm the particular person as real, and the true self as no-self in the sense of not being reducible to a general or abstract, substantive or unchanging definition.

Traditionally, Christians have understood their true self as hidden with Christ in God,[145] and as known only in discovering the will of God. The problem arises when trying to discern God's will for one's life. The tendency may be to assumes one's true self in God is a particular *thing* that is somehow already *there* somewhere, a secret that God is withholding until one has surrendered enough ego to be told. This way of conceiving of the true self hidden in God carries exactly the same sense of substantiality that Zen Buddhism warns against. But there are no preexistent marching orders, nor are they in any envelope.

One discovers one's true self and God's will for one's life by negation and intuition. For example, Merton tried to be a novelist, and, faced with rejection, he pursued his religious interest, staying with *that* uncertainty rather than the uncertainty of a novelist trying to get published. He surrendered that identity, negating it, in order to stay with his intuitive search. This was the reach of a blind man among clouds of unknowing. As soon as God's will or one's self becomes a fixed, identifiable *thing*, one has lost the essence, which is freedom.

In Christianity, the Son of Man (Jesus) has no place to lay his head; in Zen Buddhism, the monk is *unsui*, cloud and water. The true self is homeless and empty because it is constantly pouring itself out in order to receive. No fixed essence. No nest. No hiding place. No security. The more one recognizes this emptiness as the actual place of divine activity, the experience of emptiness is transformed from an experience of loss to an experience of fulfillment, and we are transformed into increasing viscosity.

The only way to get there, Merton said, is by affirming one's own nothingness and helplessness. As Zilboorg pointed out in no uncertain terms, this was hard for Merton to do, but his direction was clear.

Journeys into Emptiness

Emptiness as Dread

Merton's "lost middle years" continued into the experience of emptiness as dread, because in fact, the experience of helplessness and nothingness induces dread, and if we are not experiencing dread, we are probably not really experiencing helplessness and nothingness. In this process of purgation, Merton discovered his own temptation to cling to images and things that are designed to hide one's interior emptiness. Faith is required to be able to face one's emptiness. The attempt to use images and concepts can actually be dangerous because it is the ego's attempt to reestablish its hegemony over the self and over God, ending in "the dislocation of one's entire moral and intellectual existence."[146]

It is at this point that the possibility of "dread" arises as one becomes aware of the possibility that one may not be faithful in pursuing one's experience of emptiness, that one may actually run away from it, deny its significance, drop the baton. In dread, we experience our own powerlessness to choose the good and our greater tendency to choose the lesser good.

> The real import of dread is to be sought in an infidelity to a personal demand of which one is at least dimly aware: the failure to meet a challenge, to fulfill a certain possibility which demands to be met and fulfilled. The price of this failure to measure up to an existential demand of one's own life is a general sense of failure, of guilt. And it is important to remark that this guilt is real, it is not necessarily a mere neurotic anxiety. It is the sense of defection and defeat that afflicts a man who is not facing his own inner truth and is not giving back to life, to God and to his fellow man, a fair return for all that has been given him.
>
> The worst emptiness is the emptiness of the faithful Christian…who sees that no virtue of his own, no good intentions, no ideals, no philosophy…can rescue him from the futility, the apparent despair of his emptiness without God.

At the same time, he seems to lose the conviction that God is or can be a refuge for him. *It is as if God himself...had become emptiness,* and as if all were emptiness, nothingness, dread and night.[147]

●

Dread is an expression of our insecurity...a realization that we are never and can never be completely "sure" in the sense of possessing a definitive, and established spiritual status. It means that we cannot any longer hope in ourselves, in our wisdom, our virtues, our fidelity....we no longer rely on what we "have."... We are open to God and...his grace, which will support our liberty in the emptiness where we will confront unforeseen decisions. Only when we have descended in dread to the center of our own nothingness, by his grace and guidance, can we be led by him, in his own time, to find him in losing ourselves.[148]

Emptiness as dread performs a liberating function: it enables us to find the fulfillment of our life not so much in *having* or *doing* as in *being*.

...dread divests us of the sense of possession, of "having" our being and our power to love in order that we may simply *be* in perfect openness (turned inside out), a defenselessness that is utter simplicity and total gift.
...the full maturity of the spiritual life cannot be reached unless we first pass through the dread, anguish, trouble and fear that necessarily accompany the inner crisis of "spiritual death" in which we finally abandon our attachment to our exterior self and surrender completely to Christ.[149]

By persevering and not running away from his own experience of emptiness as dread, or even, nota bene, by acknowledging that he was not squarely facing emptiness as dread, and at the same time remaining aware of that failure, Merton experienced a radical transformation.

> The truly sacred attitude toward life…does not recoil from our own inner emptiness, but rather penetrates into it with awe and reverence, and with the awareness of mystery.
>
> This is a most important discovery in the interior life. For the external self *fears* and recoils from what is beyond it, and above it. It dreads the seeming emptiness and darkness of the interior self….The whole tragedy of "diversion" is precisely that it is a flight from all that is most real and immediate and genuine in ourselves. It is a flight from life and from experience—an attempt to put a veil of objects between the mind and its experience of itself. It is therefore a matter of great courage and spiritual energy to turn away from diversion and prepare to meet, face to face, that *immediate* experience of life which is intolerable to the exterior man. This is only possible when… we are able to see our inner selves not as a vacuum but as an *infinite depth,* not as emptiness but as fulness. This change of perspective is impossible as long as we are afraid of our own nothingness, as long as we are afraid of fear, afraid of poverty, afraid of boredom—as long as we run away from ourselves.[150]

The positive benefit of facing emptiness as nothingness and dread, Merton discovered, was that thereby, and only thereby, could he get rid of his false selves. In so doing, Merton experienced his own self as empty, similar to the experience of Dōgen Further, paralleling Nāgārjuna's position, Merton discovered that the emptiness he experienced at that point was not a dreaded vacuum (or *nihil,* as above, 34–35), but a fullness as infinite depth.

Emptiness as Union with God

Finally, Merton achieved a resolution of sorts[151] by 1955. He resumed writing poems after an eight-year hiatus. He began writing with a new authority, including the capacity to criticize the church and monasticism. He found his voice and his language.

There are several dimensions of this maturation. He was beginning to experience the benefits of contemplation as a path to his true self and to God, as distinct from his conflicts with superiors in the order both at Gethsemani and abroad. In contemplative prayer, Merton focused on the experience of emptiness as an apophatic direction. This attention to the self served, psychologically, to bring more cohesion to his self as he experienced his own reality and the reality of God in contrast to his encounters with others.[152] This gave him a confidence evidenced in *The Sign of Jonas,* and—in contrast to the rejections he had received for his novel, *The Labyrinth*—he had successfully maintained his insistence on and arguments for the publication of *Jonas* against considerable objections from his superiors. He had also been given a compromise to his urges to move outside the monastery, in the form of "St. Anne's," an abandoned toolshed set in the woods, which he could use as his own place for solitude. In addition, he seemed to have revised his wish to be a saint, evidenced by an increasing satisfaction in both contemplation and writing and an expanding communication with people outside the monastery.

In Merton's new language there is no longer a dichotomy between the monastery and the world, nor between his role as a writer and a priest. The new language speaks out of a universally human perspective, rather than the narrowly understood Catholic perspective. A standard was found for judging the authenticity of political, national and institutional life, as well as personal, spiritual life. Without leaving the monastery, Merton found the monk's place in the world: It is precisely the monk's life of emptiness and his testimony regarding the experience of emptiness that constituted the monk's primary contribution to the world, calling people to a true self that was easily lost in an impersonal, one-dimensional, technological, war-driven society. The mature Merton thus maintained a very active involvement in the events of the world by his correspondence and writing, but the central stance from which he derived his perception of what was going on in the world was his reflection through contemplation on his own experiences of emptiness.

By descending deeply into that inner darkness, Merton had a "vision" of God that was not really "seeing."

Journeys into Emptiness

> In this last ecstatic act of "unknowing," the gap between our
> spirit as subject and God as object is finally closed, and in the
> embrace of mystical love we know that we and He are one.
> This is infused or mystical contemplation in the purest sense
> of the term.[153]

Here, finally, Merton reaped the reward for facing the negative
aspects of the experience of emptiness. To persist in facing each
aspect of the experience of emptiness is to gain an increased sense
of personal authenticity, to lose fear and to be united in our
humanity with others and with God.

Merton experienced this unity in what has since become
known as the "Louisville vision" on March 18, 1958:

> Yesterday, in Louisville, at the corner of 4th and Walnut, I
> suddenly realized that I loved all the people and that none of
> them were, or could be, totally alien to me. As if waking from
> a dream—the dream of my separateness, of my "special" voca-
> tion to be different. My vocation does not really make me dif-
> ferent from the rest of men or just one in a special category,
> except artificially, juridically. I am still a member of the
> human race—and what more glorious destiny is there for
> man, since the Word was made flesh and became, too, a
> member of the Human Race![154]

Here is the distinctive contribution religious practice can make to
the discovery of the true self. In contrast to psychotherapies that
focus on personal interaction, the practice of meditation on the experience of emptiness, whether contemplative prayer or *zazen* (or a
name from another tradition), leads to the meeting point between the
true self and God, and at that junction, a sense of oneness pervades
and prevails over a tendency to make the 'I' a separate place from
which to view as separate everyone and everything else.

To what extent Merton felt he himself achieved a full union with
God is, like much of his life, open to question and interpretation. In
1965, he wrote,

What has been so far only a theological conception, or an image, has to be sought and loved. "Union with God." So mysterious that in the end man would perhaps do anything to evade it, once he realizes it means the *end* of his ego-self-realization, once for all. Am I ready? Of course not. Yet the course of my life is set in this direction.[155]

While in India, Merton met Chatral Rimpoche,

the greatest rimpoche I have met so far and a very impressive person....We must have talked for two hours or more...dharmakaya...the Risen Christ, suffering, compassion for all creatures, motives for "helping others"—but all leading back to dzogchen, the ultimate emptiness, the unity of sunyata and karuna, going "beyond the dharmakaya" and "beyond God" to the ultimate perfect emptiness. He said he had meditated in solitude for thirty years or more and had not attained to perfect emptiness and I said I hadn't either (November 16, 1968).[156]

Emptiness as Anima/Animus Failure

This category did not exist in Merton's conscious thought, perhaps because it represents the central area of lifelong inner conflict for him that he did not quite know what to do with. He read Jung, but Jung's thought didn't "grab" Merton the way Freudian categories did. Yet this very fundamental inner woundedness went back to his earliest childhood, to those months between which he enjoyed being held and those in which he "never wanted to be rocked and never wanted to be 'held.'"[157] In his conscious memory, this form of emptiness was the inner image he had of his mother as cold, distant, perfectionistic and critical.

It must be kept in mind that, because Merton's mother died when he was so young, he did not have a chance to experience other aspects of his mother's ways of being. Nuance and variety is lost when memory is reduced to one aspect of a person. This limitation was not helped by Merton's attendance at all-boys' schools, including the Columbia of that time. With the exception of his "dear Aunt Maud," Merton did not feel much contact with women and was in their presence infrequently. This left him vacillating wildly between an idealization,[158] common for some adolescents, which caused him to be totally out of touch with the other person's reality, to a use of women as objects for sexual gratification,[159] to whom he was equally unrelated as persons. As Merton began to publish, he developed relationships with women that were largely intellectual, and thus, equally emotionally distant.

This inner image was his actual anima for the first forty years of his life, and dominated his consciousness as an internal witness (and therefore critic) to everything he did. Ann and Barry Ulanov describe this inner image:

> The anima/animus is an image produced by the unconscious, usually of the opposite sex and always contrary to our conscious gender identity, that connects us to our inner life. The person reaching toward wholeness is a contrasexual person, looking to join within himself or herself the energies of both masculine and feminine modes of being human.[160]

As the path of entrance to the unconscious, and therefore to the true self, one's anima has the power of a guardian at the gate. And if, as a matter of one's spiritual beliefs, the ultimate consciousness is of a loving God, a predominantly critical, cold and unresponsive anima is a barrier to spiritual attainment. Willy-nilly, therefore, everyone who embarks on a spiritual path will have to come to terms with his anima/her animus figure and work it through to get beyond it to the transcendent reality to which one aspires and to which it forms a threshold.

The beginning of the transformation in Merton's anima was in his reading of the Russian mystics in the latter part of 1956. In July of that year he had had his initial "dressing down" by Gregory Zilboorg, M.D., in which he had been faulted for being a "narcissist," for being "stubborn," a "gadfly to your superiors," and "afraid to be an ordinary monk in the community."[161] For several months, and with some additional meetings with Zilboorg, Merton wrestled with the charges and questioned the validity of his own vocation. With this challenge to his core personality in the background, Merton found solace and inspiration in the personification by Vladimir Soloviev in Egypt of "Holy Wisdom as *Hagia Sophia*," and the idea of "Cosmic Play."[162]

In July of 1957, Merton studied carefully Bulgakov's "sophianology" and, in his journal, tried to think through an aspect of the Russian's thought he did not understand:

> The divine nature is distinct from the 3 Divine Persons, but is not therefore a 4th principle superadded to make a "quaternity." No one imagines that it does. When the same nature is regarded as "Sophia"—why should that constitute a 4th person?
> ...[quoting Bulgakov] *"La nature de Dieu en tant que contenu absolu de la vie de Dieu est ce qui est appellé par la Parole Divien* (Prov.VIII)." La sagesse de Dieu, p. 22.
> "La Sophia est le plerôme...."
> (...God loves in me His own wisdom. His own wisdom in one is love, uniting us to Him in the 3 Divine persons.)[163]

In this all-too-brief entry in his journal, Merton is struggling to come to terms with the central struggle of his spiritual and emotional life, his own anima. He is doing it at this point from a theological perspective, trying to understand the Russian's elaboration of *Sophia* as divine wisdom as a central point of entry into understanding the human/divine/cosmic connection. As a feminine figure, *Sophia* offers an alternative image of the anima, an image that is directly related to God and is, in Bulgakov's theology, of the essence of God.[164]

Merton's effort to understand the question of "quaternity" was prompted by two other considerations that are not articulated in his journal. The first is the fact that in 1950, Pius XII issued a papal bull, entitled *Munificentissimus Deus*, making the assumption of the Blessed

Virgin Mary a formal part of Catholic doctrine. The second reference is to the implication of this act according to Carl Jung. For Jung, the doctrinal change meant that the West had finally recognized the absolute necessity for including the feminine in the Godhead. Mary thus joined the Trinity to make a quaternity, which, for Jung, was a symbol of wholeness heretofore lacking in the Trinity.

> ...the Pope has recently announced the dogma of the Assumption Mariae, very much to the astonishment of all rationalists. Mary as the bride is united with the son in the heavenly bridal-chamber, and, as Sophia, with the Godhead.
> This dogma is in every respect timely. In the first place it is a symbolical fulfilment of John's vision. Secondly it contains an allusion to the marriage of the Lamb at the end of time, and thirdly, it repeats the Old Testament anamnesis of Sophia. These three references foretell the Incarnation of God. The second and third foretell the Incarnation in Christ, but the first foretells the Incarnation in creaturely man.[165]

Merton did not conceptually grasp what Bulgakov, much less Jung, was trying to say. Nevertheless, Merton intuited the central importance of *Sophia* for theology and continued working with it in his thought, and in his inner life.

On February 28, 1958, before his "Louisville Vision"[166] Merton had a dream:

> On the porch at Douglaston I am embraced with determined and virginal passion by a young Jewish girl. She clings to me, and will not let me go, and I get to like the idea. I see that she is a nice kid in a plain, sincere sort of way. I reflect "She belongs to the same race as St. Anne." I ask her name and she says her name is Proverb. I tell her that is a beautiful and significant name, but she does not appear to like it—perhaps the others have mocked her for it.
> When I awake, I rationalize it completely: *"Sapientiam amavi et quaesivi eam mihi sponsam assumere"* ["I loved wisdom and sought to make her my wife"]. Sophia (it is the *sofa* on the back porch...etc. etc.).[167]

However much he discounted the dream at first, his next journal entry is addressed "Dear Proverb," and is a love letter expressing his gratitude for her presence in his life.[168]

In April of 1958, Merton wrote his literary agent, Naomi Burton, for a copy of Boris Pasternak's *Dr. Zhivago*, a book whose primary theme is about anima love and how to reconcile it with everyday life. To this author's knowledge, Merton never made the conscious connection between his own experience of his mother's death and the opening pages of *Dr. Zhivago*, which contains a fictionalized account of Pasternak's mother's death when he was about the same age as Merton. Yet Pasternak and Merton recognized each other as kindred spirits, and Merton was so excited by their correspondence that he began studying Russian and dubbed Pasternak a "Christian anarchist."[169] Certainly, for both writers, the death of the mother at an early age was determinative, an experience of emptiness that opened up deep questions about the meaning of life and death, an experience that carried an inner imperative to seek and to find, through words, a meaning of universal significance. Pasternak resolved his experience in the character of Lara, a quintessential anima figure. Merton resonated with the Lara of *Dr. Zhivago* as a reflection of what he was experiencing as *Sophia*, the feminine principle of wisdom.

On April 23, 1959, Merton visited his friends, Victor and Carol Hammer, at their home in Lexington. His impressions of their house are recorded in his journal, but the most important part of his experience was only revealed in a letter to Victor Hammer on May 14, in which Merton described his impression of a triptych entitled *Hagia Sophia*, and tried to explain to Hammer its relation to Russian mysticism.[170] What Merton reported and elaborated later in his gift to Hammer of the prose poem, "Hagia Sophia," was the importance of the feminine presence, Mary as Mother of Jesus and as *Sophia*, the Wisdom of God. Looking at the picture as part of his internal process of coming to terms with his anima, and his need for the healing of narcissistic wounds derived from a distant, cold and critical mother, however, it is clear that the central theme of the picture is not the female per se, but her relationship to the son, whom she is crowning "with glory." Mott reports that the evening Merton saw this, he kept leaving the dinner table to return to look at the picture, clearly moved by it, so moved that he could not put it into words in his journal. What he was experiencing was not only the integrating of a truly loving mother imago, replacing his critical mother image, but also the bestowing on himself as the son, of a crown, a symbol of complete approval, acceptance and authority, an approval, as he said years before, which he never got from his mother. This event marks a turning point in Merton's writing.

By July of 1960, Merton was discovering his own inner feminine as would ultimately be expressed in "Hagia Sophia,"[171] a brief prose poem dedicated to the feminine principle of wisdom in the Russian mystics. From the hospital he wrote:

> There is in all visible things an invisible fecundity, a dimmed light, a meek namelessness, a hidden wholeness. This mysterious Unity and Integrity is Wisdom, the Mother of all, *Natura naturens*....This is at once my own nature, and the Gift of my Creator's thought and Art within me, speaking as Hagia Sophia, speaking as my sister, Wisdom.
> ...we do not hear the soft voice, the gentle voice, the merciful and feminine.

His next major publication was *New Seeds of Contemplation*, an updating of the earlier *Seeds*, with much different language. In this new version, in a chapter called "The Woman Clothed with the Sun,"[172] Merton unites the new feminine presence and the theme of emptiness and nothingness.

> Mary's chief glory is in her nothingness....retaining nothing of a "self" that could glory in anything for her own sake, she placed no obstacle to the mercy of God....

That God should assume Mary into heaven is not just a glorification of a "Mother Goddess." Quite the contrary, it is the expression of the divine love for humanity....And we will most truly possess Him when we have emptied ourselves and become poor and hidden as she is, resembling Him by resembling her.

...and the most precious of all the gifts of nature or grace is the desire to be hidden and to vanish from the sight of men and be accounted as nothing by the world and to disappear from one's own self-conscious consideration and vanish into nothingness in the immense poverty that is the adoration of God.

This absolute emptiness, this poverty, this obscurity, holds within it the secret of all joy because it is full of God.[173]

Here Mary as anima mother shows Merton the way to God and to the *fulfillment* of his experiences of emptiness, that toward which they have been aimed all along. It is also in this book that Merton outlines more clearly than ever before the relationship between the true and false self. In chapters 5 and 6, he describes how our true self is unknown to us because it is hidden in God, and we may only come to know it by emptying ourselves of all that we think we are.

Everyone of us is shadowed by an illusory person: a false self.

My false and private self is the one who wants to exist outside the reach of God's will and God's love....

The secret of my identity is hidden in the love and mercy of God.

Therefore there is only one problem on which all my existence, my peace and my happiness depend: to discover myself in discovering God.

In order to become myself I must cease to be what I always thought I wanted to be, and in order to find myself I must go out of myself, and in order to live I have to die.[174]

Although Merton began "Hagia Sophia" while in the hospital in 1960, it presages his actual experience nearly ten years later, being visited by a student nurse, awakened by her "soft voice."[175] The clear connection between his body's revolt against neglect, and the hospital as the place where feminine caring could happen is evident.

In 1966, an embodied *Hagia Sophia* entered Merton's life, and all that he had learned about the experience of emptiness was consciously called upon in order to effect yet another transforming movement in his emotional and spiritual life and in his identity as a monk. This was the episode of his falling in love with Marjorie Smith.[176] The entries in his journal in which he reports this experience are among the most poignant, raw revelations of the man in his struggle that exist in all his writings.

Shortly after his move into the hermitage[177] where he could be alone on a full-time basis, Merton began reflecting on a certain residual flaw or limitation in his faith in God and related it to "the *refusal* of woman which is a fault in my chastity." Griffin reports that Merton

> saw chastity as his most radical poverty, and his lack of poverty in accumulating things "as a desperate and useless expedient to cover this irreparable loss which I have not fully accepted. I can learn to accept it in the spirit and in love and it will no longer be 'irreparable.' The cross repairs it and transforms it. The tragic chastity which suddenly realizes itself to be mere loss, and fear that death has won—that one is sterile, useless, hateful. I do not say that this is my lot, but in my vow I can see it as an ever present possibility. To make a vow is to be exposed to this possibility. It is the risk one must run in seeking the other possibility: the revelation of the Paraclete to the pure heart."[178]

Solitude was necessary to reach new depths, depths filled with old wounds for Merton. The "fault" in his chastity was not that he still experienced women as attractive, though that was true. The fault lay in the connection between the inner image of the critical, distancing mother and his ability to feel loved. There was a gap between the developing inner image of *Sophia* as divine feminine wisdom at play and the part of himself connected to the critical mother that still felt unloved. As he began to experience his solitude more completely, he felt changes inside himself. "Each day, a little, I realize that my old life is breaking loose and will eventually fall off, in pieces, gradually. What then?"[179]

He became increasingly aware of his physical vulnerability. As suggested above, Merton's body sometimes forced him into a vulnerability his mind would have rejected. Perhaps because of this, he began to meditate on death more and more: "Death is flowering in my life as a part and fulfillment of it."[180] In March 1966, he wrote, "...how impossible it is really to grasp the fact that one must die. And what to do to be ready for it?[181]...Yet I know I have to die sometime and may this not all be the beginning of it?"[182]

This increased awareness of his own finitude, vulnerability and mortality was emotional and psychological preparation for what happened to him in the hospital.

At the end of March, Merton had a cervical fusion performed and remained in the hospital in Louisville to recover. He began conversations with a nurse named Marjorie and discovered that he looked forward to her visits. After a few days, he began to call her by her first name, "...the person whose name I would try to use as magic to break the grip of awful loneliness on my heart."[183]

Merton dreamed of her, of the two of them going to a city "where we could not find our way to the center that was 'real.'"[184]

It reached the point where Merton felt forced to admit he was in love with her. This created a great crisis for him.

> To seek happiness in human love now would be as absurd as a fish getting out on the beach to walk....My chastity is not merely the renunciation of sin or of sexual fulfillment but the renunciation of a whole mode of being, a whole conception of life and of myself.[185]

Yet they continued to see each other after Merton returned to the monastery. They talked by phone, met whenever Merton could find an excuse to leave, exchanged love letters, which Merton designated as secret to his editor, calling them the "Menendez file," a name that could be passed off as fiction, should the letters ever be exposed.[186] They struggled to find a way of understanding what was happening to them that would honor the best without dishonoring Merton's vows. He was also concerned for what all this meant to her, and the futility for her of having a relationship with a monk. Merton tried to understand what was happening as providential.

> He realized that his own deepest capacities for human love had never before been tapped, and that he too could "love with an awful completeness."...He struggled to fit his longing for her into the heart of his vocation to solitude, his way of emptiness and unknowing.[187]

Mentioned so off-handedly in his journal that it could easily be missed was the fact that "Marjorie" was only nineteen and that she was already engaged to be married.[188] Merton was fifty-one. As an event in his emotional and spiritual life, this changes nothing. It does, however, weight the importance of this encounter more heavily as an inner, psychological issue for her and Merton rather than a realistic possibility that they might consummate the relationship by his leaving monastic orders and getting married. Also, the failure of Merton and Marjorie to discuss seriously the import of their relationship for her engagement meant that *they* were not taking their own relationship seriously as an external event, but were entirely absorbed with its internal meaning for each of them.

After several attempts to break off, which neither of them could keep, Merton made a phone call at one point that was obviously likely to be overheard by the monk who connected the call. The monk reported it to the abbot and Merton went in and confessed to the relationship. The abbot told him a complete break was necessary, and blamed it all on Merton's hermitic solitude.

During a difficult and tormented night of dreams and frequent wakenings, Merton allowed himself to drift to the very heart of loneliness, dimly aware of the long hours in the darkness of the hermitage, in the stillness and silence of the surrounding forest, until the loneliness was total and desolate of every human consolation. He waited, abandoning himself to the emptiness, until loneliness transformed itself into solitude.[189]

A few nights later, he awoke again, unable to sleep, and imagined Marjorie at his door, knocking. The thought was so painful to him that he got out of bed and went for a walk in the night woods.

There he tried to empty his thoughts of everything except what was right in front of him: trees, fireflies, stars, and nothing, nothing, nothing. He waited, fixing his attention to the south on the huge sign of the Scorpion and the red eye of Regulus, until the nothingness filled with a sense of presence, totality and peace. Nothing became everything.

"What is there to look for or to yearn for but *all* reality here and now in whatever I am?" Merton wrote.[190]

A few nights later, June 24, Merton had a dream:

...he saw a tangle of dark briars and light roses. His attention fixed on one beautiful rose, which became luminous in a way that revealed the silk texture of its petals. His mother's face appeared behind the roses and the roses vanished.[191]

Though all contact with Marjorie was not over and certainly he continued to have fantasies of being with her, the inner separation was effected. In early September, Merton made a retreat, which he ended by making a new, lifelong vow to his vocation of solitude. For her part, Marjorie married the man to whom she was engaged and had children.[192]

From his experience of falling in love, Merton gained two crucial lessons, each of which was dependent on the other. He learned

> that he himself had the capacity to love fully....He now knew
> that he possessed an authentic potential for love and that his
> religious commitment was not the subtle disguise of an emo-
> tional cripple. This provided an inner liberation, which gave
> him a new sense of sureness, uncautiousness, defenseless-
> ness in his vocation and in the depths of himself.[193]

The new level of confidence in his vocation to solitude would
not have been possible without Merton's both facing the force of
his love for Marjorie and facing the emptiness of life without her.
All his experience with emptiness beforehand was needed and
called upon to clarify the meaning of his relationship with her. By
following through on his experience without forcing it to yield to
personal whim, deep desire or monastic rule, Merton effected a
great transformation in his own ability to love that is simultane-
ous with his ability to suffer in that love without requiring anything of it other than its factuality. By staying with his experience
of emptiness, he was able to accept reality—the stars, trees and
darkness—and let himself be transformed into a wiser, more loving
person. Such is the experience of emptiness in the process of self-
transformation, that what began as a deep, personal wound for
Merton, namely, the loss of his mother, was a driving force that led
him on his own spiritual journey and became a positive experience when its universal significance was grasped in the discovery
of himself as lovable and able to love, irrespective of whether he
would live it out in an ongoing relationship with his beloved.

And yet...one wonders how well Merton truly survived this
true love of his life. To what extent did he make his decision out
of concern for his followers and the impact on them had he suddenly renounced monkhood? To what extent did he, in effect,
swallow his pain out of consideration of the huge cost to him of
his vocation, rather than being transformed by it? These are
extremely subtle and difficult questions even to ask, in the face of
his prodigious contribution to the world. Although one outcome
of his experience with Marjorie was the writing of the essay, "Love

and Need–Is Love a Package or a Message?",[194] another outcome was the poem entitled,

Antipoem I

O the gentle fool
He fell in love
With the electric light
Do you not know, fool,
That love is dynamite?

Keep to what is yours
Do not interfere
With the established law

See the dizzy victims of romance
Unhappy moths!
Please observe
This ill-wondered troth.

All the authorities
In silence anywhere
Swear you only love your mind
If you marry a hot wire.

Obstinate fool

What a future we face
If one and all
Follow your theology

You owe the human race
An abject apology.

From the benefit of hindsight, it is difficult not to see this poem, written at the beginning of 1967, as making a connection between Merton's affair with Marjorie and his death, not quite two years later–which is the proverbial time for unresolved grief to be manifested in bodily illness or death—by electric shock. This is certainly not to say that Merton planned his own death, but the symmetry is definitely uncanny, just as his opening scene in "Hagia Sophia," in which he is attended by a nurse and is brought into health by her wisdom and love, uncannily presages his encounter with Marjorie. Was his death an unconscious reach for the "hot wire," a self-punishment for the depth of his need for love, or is "Antipoem" merely putting in brazen terms the sacrifice of self that the desire to see God demands?[195] Was his dream of his mother and the roses a transformation of the distant, critical and cold mother into loving acceptance, or was her critical face pushing through the fading roses a reassertion of her critical judgment and her victory over Merton's attempt to find love? We only read it was his mother's face, not what her mien was. These questions cannot, perhaps, be answered. Like Rilke's advice to a young poet, such questions are best lived—brought into our own lives for personal significance.

But is this not, after all, what so fascinates and intrigues us about Thomas Merton: that he is open enough with and to his own contradictions and is so forthright in his self-searching that we find our own complexity mirrored in him, a complexity we would usually prefer to simplify into an ideal goodness? He who was so early without a mirror has become a mirror for thousands after him. And is it not thus that we find ourselves encouraged in our own journey, to face the contradictions, limitations and untidiness that we see in this man, who was, after all, born under that most fluid of signs, the Water Bearer?

One of the important questions raised by this examination of Merton's changing anima is to what extent is anima failure the primary basis for the experience of emptiness? If one had, for the sake of argument, "good enough mothering," in Winnicott's language, would one experience emptiness as it has been discussed here? Clearly there would be a difference between those whose loss was both early and severe and those whose loss of important figures occurred at a more common time in the life cycle. Yet, death and change are inevitable, and this would be the Zen Buddhist point: Impermanence is written into every aspect of our experience of life, and a serious consideration of that fact very often leads one to follow the thread of the experience of emptiness in the directions we have been discussing.

Certainly, for Merton, it was necessary for him to go through the transformation of his own anima in order for him to be ready to experience emptiness in all reality as the basis of compassion.

Emptiness as Constituent in All Reality as Basis of Compassion

The choice of this rather cumbersome title for an experience of emptiness is taken directly from Merton's writing while in Polonnaruwa, Ceylon, in December 1968, just a few days before he died. It is the closest Merton came to being able to apply the concept of emptiness from Buddhism to something beyond personal experience.

> ...there is no puzzle, no problem, and really no "mystery." All problems are resolved and everything is clear, simply because what matters is clear. The rock, all matter, all life, is charged with dharmakaya...everything is emptiness and everything is compassion....I have now seen and have pierced through the surface and have got beyond the shadow and the disguise.[196]

In Zen Buddhism, emptiness is the fundamental nature of all reality, not just a kenotic action within the disciple surrendering his ego to God's will. For Dōgen, the emptiness of insentient beings was experienced as complete realization:

> Mountains and waters right now are the actualization of the ancient buddha way. Priest Daokai of Mt. Furong said to the assembly, "The green mountains are always walking; a stone woman gives birth to a child in the night."[197]

Journeys into Emptiness

In this entry at the end of his last journal, Merton appeared to have understood this in a new way, certainly in a way that inspired and moved him. It represented a very profound and significant shift in his understanding of emptiness, which heretofore had always been applied in his writings to oneself and one's relationship with God. The idea that what we call inanimate matter was also "empty" never appeared in Merton's writings before this note in his journal. Certainly he had no time to integrate the implications that this would have several years later for getting beyond an anthropocentric understanding of ecology, an appreciation for which was an increasingly important theme in his unpublished notebooks of the 1960s. Along with Dōgen and Merton, Jung also viewed stones and water, pots and pans, as, in some sense, alive. Merton's linking of "emptiness" with "compassion" is certainly in accord with the Zen Buddhist experience and may perhaps be understood as an essential aspect of what might be called the "mystical" experience. All three people studied here have been, rightly or wrongly, called "mystics." What does this mean, other than to see into the intrinsic interconnectedness of all things? And it is the experience of all who see this that they feel compassion both to and from all things, inanimate as well as animate.

The Emptiness of Emptiness

This phrase is taken, not from Merton, but from Nāgārjuna[198] and is carried on into Zen in the insistence on "mind to mind transmission, outside of words and letters." In this final experience of emptiness (which remains, nevertheless, merely one more door into whatever is next), all concepts, including 'I' or "experiencing" or "emptiness," are left behind, and one experiences "*tathata*," "suchness," "reality-itself," without thought or concept.

While Merton understood this concept of the emptiness of emptiness intellectually, it is the judgment of this author that he was never able to relinquish the inner witness to his own experience. He could never escape being the observer (and, to be sure, the recorder) of what he experienced. This fact carried fundamental significance for Merton's psychological and spiritual growth process, and is the key linking two of his lifelong conflicts, the conflict of his identity as a monk versus his identity as a writer, and the conflict he experienced in the need for greater solitude than was afforded him at Gethsemani contrasted with his constant urge to go elsewhere: either to join a new order, or to found a new monastery—or to invite people over to his hermitage!

The primary problem Thomas Merton struggled with throughout his adult life was self-consciousness: always being aware of himself doing what he was doing, writing what he was writing, even praying what he prayed as if he were always on stage, and even his earnest desire to get off stage became part of the performance. The appeal to Merton of the idea of emptiness in Zen was in its potential as a key to unlock the prison of his self-consciousness.

However badly Zilboorg handled his meeting with Merton, he was basically correct in his assessment. Merton was his own worst enemy in terms of the burden of self-consciousness—and he knew it. More importantly, however, he wrote about it with an honesty that makes him very valuable to us today.

Mott sees this conflict as apparent before Merton entered the monastery.

> By 1935, the chief struggle of Merton's life had emerged. It was a battle with a kind of self-consciousness that could be agonizing under certain conditions. Merton's courage shows itself in the fact that he chose to engage the struggle precisely where it was most acute; that was, in his approach to his own writing and in the public aspect of religion. In his writing, especially in his journals, he sought the ground of his own being beyond everything else that was false.[199]

It is here that a fundamental difference between emptiness as *kenosis* according to the apophatic tradition in Christianity, and emptiness as *sunyata* in Zen Buddhism becomes crucial and apparent.

Journeys into Emptiness

Throughout Merton's writings, his actual use of the concept of emptiness functions apophatically and kenotically to denote the total reduction of ego and individual personality to "nothing" in order to make way for God. On this subject, Merton quoted Eckhart to the effect that we must become so small that not even God could find a place in us. This is the shared experience of the desert fathers and the English and European Christian mystics. In this form of "emptiness," one becomes more and more "nothing" in order to be "in" and "at one with" God, without separation or division. What is left from this experience of emptiness is God, "who is in all and through all." One might say, though the actual experience is beyond words, that in the ultimate experience of emptiness in Christian mysticism, one becomes nothing that God may be everything.

To put it this way is, from a Zen perspective, immediately to set up a dualism from which it is impossible to escape. The antinomy between God and self remains, however much self is "emptied" into union with "God."

In Merton's actual practice, as near as this author has been able to determine from his writings, Merton never got beyond this. David Cooper has given an excellent account of what he called Merton's "failed mysticism," showing the shift for Merton between trying to be a genuine mystic to his accepting the limitations of his ideal self and turning his attention to the world, thereby becoming, in Cooper's view, a "radical humanist."[200] From this author's point of view, Merton failed to be a saint, but his vision was mystical, however limited it was by his self-consciousness. Merton's limitations were on three levels: (1) His fundamental narcissistic wounds, suffered from his earliest childhood and compounded by the deaths of his parents, made him captive to the grandiose ideal self that Gregory Zilboorg accused him of; (2) his method of writing remained hampered by his stage-consciousness; and (3) his spiritual aspiration was limited by a method inadequate for the task of losing self-consciousness. It is not that his aspiration was misdirected by its grandiosity, so much as it was that his inner wounds were deeper than any method available at the time to deal with them.

Intellectually, Merton saw from his readings in Zen that there was yet a further step to take. But without an actual teacher, he was left to figure it out for himself by reading, which, in Zen, as in depth psychology, is impossible.

In this regard, one wonders to what extent Merton was ever able to let himself learn directly from another person, which would have required his becoming a vulnerable child again. Did this man, who suffered such repeated early failures from parents and authorities, *ever* let anyone be an authority for him?[201] With the exception of the nurse, did Merton ever let anyone *in*? To what extent did he ever allow himself to be affected by another person's concrete reality (such as someone's crying or needing a bedpan carried out) and moved thereby to direct, personal compassion? From whom, besides the nurse, did he ever experience such compassion for himself? And if Merton had such trouble letting in human beings, what does that say about the way he really experienced, rather than thought about, God?

Merton's ability to intuit this further step in the experience of emptiness was remarkable and indicative of his inner honesty and integrity. Because he sensed this, he was constantly trying to learn more about Zen. Yet some things need to be noted that would escape most Western readers.

Merton's primary knowledge about Zen came from two people, D. T. Suzuki and John Wu. D. T. Suzuki was not, contrary to what many Merton biographers assume, a Zen master. He was not a person who had received "mind to mind transmission." He was a brilliant intellectual articulator of Zen thought and experience into English and Western culture, but he was not a Zen teacher. Similarly, although John Wu was Chinese and obviously, based on his book, *The Golden Age of Zen*,[202] knowledgeable *about* Zen, he was nonetheless an intellectual who studied Zen texts, not someone who practiced Zen (or, in Chinese, *Ch'an*); indeed, he was a convert to Catholicism. In addition—and most poignantly, from the perspective of the concern with self-consciousness—the book Merton loved the most was the translation he did with John Wu of *The Way of Chuang Tzu*, and Chuang Tzu was a Taoist, not a Chan Buddhist! While Buddhism absorbed significant elements of Taoism in its development of Zen, one of the most important differences between them is Zen's emphasis on mind to mind transmission, which can only happen in a personal encounter between a qualified teacher and a student. This Merton was unable to experience, because the only teachers in America at the time were in California, and Merton had not even heard of them.

The importance of having a qualified teacher in order to *experience* Zen was underscored by Heinrich Dumoulin in his correspondence with Merton in 1964. Dumoulin told Merton that the only way really to understand Zen was to experience it under a qualified teacher, and therefore Merton should come to Japan to study.[203] Abbot Dom James refused to allow him to go. This must be considered the severest failure on the part of the abbot to serve Merton's personal spiritual growth needs, a failure with vast ramifications for the rest of Merton's life and career. It is not that the failure was malicious or knowingly withholding. Dom James had decided, with Zilboorg's support and Dom James' superiors' concurrence, that Merton's urges to travel were entirely neurotic. To forbid travel was therefore to maintain his consistency in keeping that urge reined in. In retrospect, however, this was an instance where Merton's spiritual need was not fathomed because of the inadequacy of training of his own spiritual teachers. No one in American Christianity at the time could have any idea of the importance of a spiritual process that would liberate one from self-consciousness.

Lastly, apart from some Zen koans and the texts used in John Wu's book, Merton did not have access to the primary sources of Zen Buddhism because they were not yet available in English. In the 1960s, even Dōgen was just beginning to be appreciated for his philosophical profundity in Japan.

Merton experienced his problem of attachment to self-consciousness on the psychological level as an inability to get away from his performer self. As mentioned above, Merton's earliest experience of his mother was of her observing him, writing about him. Merton's writing became, therefore, his own act of observing himself, as well as his act of presenting himself to others. It was also, most importantly, his way of keeping the only mothering presence he knew between him and an absolute void in which he would psychologically disappear. There remained, perhaps inescapably, once *Seven Storey* was published and he became famous, an awareness that everything he wrote would be read. However well he explored thoughts and experiences by writing about them, there remained a self-consciousness about being a writer that never entirely left him. His own assessment expresses residual ambivalence as late as 1967:

> I myself am open and closed. When I reveal most I hide most...I think I have finally got away from self-consciousness and introversion. It may be my final liberation from all diaries. Maybe that is my one remaining task.[204]

Merton's linking of "self-consciousness" and "introversion" suggests that he saw them as synonymous. One wonders, therefore, whether he thought that, by being more extroverted, he could overcome his self-consciousness. This is a common mistake that often deflects people from their inner journey. Was this one motivation for Merton's becoming more socially active at this point in his life (1965 and after)? Did he, in essence, hit an inner wall that his methods of writing and contemplative prayer could not get past? Thus seen, his "guilt" as a "bystander" simply underscored his continuing self-consciousness and shows, in spite of his words in his introduction to *Chuang Tzu*,[205] that he had not yet integrated the

Taoist concept of *wu-wei*, nonaction, into his personal circumstance as a monk.

It is only recently that a method called proprioceptive writing[206] has been developed by which writing can be used to access the deepest parts of the self. It was not really known at the time.

Thus, while Merton strove mightily to reach toward his true self and let go of all falseness, he never quite succeeded in reaching deeper into the spontaneous self that preceded his mother's observing status. This is a methodological failure psychologically as well as spiritually. Although no notes appear available regarding his psychotherapy work with John Wygal, M.D.,[207] it is apparent that their relationship developed into a friendship,[208] making depth psychological work practically impossible. Here, once again, a methodology that might have been expected to bring deeper healing failed him. As with Zen, the psychiatry and depth psychology of 1965 in America was not yet ready to deal with the level of narcissistic dynamics for which Merton needed help.[209]

It is from the perspective of Merton's unmet inner need to go deeper into himself than his own method of contemplative prayer allowed him, a level that would liberate him from the vestiges of the false self still needing the observing mother (read Gethsemani and all Merton's readers), that his perpetual restlessness and longing for greater solitude, as well as the conflict between writer and monk, must be seen. A person still psychologically wrestling with a critical mother for whom everything was a performance is desperate to have an experience that he can call uniquely his own. So thoroughly has he been trained to please the mother as a life source that it is only by literal and inner solitude that he is able to hear his own voice and know it is not the voice of the child trying to get the mother's attention. This is a problem endemic to religious life because both the actual religious authority and the projected authority (as God or Buddha, etc.) are seen and experienced as observing one, and one wants to please them. But to please them is to not be true to oneself.

Therefore a method has to be devised in which the original, spontaneous self can be recovered.

For Merton, that could only be approached in solitude, and the many concerns of the Gethsemani community and the need to be accountable to and interacting with the community, apart from the support and renewal of communal worship, were experienced by him as impingements—as intrusions from the outside that required an adaptation in attention and behavior that stole time, energy and focus from his learning to listen to his true self. Merton's desire to move away from the Gethsemani community must not be understood as a misanthropic one, but rather as a reflection of the fact that there was evidently no one in the community who matched the breadth and depth of his spiritual, emotional and intellectual quest, who could have, by mirroring him, enhanced his inner journey.

In the same vein, when Merton entered Gethsemani and asked to be told to stop writing, he had, in fact, a good idea, a healthy impulse. It was his desire to be allowed off-stage. Psychologically, it would have allowed him to experience himself without the observing mother, which his writing long may have represented. Only such an experience would have allowed him to actually contact, experientially, his deeper, true self and to experience it without having to write about it for validation. The abbot's insistence that he keep on writing, while well intended, only served to sink Merton deeper into his writer/performer self and to lock in his mother's critical eye. Here again, in Zen practice, certain times are set aside when writing and reading are forbidden precisely in order to enter more deeply into one's self. It is a great pity Merton never had the chance to experience such a method.

Likewise, Merton's constant wish to go somewhere else where he could be more solitary had an important health-seeking motivation behind it, namely, the recovery of his true self. When William Shannon quotes Merton—"Our real journey in life is interior"[210]—to gloss over Merton's urges to leave the community, he is overlooking the fact that we often have to travel a great deal in order to find the people who will help us learn from ourselves and teach us about the inner journey. Merton, after all, left New York, not to mention France and England. Dōgen left Japan to go to China. Jung went to Freud, then left Freud and traveled around the world to observe different cultures. It is the position of this author that Merton would have been better served by either an extensive depth psychological analysis or/and an extended study in Japan (or California) with a Japanese Zen master.

To have changed places without such a mentor, though, would not have served him, because the need for solitude clearly reflected only one side of his personality. The other side was outgoing, and it was from this side that he wrote. Further, it should not escape notice that once he received the permission to be a hermit, he began a very active social life, both at the hermitage and in trips to Louisville, under whatever pretext.

Part III

Merton's Understanding of Emptiness and His Contribution to the World

For Thomas Merton, the experience of emptiness was a multi-colored thread that led him from the deepest pains, wounds and loneliness of life to an understanding of the vacuity and shallowness of much of human striving, to an inner meeting where the true self is hidden with Christ in God, and the self encounters the God who cannot be named. This is the self relieved of the burden of having to determine its own fate by will power, consciousness, knowledge or any other form of power. The self thus experiencing emptiness on this level is liberated to be free for God, to be free for others and to be free for whatever God wills. This is the understanding of emptiness that was the ground for Merton's critique of society, the ground on which the guilty bystander stands. The experience of emptiness was not, therefore, for Merton, an isolated and isolating personal experience, but, on the contrary, was the basis on which he understood himself as simply human and knowing what that meant. The experience of emptiness, followed in its multicolored strands, led Thomas Merton to God, to his true self and to membership as an ordinary person in the human community.

From the time of his conversion, Merton kept exploring his experiences of emptiness until it took him, literally, around the world. Had he not gone to Gethsemani, and remained at Columbia for a Ph.D., he might well have become, as he imagined, a writer for the *New Yorker* or a teacher at Columbia; but he probably would have also become an alcoholic and would have dissipated his talent and energies without achieving anything of significance. Once in the monastery, he might well have become (were he someone else!) a complacent monk, dutifully carrying out his duties, and might even have been made an abbot, but he would not have produced the many books, articles, letters and speeches for everyone's edification that came from his working through his experiences of emptiness.

There were three points, at least, at which a case could be made that Merton backed away from the experience of emptiness and retreated into the security of the known rather than venture forth further into untrod territory. The first was in 1960, when Merton finally decided to try psychoanalysis with James Wygal, M.D. In this case, Merton's own charisma doubtless interfered, defensively, and unfortunately also successfully, to deflect serious analysis. Merton made his request to see Wygal in January of 1960, and by July he was listening to jazz in Wygal's house.[211] As discussed above, Merton was not accustomed to relying on anyone else to understand himself and, as with most people entering psychotherapy or psychoanalysis, his desire for help competed with his dedication to preserving the autonomy of his own ego.

Journeys into Emptiness

The second refusal to enter his experience of emptiness more fully was in 1964 (as mentioned earlier), when Dumoulin invited him to come to Japan to study with a Zen master. Merton asked for permission to go and was refused. Since he had made many such requests to travel, as well as to join other orders, the abbot probably saw no reason to give this request any special consideration. Merton himself seemed not to recognize this opportunity as something worth holding fast to and fighting for, which he was quite capable of doing. But here again, his unconscious resistance to accepting someone else's influence on his inner life interfered, and he did not protest.

The third instance of his backing away from emptiness might be considered his affair with Marjorie. Quite apart from any objective assessment of the ability of these two people to sustain an intimate relationship, from the point of view of Merton's inner journey, to leave monastic life in order to fully experience the vicissitudes of a real human relationship might be considered an appropriate "Zen" leap from a hundred-foot flagpole, a deliberate leave-taking from security and the familiar. From both a Zen and a psychological point of view, such a leap into the void of the unknown might well have been considered a deeper entry into emptiness than Merton's staying where he could be fed and famous. Merton considered this possibility carefully.

But it is exactly here that Merton's decision has something to teach us about the experience of emptiness. From every perspective studied here—Zen Buddhism, Christianity and analytical psychology—the experience of emptiness does not carry an absolute value in itself, but is essential only insofar as it is a process of winnowing within the self, so that the superfluous and extraneous may be relinquished in order that the true self may be manifested. If we follow the meaning of our experiences of emptiness, they ultimately lead us to our life task and our destiny. We walk forward through the experiences of emptiness until we find ourselves manifesting our deepest modes of presence, knowing and acting, and then discover that we are met by limits both within and without, constraints of character and the historical moment. To defy those limits would be to try to be—in an oversimplified phrase—other than who we are. But we cannot know who we are, really, until that time comes when our identity is revealed by our acceptance of both ourselves and our time as somehow "given," over which we have neither choice nor control, and we simply "do" who we are.

Jung expressed such an attitude this way:

> I might call it an affirmation of things as they are: an unconditional "yes" to that which is, without subjective protests— acceptance of the conditions of existence as I see them and understand them, acceptance of my own nature, as I happen to be....when one follows the path of individuation, when one lives one's own life, one must take mistakes into the bargain....how important it is to affirm one's own destiny.[212]

Merton's time with Marjorie must be considered of inestimable value not only for himself, in teaching him to accept love and that he could love, but as made possible because of his earlier explorations of his experience of emptiness. Had he refused those earlier parts of his journey, he would have treated Marjorie as he had treated the women he met before he entered the monastery, as objects for his personal gratification or for his refusal. Instead, with Marjorie, he learned he could love, could be emotionally vulnerable and present. One hopes that the experience also enabled her to better fulfill the subsequent part of her own life in marriage and family.

Thomas Merton did not reach his stated goal of becoming a saint. Instead, by pursuing his own experiences of emptiness into his own tasks and destiny, he bequeathed to subsequent generations a rich record of what it is like from the inside to wrestle with the experience of emptiness in all of its rough edges. He was, in many ways, a quintessential Euro-American, bridging cultures, nations, histories, races and religions. As Anthony Padovano has noted, he was the "symbol of a century."[213] He alerted not just Catholicism, but all Christianity to its obligation to the world at large, its obligation to spiritual depth and social engagement. He mapped out the territory of emptiness on both personal and social levels in a way that alerted Americans to their propensity for destruction and loss of religious faith. He articulated the depth dimension that Christian faith brings to a humanism that otherwise declared God dead. He demonstrated by his essays, letters and poetry the continuing relevance of a spiritual dimension for scientists, writers, philosophers, artists and government leaders around the world. He initiated dialogue among Christianity, Buddhism and other religions that continues on to the present day. He made contemplative prayer a way for others to join him in exploring their own experiences of emptiness en route to their true selves. These are the gifts he brought back from his own "dark path," his explorations into the experiences of emptiness.

Jung

Chapter 3

THE EXPERIENCE OF EMPTINESS IN DEPTH PSYCHOLOGY

Depth psychology is an important tool for understanding the experience of emptiness because it studies the structure and dynamics of the psyche,[1] with particular regard for the role of the unconscious in all human experience. Through depth psychology the dynamics of the psyche may be seen to determine, to a large degree, the scope and the reach of the experience of emptiness. The psyche is understood as having its own rules, its own needs and its own ways of perceiving, creating and responding to its experience in the world. Without a deliberate grounding of awareness in one's own unique psyche, including one's personal history, the experience of emptiness will be shaped and limited by inner dynamics, about which one will remain unconscious. To the extent that one is unconscious, one is, in religious terms, subject to illusion (Buddhism, *maya*) or sin (Christianity, *hamartia*, "missing the mark"), to mistaking the unreal for the real. In its ambition to resist unconsciousness by understanding the psyche, depth psychology offers valuable insight into the experiencer as well as the experience of emptiness in a way that is not only iconoclastic but hope-giving and helpful to the self in the process of transformation. For this reason, depth psychology as represented primarily by the work of Carl Gustav Jung, with some additional consideration of Donald W. Winnicott and Heinz Kohut, can contribute to our understanding of the experience of emptiness based on its understanding of the psyche.

Carl Gustav Jung, son of a Reformed Protestant pastor in Switzerland, became a psychiatrist and early on focused on the problems of people with schizophrenia. For more than six years[2] a close friend and protégé of Sigmund Freud, Jung reached a point of irreconcilable differences with Freud over the nature of the psyche—especially over the unconscious and libido, and consequently, the meaning of religion—and they broke off both their personal and professional relationship. For Freud, the elements of the unconscious that we can retrieve into consciousness were derivatives of personal contents, cultural and societal values, and instincts, including *thanatos*, the death instinct. For Jung, the unconscious bore crucial information about the individual as well as the collective psyche that seeks to aid both the individuation[3] process for the individual and for the larger life of society and culture across time. In Jung's view, the person who accepts the path of individuation does so, in effect, on behalf of the community and brings back what is learned for the common welfare. This is true, he maintained, even when (or especially when, as in the case of prophets and reformers) what the individual has brought back challenges or confronts the collective[4] unconscious values. Without such a challenge, people remain subject to the ruling images and ethos of the collective, or objective, psyche.[5]

The Experience of Emptiness in Depth Psychology

The viability of any particular religion, in Jung's understanding, lay in its provision of symbols and rituals to enhance the growth and development of the self. Such symbols and rituals take their form from the collective unconscious and are shaped by contemporary culture. Through these symbols and rituals, the archaic objective psyche is mediated to the ego, thus integrating and strengthening the entire psyche. Symbols and rituals in this way can be seen as connecting links between the realm of the psyche and the realm of the spirit.[6] For Jung, the psyche could find its wholeness (however provisionally) in a vital contact with the realm of the spirit as mediated through symbols and symbol making, often in religion. However, he also felt that no given institutional or collective form of religion could be assumed to be sufficient to meet the full life possibilities of any given individual, generation or society on its own.

For Jung, an understanding of the psyche was essential to understanding religion in much the same way that the laws of mass and energy are important for locomotion: One can mentally deny such laws or avoid learning about them, but one will nonetheless be bound by them; conversely, understanding them will offer more possibilities for achieving one's goals. Understanding the nature of the psyche is of importance, therefore, in evaluating the contribution of religion to the transformation of the self. Thus, through depth psychology, the way in which each religion approaches the experience of emptiness and uses it either for healthy or for pathological possibilities can be identified and appreciated.

Depth psychology also studies the ways in which the potentials of each person to be him-/herself is aided or hindered by the given psychological dynamics of a situation. With regard to religion, it offers a critique not just in terms of a religion's service to the individual and to community, but in terms of that religion's service to its own source and telos, whether it is called God, Buddha or the ground of being. It is precisely because Jung provides us with such a strong model for relating the spiritual and psychological dimensions of the life of the self that he has so much to offer to this study.

Part of Freud's discomfort with Jung was Jung's attention to occult and religious phenomena. Whereas Freud had dismissed religion as an illusion devised by people too afraid to face the harshness of reality and the pressures of the unconscious, Jung saw in religion the attempt of cultures to enable the process of individuation by which the self becomes actualized. In the process of individuation, the collective psyche is enhanced by the work of each individual self, which constitutes an offering that, were it to be withheld, would inhibit and throw off balance the vitality of the collective. This holds true, for Jung, in psychological matters as well as more obvious realms of creativity such as the arts, education, government and science. Thus each person's assumption of responsibility for his/her own psychological journey makes a positive contribution to the psychological well-being of all.[7]

Donald W. Winnicott and Heinz Kohut, representing the two additional schools to be considered here (respectively of object relations theory and self psychology) will also be considered for their contributions from the depth psychological perspective on the experience of emptiness. Although their personal biographies and self-reflections will not be considered in the way that Jung's will be, they will be presented for the specific points they contribute to our understanding of the experience of emptiness and its role in the transformation of the self.

In Winnicott's view of true self and false self phenomena, several changing phases of emptiness can be seen. For example, according to Winnicott, (1) emptiness that comes from a false self mode of living leads to a different kind of emptiness from (2) that which is experienced when letting go of the (seeming) security of false self living, which leads to (3) a third kind of emptiness that is experienced in true self life. Furthermore, Winnicott's idea of transitional space[8] may constitute a direct elaboration of the experience of emptiness (while, paradoxically, full of symbols of self, other and culture), and his idea of transitional objects[9] may be seen as having ambivalent status in living with the experience of emptiness, carrying both creative and limiting possibilities.[10] Thus, images of God and other religious figures may be viewed as transitional objects and must be explored for ways in which such images can be both creative and limiting for a given individual in the experience of emptiness. Winnicott's understanding of transitional phenomena suggests ways to work with, engage and even revise one's internal images, both those that are inherited from religion and the more idiosyncratic ones that appear in prayer and meditation. Such work can be crucial when attending to experiences of emptiness in order to facilitate one's psychological growth.

Kohut, in addition to contributing significantly to the methodology of this study, will articulate the role of the experience of emptiness in the developing of cohesion within the self and the fact that a cohesive self, though required for full maturity and functioning, can never be assumed. Major problems arise both from the failures to work through the experience of emptiness in order to form a cohesive self and out of the effort to compensate for and to heal the wounds and deprivations suffered before a cohesive self can be achieved. In effect, Kohut's position parallels the thesis of this study in his contention that the experience of emptiness signals very real and significant narcissistic needs that, if unattended, will severely attenuate one's capacity to function in the world and to undergo whatever transformation that self-realization may require.

Part I
Carl Gustav Jung and Analytical Psychology

HERITAGE

Carl Jung's lifelong interest in both psychiatry and religion was preceded by the substantial careers of each of his grandfathers in those fields. To the young Carl, his father was overshadowed by the stature of both grandfathers. Carl's father's father, referred to, after young Carl's birth, as Carl Gustav I (1794–1864),[11] was a medical doctor on the faculty of the University of Basel who created Friedmatt, a psychiatric clinic, as well as the "Home of Good Hope," for retarded children.[12] Carl I was somewhat jokingly referred to as an illegitimate son of Goethe, a "myth" which the later Carl was evidently fond of repeating. While this does not appear true, it certainly bespeaks a self-image that the younger Carl was glad to cultivate, no less grand for being untrue.

Significantly, grandfather Carl I was converted from Catholicism to Protestantism under the influence of Friedrich Schleiermacher.[13] Schleiermacher was renowned for the importance he attached to personal experience in religious belief and life and must have, for Carl I, represented a vitality then lacking in Catholicism.

Young Carl's grandfather on his mother's side, Samuel Preiswerk (1799–1871), taught Hebrew and literature in Geneva before he became a pastor in Basel. Considered the "dean of the Basel clergy,"[14] he also called for the "restoration of Palestine to the Jews and thus is considered a forerunner of the Zionists."[15]

The grandson's lifelong effort to dig into the vital foundations of religions, most especially of Christianity, must be understood, therefore, as the carrying-on of at least a three-generational conscious wrestling with religious meaning[16] on both sides of his family.

Jung's paternal great-grandfather, Franz Ignaz Jung (d. 1831), married Sophie Ziegler, who reportedly suffered from mental illness, which the young Carl took pains to investigate.

> Sophie-Ziegler Jung's mental illness has absorbed me again. The only documents relating to this are some letters of hers in my possession. The handwriting shows no schizophrenic traits but rather, for all its character, an emotional ravagement such as can be observed in psychogenic melancholias.[17]

On the maternal side of the family, Grandfather Samuel Preiswerk distinguished himself further in that he maintained an active belief in ghosts.

> In his study he kept a chair for the spirit of his deceased wife, Magdalene. To the annoyance of his second wife, he set aside a certain time of every week for intimate conversation with Magdalene's ghost.[18]

In addition, Pastor Preiswerk required his daughter, Emilie, Carl's mother, to stand behind him while he wrote sermons in order to keep ghosts away,[19] serving as a sentinel between two aspects of transpersonal reality: God and the Holy Ghost on the one hand, and the ghosts of ancestors on the other. Insofar as ghosts represent dissociated or unintegrated pieces of the psyche, these stories confirm that some degree of mental illness was evident on both sides of young Carl's family for the prior two generations and constituted an important aspect of his own experiences of emptiness.

Family Tree

Jung (paternal) side

Franz Ignaz Jung (physician, d. 1831)—Sophie Ziegler

Carl Gustav Jung (physician, 1794–1864)—Sophie Frey (daughter of Basel mayor)

Johann Paul Achilles Jung (pastor, 1842–96)

Preiswerk (maternal) side

Samuel Preiswerk (pastor, 1799–1871)—Augusta Faber (1805–65)

Emilie Preiswerk (1848–1923)

Carl Gustav Jung (1875–1961)—Emma Rauschenbach (1882–1955)

Agatha (12/04), Gret (2/06), Franz (11/08), Marianne (8/10), Helene (3/14)

The scene in which Carl's maternal grandfather routinely talked to his dead first wife with his living wife's knowledge and demanded that his daughter, Emilie (Carl's mother), stand behind to protect him against ghosts prefigured at least two developments for the younger Carl: It may well have set a background for his formulation of the technique of active imagination, in which objects and images from the psyche were to be engaged in dialogue to see what they had to say. It also prefigures the young Carl's psychological position vis-à-vis women in his life, in which he maintained one as a wife who was stable, reliable and "there," and another (first Sabina Spielrein, then Toni Wolfe[20]) who served as a more engaging and inspiring, almost ethereal personality by which his own creativity was encouraged.[21]

The Experience of Emptiness in a World of Unreliable or Inconsistent Models

Carl Jung was born in the shadow of an experience of emptiness that was not his own. His own birth in July of 1875 was preceded by that of a brother, Paul, in August of 1873, who died within a few days.

The birth and death of this older brother is given a single sentence in almost all of Carl Jung's biographies.[22] No one says or wonders how the infant died. The significance of the sudden early death of her firstborn for the mother, Emilie, had to have been enormous, and may have triggered the acute episode of mental illness that led to her hospitalization. For the father, Johann Paul Achilles,[23] the loss of his first son surely contributed to the feelings of sentimentality and powerlessness[24] that the second son, Carl, saw in him. Naturally, the experience also had a strong and lasting impact on the subsequent relationship between the mother and father in their marriage. Yet, the indirect impact of the elder brother's death on Carl, based on how his parents were affected, and the direct impact on Carl of living under the shadow of a dead brother has not even been considered important enough to warrant speculation, much less research. This seems to be an extremely striking omission in the mounting biographical corpus of a psychotherapist by many otherwise psychologically attuned writers. It is even more striking that Carl Jung does not even mention his brother in his autobiography.[25]

The death of a child casts a pall over the entire family, from which the family rarely entirely recovers, and subsequent children may often feel they live in the shadow of a ghost who can never be exorcised. The divorce rate for couples who experience the death of a child is significantly greater than the norm, because issues of guilt and grief often devolve into blaming that is passed back and forth between mother and father like a hot potato. Each is so wounded that little energy is left to offer succor to the other even when wishing to do so. In the context of the loss of their first son, the marital difficulties of Carl Jung's parents would seem, in retrospect, inevitable, no matter how well they otherwise related to and loved each other.

It is certainly significant that the first son was named after the father, and it may well have been infant Carl's salvation that he was named after his grandfather. Names, as was noted above in discussing Thomas Merton, are important both as designations of parental expectations and as signifying some essence of personality. For Carl to have carried his noted grandfather's name rather than that of his father, whom he saw as powerless, may have offered him a much needed strong self-image by which he could see himself transcending his personal history.

Carl Gustav Jung was born July 26, 1875, the second child of Johann Paul Achilles (1842–96), a Reformed Protestant pastor, and Emilie Preiswerk Jung (1848–1923) at Kesswil, Canton Thurgau, Switzerland. Six months after Carl's birth, his father took a parish in Laufen, Canton Zürich, where he served until 1878. This was the place of young Carl's earliest memories. In 1879, after Emilie was hospitalized for depression for several months, they moved to the parish of Klein-Hüningen. In addition to Johann Paul's parish duties, from the 1880s on, he served as chaplain at Friedmatt, the insane asylum in Basel that his father-in-law had been instrumental in founding.

It was almost exactly nine years after Carl's birth that his sister was born, July 17, 1884. Although she was apparently important to Carl and they enjoyed a good relationship, their nine-year difference in ages meant that, by the time she came along, Carl had already developed a basic sense of himself. With such a difference in their ages, she was not able to be a peer or companion to her older brother in his childhood. Thus, Carl saw himself, fundamentally, as an only child.

According to Carl Jung's autobiography, his earliest memories were quite bright and positive. The one he considered earliest occurred when he was in a pram, having "just awakened to the glorious beauty of the day," and the next one was his recollection of sitting in a high chair and experiencing the pleasant taste and smell of milk.[26] One's earliest memories, however detailed or vague, are important on several levels. As the first consciously remembered experiences, they give a quick picture of how a person feels being in the world, whether it is basically a positive experience or not, and this can provide a resource and a reservoir for later life's difficulties. It is questionable whether one can remember much without a basically healthy beginning. The extent of people's capacity to remember back into infancy or childhood varies tremendously. For the most part, uncertainty—the sense of a tenuous or threatening world—and actual trauma are repressed. Only if there is a basic sense of trustworthiness is there very early memory.[27] From this point of view, Carl Jung's ability to remember back to his days in a pram would suggest that, at least initially, he felt a basic security in the world.

The Experience of Emptiness with a Mother Both "There" and "Not There"

Carl Jung's first *conscious* experience of emptiness occurred when his mother was away in a psychiatric hospital for several months because of depression, when he was three years old.

> I am restive, feverish, unable to sleep. My father carries me in his arms, paces up and down, singing his old student songs. I particularly remember one I was especially fond of and which always used to soothe me, "*Alles schweige, jeder neige….*"[28] To this day I can remember my father's voice, singing over me in the stillness of the night.[29]
>
> I am suffering, so my mother told me afterward, from general eczema.[30] Dim intimations of trouble in my parents' marriage hovered around me. My illness, in 1878, must have been connected with a temporary separation of my parents. My mother spent several months in a hospital in

Basel,[31] and presumably her illness had something to do with the difficulty in the marriage.[32]

Jung continues on the same page to elaborate on the effect on him of his mother's absence.

> I was deeply troubled by my mother's being away. From then on, I always felt mistrustful when the word "love" was spoken. The feeling I associated with "woman" was for a long time that of innate unreliability. "Father," on the other hand, meant reliability and—powerlessness. That is the handicap I started off with.[33]

There is a great deal of history, family dynamics and interpretation compressed into these brief excerpts—so much so, that one wonders if there was some later family editing of the original manuscript.[34] The occasion of a fever-induced restlessness was connected to the emotionally heavy-laden experiences of emptiness in a world of unreliable or inconsistent models. This world flooded the young Carl with feelings of instability triggered by several aspects of family life: living with a mother who, due to her mental illness, was often "there" but "not there"; being abandoned by her, literally, when she was hospitalized; his sense of his father as being alternately powerful and "powerless"; and his vague awareness of a conflict between his parents.

In Jung's earliest conscious experience of emptiness, therefore, several elements converged in his memory as a string of associations from that period of at least several months during his third year, more so than the isolated aspects of a single episode in his life. As was noted above in looking at Thomas Merton's repeated experiences of emptiness,[35] one experience by itself may not impact personal development significantly, but it is rather the accumulation of repeated experiences of emptiness piling on top of each other like a stack of skewed coins that make for psychological vulnerability. The determining factor in all of these was the fundamental fact of his mother's mental illness. The exact nature of the illness is difficult to determine on the basis of Jung's autobiography.[36] What he does say clearly is that she had "two personalities."

> My mother was a very good mother to me. She had a hearty animal warmth, cooked wonderfully, and was most companionable and pleasant. She was very stout, and a ready listener. She also liked to talk, and her chatter was like the gay plashing [sic] of a fountain. She had a decided literary gift, as well as taste and depth. But this quality never properly emerged; it remained hidden beneath the semblance of a kindly, fat old woman, extremely hospitable, and possessor of a great sense of humor. She held all the conventional opinions a person was obliged to have, but then her unconscious personality would suddenly put in an appearance. That personality was unexpectedly powerful; a somber, imposing figure possessed of unassailable authority—and no bones about it. I was sure that she consisted of two personalities, one innocuous and human, the other uncanny. This other emerged only now and then, but each time it was unexpected and frightening. She would then speak as if talking to herself, but what she said was aimed at me and usually struck to the core of my being, so that I was stunned into silence.[37]

Jung is describing here a severe case of splitting,[38] or dissociation, that was evidently characteristic of his mother all his life. Emilie's tendency toward dissociation needs to be seen in the context of her personal history. A brief summary of what is known of her would call attention to the facts, as mentioned above, that she was the daughter of a prominent Protestant pastor by his second wife. As a child, her father required her to stand behind him while he wrote sermons to keep away ghosts. At the same time, her father kept a chair in the room for his first wife's ghost, with whom he talked regularly. Emilie then married a man who became a pastor. Their first child died a few days after being born. There was conflict in the marriage. Three years after her second son was born, she was hospitalized for mental illness for several months. For at least the subsequent eighteen years, she evidenced a split in her personality that made her behavior unpredictable. Looking at these facts suggests some of the dynamics involved for Emilie that set the stage for young Carl's own experiences of emptiness.

Right after Jung's description of his mother's two personalities in his autobiography, he describes the first time he experienced her divided self, a time when he was six years old, two years after they had moved to Klein-Hüningen.[39] His mother had been making frequent remarks about neighborhood children who were better off financially and better dressed than Jung himself was, and she made repeated invidious comparisons, of how nice the neighbor children looked and behaved in contrast to Carl himself, much to young Carl's consternation and humiliation. He decided to take out his aggression on a boy his age, "to give the boy a hiding—which I did." After he pummeled the neighborhood boy, the boy's mother raced to Carl's mother in protest, whereupon she launched into a criticism of him with her "powerful" personality. He recalled the power of her "lecture, spiced with tears, longer and more passionate than anything I had ever heard from her before." The young Carl was taken aback, because he felt he had just "made amends for the incongruous presence of this stranger in our village." "Deeply awed by my mother's excitement, I withdrew penitently to my table behind our old spinet...."

What happened next was perhaps such a recurrent pattern as to seem unremarkable to the author in his memoirs. A few minutes later, Jung describes his mother as "muttering to herself" after he had withdrawn behind the piano. Then he relates how she suddenly said loudly, "Of course one should never have kept a litter like that!" At six years old, Jung made the tangential connection between "litter," his mother's brother who raised "litters" of dogs, and the neighborhood children now being referred to as "inferior whelps." From this he deduced relief, realizing his mother's outburst was not to be taken seriously, because she in fact agreed with his own assessment of the neighbors, but also would not have admitted it directly to him.

This is an extraordinary piece of mother/child interaction. The six-year-old has just experienced a new level of traumatic assault from his mother, "longer and more powerful than anything I had ever heard from her before," that prompted him to "withdraw penitently...." He is stopped from internalizing her criticism completely (i.e., dwelling on his guilt and considering himself "bad") by observing her subsequent soliloquy, which he translates, perhaps correctly (thus evidencing an intimate, intuitive sense of the way his mother's mind worked), by following a quite circuitous—what would clinically be called "loose"—series of associations in which she reveals that she basically agrees with her son. The son, realizing she did not really mean the castigation she just delivered, forgets her betrayal of him (i.e., the fact that only moments before she had castigated him for his violence and now is conceding that she agrees with his assessment of the neighbors) in order to accept her (unstated) identification with his point of view. The son has seen the split within the conventional critical mother, cow-towing to another mother's distress and social code, and, by a mental stretch, also sees her secretly agreeing with him. So relieved is he by the second part that he overlooks his own narcissistic wound effected by the first part. Thus, though he survived well psychologically by keeping both aspects of his mother's (and his own) personality in awareness, the wounded part of him was repressed and may have contributed to his later relations with women other than his wife.

In this very brief incident, the mother's own propensity toward dissociation is manifested, as well as the son's ability to follow the loose associations in order to construct meaning. This episode surely reflects a process of Carl's own psyche having learned, through empathic attunement to his mother's psyche, how to function. His very mind, therefore, had already been shaped to fit his mother's psychic splits.[40] The point was made earlier that Thomas Merton's *behavior* was to a large degree shaped by his effort to please his mother and thus constituted a false self. In the case of Jung, his very *psyche* was shaped by his attunement to his mother's psyche thus constituting a more elementary basis for the false self.

This incident of his mother's dissociation and inconsistency when Jung was six was repeated in various ways throughout her life. When he was eleven, his mother told him something about his father that upset Jung greatly, so much so that he went into town to consult with one of his father's friends. The friend wasn't home, so Jung returned still worrying, only to be met, later, by his mother's rendering an entirely different picture of the situation than originally. Jung castigated himself for having believed her in the beginning and for nearly provoking a conflict. "From then on I decided to divide everything my mother said by two."[41]

Though it is a report from later years, Ruth Bailey, Jung's housekeeper for some time, remembered his mother in the following way:

> She used to have...mental aberrations, she would go shopping for one thing and come home with another....She would go [looking] for something like a dish cloth and come home with a netting to keep the birds off, something vaguely connected but quite the wrong thing.[42]

In a way that is clearer than it is with any of the people heretofore studied, Carl Jung's earliest experiences of emptiness clearly not only impacted him, but formed the very shape of his developing psyche. It is one thing to be affected by the impact of one object upon another object that is already in existence; it is quite another thing for something that has yet to be distinctively formed to be molded by the shape of that which already existed.[43] Every child is,

The Experience of Emptiness in Depth Psychology

of course, molded by his/her parents through the natural process of introjection and identification.[44] What is unique in this early, elementary formative experience for Jung is that he is taking in (introjection) and identifying with, as well as trying to relate to, a mother who has two clearly distinct modes of being in the world.

On this level of psychic development, Jung's identification with her may be seen as so encompassing that there was very little room for him as a separate person, except as an observer of his mother. In the terms of Kohut's self psychology, Jung was often a self-object[45] for his mother. She looked to him for an understanding and support that she wasn't getting from his father.[46]

There remained a part of his own psyche that was not included in the identification, nor supported by nor evoked by his mother. This included everything that went into making him a separate person from her, a process supported by his father in objective, concrete ways (holding, carrying, teaching and enabling him to go to university. See pages 213–14 in this chapter). This was also the part of him that felt connected to the maid who took care of him, with associations of

> black hair...olive complexion...darkly pigmented skin....This type of girl later became a component of my anima. The feeling of strangeness she conveyed, and yet of having known her always, was a characteristic of that figure which later came to symbolize for me the whole essence of womanhood.[47]

This hidden part of himself was called forth later in his encounters with Sabina Spielrein and Toni Wolfe.

When, therefore, the six-year-old Carl observes his mother muttering to herself and interprets her remarks in a way that comprehensively explains her view of the neighbors, her critical response to him and her basic agreement with him he is, in essence, *being her*, being her own psyche, knowing what is unstated but intended, knowing secret feelings and knowing her view of the world. What we call intuition is often, as in this instance, very primitive identification. Though most children try to "guess" or intuit what makes their parents "tick" in order to have some power in the relationship, not all children have to deal with a parent whose verbalizations may have large gaps consisting of loose references, nonlinear logic or outright contradiction.

The later genius of Jung's association experiments with schizophrenia at Burghölzli, as well as his ongoing work in relating dreams and myths from different eras and cultures, was in essence an elaboration of what he was doing with his mother at least by the age of six—tracking very loose associations and constructing implied meanings from them.

There was another aspect to her that, while it may have been heard by young Carl as the expression of the "powerful personality" or what is sometimes referred to as "mana personality,"[48] constituted a crucially different impact on him. This was the aspect of her personality that was not directed at him at all, even though he was physically present. Jung acknowledged that she would sometimes speak "as if talking to herself," but then he blithely goes on to assume—as only an abandoned and frightened child would, by creating a truth counter to external reality—that "what she said was aimed at me...."[49] Though he was referring to a later period in his childhood after his mother's hospitalization, it is fair to assume that, at least to some degree, this pattern was evident before she was hospitalized. The truth was, she was *not* talking *to* him. Jung's assertion that "what she said was aimed at me" was Jung's active use of projection, intuition and identification to protect both him and her from the devastating experience of her manifest failure to relate directly to her son.

In similar fashion, years after the boyhood pummeling, Jung's mother made a remark shortly after his father's death in 1896, when Carl was twenty-one and just beginning medical studies, that he again took as intended for himself and applied his own interpretation.

The Experience of Emptiness in Depth Psychology

Once my mother spoke to me *or to the surrounding air*[50] in her "second" voice, and remarked, "He died in time for you." Which appeared to mean: "You did not understand each other and he might have become a hindrance to you."[51]

What is in question is not whether Jung's mother intended such remarks for him, nor whether he rightly intuited their meaning. What is to be noted is that Jung's mother spoke at significant points in his life in such a manner of indirection with such a paucity of concrete information that Jung repeatedly had to reach both inside his own reasoning and inside what he imagined to be hers, to construct a meaning and to appropriate it to himself in a way that would not have been obvious to a third party observing the interaction. While this is good training for a psychotherapist, it is a starving experience of emptiness for the person having to do so much work in order to feel related to. It is almost as if one is drowning in one place in the water, and her mother comes along and says "I'll save you if you'll only swim the twenty yards to get to me."

This was an experience of emptiness of such proportion that Jung himself never fully dealt with it. To have a mother who is physically "there," yet who at the same time is unrelated to oneself, is literally "mind-boggling." Young Carl's efforts to make sense of what she said and apply it to the situation in his own mind bespeaks as much for his creativity and imagination as it does for his intuition. Had he been less intelligent, intuitive or creative in constructing meaning from his mother's speeches to the "surrounding air," Carl Jung might himself have languished in a nonproductive life.

As suggested, although not really the point of Jung's telling of his "hiding" a neighborhood boy in childhood, this story reveals the essential dynamics of one of the ways children are trained to be caretakers by focusing on a parent's need, including doing the parent's thinking for them, and forgetting any injustice suffered in order to reestablish a sense of union with the parent. What gets split-off within the child is the denied part of the self that felt the sting of the original castigation, with its subsequent sense of betrayal. All of that is repressed, denied, forgotten, in order to reestablish a sense of connection and acceptance with the parent.

As Merton did, Carl Jung developed a strong false self to maintain the alliance with his mother. As Winnicott makes clear, the function of the false self is to protect the true self, which is "acknowledged as a potential and is allowed a secret life....[Further, The] False Self has as its main concern a search for conditions which will make it possible for the True Self to come into its own."[52] Jung's true self was kept hidden (as discussed below, pp. 230–31), in a pencil case with a manikin. Jung found himself so divided and self-contained that he felt he was two persons, which he named Personalities No. 1 and 2.[53] Personality No. 1 was the aspect of him that had the job of coping with the outside world, the proper function of Winnicott's false self. Personality No. 2 was in Jung's mind, himself when he was most himself, and similar in many ways to Winnicott's true self.

Carl's true self was not supported by his mother because she had never had her own true self supported. She grew up with a father who himself had chronic experiences of dissociation, in the form of ghosts, that were alleviated only by her presence. This means both that she was very close to her father and experienced his need for her, and that she grew up experiencing her father's dissociative states and his efforts to overcome them. To the extent that he required her presence, she was valued for the role she played in his psychic balance, not for herself alone, and thus her false self was reinforced. At least unconsciously, she had to have resented thus being treated like an object, which provided fuel to her own "power" states of mind. Further, as the one chosen to be the source of her father's stability, rather than her mother (who was still being displaced by the ghost of the first wife), Emilie experienced a premature and unearned Electra victory, which may have contributed to some psychic inflation of her own. She repeated the same pattern of inappropriate cross-generational intimacy with her own son by taking him into her confidence for matters too adult for his own comfort.

Carl grew up with a mother whose inner life was stronger than what she usually said, and who, when she spoke, often released her thoughts cryptically, requiring deciphering. The background for the importance he attached to his own "secrets"[54] was the experience of a mother who had many thoughts, feelings and images beneath the level of whatever she said.

One cannot but wonder to what extent Emilie's tendency toward a divided personality was triggered by the loss of her first child,[55] or, if she had been this way earlier, to what extent it was intensified and prolonged by the infant's death. However chronic a mental illness, there is usually some external circumstance that triggers an acute crisis of hospitalizable proportion. In the case of her own father, the death of his first wife was apparently a trigger to his own dissociation experience.

Some writers, following Jung's own report, have attributed his mother's mental crisis to a deteriorating marriage. But surely cause and effect are very intertwined in such a situation: Under conditions of stress from poverty, the loss of the first child in death, and (as below) Johann Paul's lack of satisfaction in his pastoral career, both husband and wife may have experienced depletion and an inability to give to each other. Given the history of the loss of the first child, it is at least possible, though admittedly speculative, that Emilie's hospitalization was prompted by the loss of another through miscarriage, or the effect on her of a lack of sex and a lack of connectedness in the marriage.[56] In a classification of personalities that Jung would later develop,[57] his parents would seem to have been very different personality types, with nothing to bridge them, so that husband and wife lived together without relating to each other in a vital way. When a marital system is out of balance, it creates stress that impacts vulnerable parts of both people, causing further problems that increase the stress. Mental illness becomes both an effect and a cause of further imbalance, further stress and deterioration of the marital system.

Thus, compressed into the memory of the three-year-old Carl's experience of emptiness in a world of inconsistent and unreliable models were Carl's experience of emptiness as his mother's "not being there" when she was "there," because of her own dissociative process, and the experience of emptiness as being physically abandoned, as mentioned above in our discussion of Merton,[58] when his mother was hospitalized. The fact that Jung's mother did not actually die made a difference in his later development, but for him, when he was three, she may as well have been dead. Her absence for several months had to have been as traumatic as if she had died, because a three year old does not understand "weeks," much less "months." Carl's father, however, *was* there for him during this time.

The Experience of Emptiness as Having a "Powerless" Father

If the anima is the contrasexual image of the "other" that connects men to their unconscious and spirituality, their inner image of their father provides the basis for their conscious identity, who they see themselves to be.

For the young Carl Jung, "Father"…meant reliability and—powerlessness.[59]

To experience such powerlessness is another form of emptiness. To experience as powerless the source on whom one relies to build one's sense of self, however—which constitutes the second aspect of Carl's experience of emptiness in a world of inconsistent and unreliable models—can be devastating, all the more so if one is still dependent on them for one's very continued existence in the world.

On the other hand, powerlessness (*wǔ nénglì*, Ch.), is one of those phrases that, as Jung later learned from the *I Ching*, is double-sided, containing a positive as well as a negative aspect.

But throughout his life, Jung mostly identified his father with the negative side of powerlessness.

The association Jung made between his father and powerlessness must most likely be seen as an association made at a much later date than when he was three. Unless there are unconscious memories behind it of which we have no knowledge, Jung's experience of his father as powerless derived from childhood, not infancy. Indeed, the memory alluded to of his father pacing, holding him and singing to him during is mother's hospitalization is hard to imagine being experienced by Carl as "powerlessness," unless he is referring to his own powerlessness to bring his mother back to him and is projecting that onto his father. In spite of his father's nurturing and acts of generosity (see pp. 213–14), however, Jung never changed this fundamental view of his father as being powerless.[60]

Jung refers, instead, with subtle indictment to the powerlessness of his father, Johann Paul, to believe in his own life and in his own religious profession.

According to Gerhard Wehr, Johann Paul suffered from such a degree of poverty that, even though he finished his doctorate in philology, he was unable to afford the fee for the official qualification. The sudden appearance at that moment of a scholarship from a dead family member for anyone who wanted to enter the ministry moved Johann Paul to become a pastor.[61] In effect, he abandoned his own unique interest and training to go into the family business.[62] This was hardly the courageous motivation of a prophet, and does perhaps bespeak a timidity or tentativeness that would have paled when compared to Emilie's numinous power.

Additionally, the fact that Johann Paul's own mother suffered from an unidentified mental illness would surely have had an effect on him, so that he reexperienced with his wife some of what he had experienced with his grandmother, Sophie Ziegler.

The young Carl remembered his father basking in memories of the past rather than meeting the challenges of his current life:

> As a country parson he lapsed into a sort of sentimental ide-
> alism and into reminiscences of his golden student days,
> continued to smoke a long student's pipe, and discovered
> that his marriage was not all he had imagined it to be. He
> did a great deal of good—far too much—and as a result was
> usually irritable. Both parents made great efforts to lead
> devout lives, with the result that there were angry scenes
> between them only too frequently. These difficulties,
> understandably enough, later shattered my father's faith.[63]

In Christianity, marriage between husband and wife is seen as
a reflection of the marriage between Christ and the church (following the universal religious formula, "as in heaven, so on
earth"). Included in the marriage vow is the promise between the
two partners that they will be faithful to each other as God is
faithful to the church (not as the church is faithful to God!), the
reward for which is a blessing on the couple and their offspring.
Jung frames their problem as stemming from their effort to be
one-sidedly good, with no room for the negative. There was a
certain kind of toughness needed in both Johann Paul's faith and
his marriage for love to endure and develop. Without such a
toughness that comes from the experience of being able to hate
without destroying oneself or the other,[64] dreams founder on the
rocks of each person's need to be a whole person. It is also plausible to imagine Johann Paul reacting with confusion and perhaps speechlessness if his wife launched an attack on him from
her "powerful" personality, all the more so if it was a repetition
of a traumatic experience with his own mother. Seen this way,
the father was perhaps simply reduced to ineptitude in the presence of a powerful outburst, in part, perhaps, out of fear that
confrontation would only make things worse. His powerlessness
was, from this perspective, not so much about being unable to
cure her as it was about his inability simply to stop her animosity.[65] Regarding the apparently frequent quarrels the parents got
into, one must also wonder to what extent each parent blamed

the other for the first child's death, in what could have been an endless round of bitterness.

It is also plausible to imagine, however, that the faith crisis and the powerlessness that the younger Carl intuited in his father may well have stemmed from unresolved grief and theological confusion over the death of his firstborn son. The Protestant tradition of that time was more focused on moralism and discipline for discipleship in a severe world; it was not inclined toward empathy. To what extent Johann Paul, the vicar, was emotionally and theologically crippled by the death of his first son is worth consideration.[66]

Further, to have experienced with his own wife a mental illness acute enough to require hospitalization and then to become chaplain to other people in such a psychiatric hospital meant Johann Paul either had to carry the subjectivity of the experience of his wife into the encounters with other patients or he had to distance himself emotionally and objectify not only the patients (which is commonly done), but his wife. Such an emotional distancing would have been seen as avoidance, and, by thus keeping energy bound up inside himself, Johann Paul would also have been experienced as boring, which is how Carl felt. To have dealt with the subjective aspect, that is to say, his own personal feelings toward his psychotic wife, and his own worldview, which required a space for mental illness in the divine economy, would have required Johann Paul to go deeper not only into his theology, but into the meaning of mental life as it relates to spiritual concerns. This he did not do. But this is precisely what his son Carl did. Thus Carl Jung took upon himself consciously the unfinished business of his father. This is one of the meanings of accepting fate and embarking on the path of individuation: to identify and consciously work with the issues that have been raised by prior generations and to develop a new perspective that adds to what was inherited.

Journeys into Emptiness

The issues of the relation between mental illness and Christian faith, which only began to be raised with the life and work of another pioneer who himself was hospitalized, Anton Boisen,[67] and developed through the Clinical Pastoral Education movement, were completely unthought of in the late nineteenth century. In short, any clergyman of that era would have felt inadequate in the face of his wife's mental illness and his professional task of ministering to the mentally ill. Most often, that inadequacy is too painful to face, and clergymen would have been more inclined to defend themselves against such feelings by intellectualization or rationalization.

Thus, what Jung meant by describing his father as powerless is not as easily understandable as many biographers assume. From the scene described in his autobiography of the father comforting the son during his mother's hospitalization, one can see a kind of maternal compassion. Carl Jung's subsequent reports about his father's failings are primarily about the father's inability to convey any sense of vitality of his own faith or experience of God as a lived presence, much less to explain basic articles of faith in the catechism.[68] The young Carl experienced his father, therefore, as powerless in the sense of someone who did not believe in his own vocation, who could not relate on an experiential basis to the transcendent, about which he was supposed to have special knowledge, on behalf of which he had to perform publicly.[69]

His father had in fact proved himself capable of scholarly work in the finishing of his thesis in Oriental languages at Göttingen University, but had not been able to secure an academic position,[70] so powerlessness was not about a lack of intelligence or ability. This failure of his father to pursue his own interest and his surrendering of passion to accepting a position in something that apparently held little conviction for him was intolerable to the young Carl. It perhaps smacked to him of not just powerlessness, but cowardice, and represented an attitude toward life that was in marked contrast to the numinosity Carl experienced in his own inner life, as well as from his mother, who was "strange and mysterious."[71] The later Carl Jung's emphasis on the task of individuation may be seen as expressive of how intolerable, perhaps even ashamed, he had felt as a child to see his father not living a life of conviction, and instead, urging his son to "Be anything you like except a theologian."[72]

Beyond Johann Paul's failure to convey convincingly the basic tenets of the Christian faith, and to take hold in some undefined way of the issues in what could have constituted a transformative way, it nonetheless appears that he was able to be very present and comforting to young Carl, evincing a modified masculinity that nowadays might be seen as exemplary.

Seen in a positive light, the other side of *wǔ nénglì*, is that Carl's father's personality may have contributed greatly to important aspects of his son's later contributions. For example, the patience and nurture embodied in Johann Paul's carrying Carl and singing to him, while sometimes it may have seemed to the son embarrassing passivity, may have also given to the son an experience of the positive power of passivity in the face of unconscious forces and external events over which he had no control, and the power of receptivity and adaptivity that is so essential to Eastern thought. His father's own powerlessness may thus have served as a model for young Carl of how to adopt a posture of emptiness, whereby he could accept and receive his intuitive experiences and learn from them. Indeed, had his father tried to assume a more common masculine rigidity and acted out his protest against the mother's illness by some form of hypermasculinity, the stage would have been set for young Carl's rejection of his own divided psyche, as well as that of his mother, and precipitated, perhaps, a complete breakdown for himself. From his father, in essence, Carl Jung received an attitude of receptivity that was absolutely crucial to his ability to attend to his own inner life and that of others, an attitude that later found complete resonance in Taoist and Buddhist thought.

Journeys into Emptiness

In addition, Jung's father was consistently considerate and generous to his son, insofar as his own resources allowed. He let young Carl use his library[73] and taught him Latin. It was by Carl's overhearing his father worrying about his illness when he was twelve years old that Carl made his own decision to relinquish malingering for an active return to school.[74] And it was by his father's sacrificing himself to pay for young Carl ("I'll stay here, it's too expensive for the two of us.") to take the train up Rigi mountain outside of Lucerne, when Carl was fourteen that he first experienced "...my world, the real world...where one can *be* without having to ask anything," which was "the best and most precious gift my father had ever given to me."[75] In such instances as these, the father manifested the clearest and most direct understanding of the son's real needs and attempted to meet them in a way that, for all her numinosity, was never manifested by Carl's mother.

Thus seen, it was *the nurturing mother within Carl's father* that was of such psychological importance for the young boy during his mother's hospitalization. In this reading of Jung's development, a somewhat tenuous ego in the infant Carl may have been managed during his mother's otherwise intolerably long absence, not only by a maid and an aunt, but by his father. It was, therefore, the mother and mothering presence *within his father* that preserved Carl's stability during those long months.

However, despite his positive qualities, whatever Johann Paul Jung may have been like in person, his son Carl, from the age of three, experienced his father as powerless in the negative sense, and never swayed from that conscious viewpoint. Compensating, perhaps, for this experience of his father as powerless, young Carl had a dream at the age of three that was of utmost significance not only in itself—as a dream that preoccupied him for decades, another "secret" he told no one before his autobiography—but as a pointer for the direction of his attention for the rest of his life.

The Experience of Emptiness in Depth Psychology

...the earliest dream I can remember...between
three and four years old.

The vicarage stood quite alone near Laufen castle, and there was a big meadow stretching back from the sexton's farm. In the dream I was in this meadow. Suddenly I discovered a dark, rectangular, stone-lined hole in the ground. I had never seen it before. I ran forward curiously and peered down into it. Then I saw a stone stairway leading down. Hesitantly and fearfully, I descended. At the bottom was a doorway with a round arch, closed off by a green curtain. It was a big, heavy curtain of worked stuff like brocade, and it looked very sumptuous. Curious to see what might be hidden behind, I pushed it aside. I saw before me in the dim light a rectangular chamber about thirty feet long. The ceiling was arched and of hewn stone. The floor was laid with flagstones, and in the center a red carpet ran from the entrance to a low platform. On this platform stood a wonderfully rich golden throne. I am not certain, but perhaps a red cushion lay on the seat. It was a magnificent throne, a real king's throne in a fairy tale. Something was standing on it which I thought at first was a tree trunk twelve to fifteen feet high and about one and a half to two feet thick. It was a huge thing, reaching almost to the ceiling. But it was of curious composition: it was made of skin and naked flesh, and on top there was something like a rounded head with no face and no hair. On the very top of the head was a single eye, gazing motionlessly upward.

It was fairly light in the room, although there were no windows and no apparent source of light. Above the head, however, was an aura of brightness. The thing did not move, yet I had the feeling that it might at any moment crawl off the throne like a worm and creep toward me. I was paralyzed with terror. At that moment I heard from outside and above me my mother's voice. She called out, "Yes, just look at him. That is the man-eater!" That intensified my terror even more, and I awoke sweating and scared to death. For many nights afterward I was afraid to go to sleep, because I feared I might have another dream like that.[76]

Journeys into Emptiness

Jung returned to this dream in the beginning of his "Confrontation with the Unconscious," his deliberate dropping down into emptiness during his creative illness (below, G., p. 260). His own associations to the dream led him (as an adult) to connect the phallus image with a slightly earlier experience he had (evidently shortly before the dream, when he was still three years old) when he saw a Jesuit walking down the road in black clothes, a sight that terrified him. He was told that it was a Jesuit, and he connected it to the "Lord Jesus" as a symbol of dark, frightening power. The hole in the meadow he associated to a grave. Jung goes on in the autobiography, discussing the ramifications for him of his views toward Christianity as something he tried hard to believe in but could never quite trust. Jung accepted his own association of the dark, underground "man-eater" to the Jesuit, thus imputing to that black-clothed figure a power Jung claimed his own father did not have. And yet, he related, two pages earlier, the fears he felt at that age to the constant death-threatening sights and sounds of the Rhine Falls, where "people drowned, bodies were swept over the rocks."[77] Jung's father often conducted the funerals resulting from these tragedies.

> My father would be there in his clerical gown, speaking in a resounding voice. Women wept. I was told that someone was being buried in this hole in the ground…[where] the Lord Jesus had taken them to himself.[78]

One wonders, therefore, to what extent Jung's memory of the frightful, dark power of the Jesuit[79] may actually have been a screen memory,[80] in which case his father was not entirely the "powerless" man Jung consciously believed. He was, on the contrary perhaps, as guardian and deliverer of bodies into the dark ground of death and the throne of "Lord Jesus," one who had unthinkable powers and connections to the world underground, a man who dressed in a (black!) clerical gown, whose voice resounded, and who could make women weep. Did the young Carl speculate that the man with such power over women and men might have, in fact, sent his own mother to the hospital, or even to her grave? It was, perhaps, utterly too frightening to allow his father to have such power over life and death, and thus Jung had to split, in his own mind, the dark power of the black-clothed vicar who sent people underground from the nurturing father who sang comforting songs while carrying the boy in his arms. In Jung's own divided mind, therefore, not only did his mother have two personalities, but his father as well. But to be at the mercy of a parent of such power might have been just too threatening to the son, so he transferred that power to the anonymous Jesuit.

A closer inspection of Jung's charge of his father's powerless-ness, therefore, reveals a father with a very power*ful* clerical per-sona in the very young child's mind. It was only later, between the ages of thirteen—when his father was preparing Jung for his first communion, and was unable to explain the Trinity—and seventeen—when he heard his father praying for a faith he did not have—that Carl came to see his father as powerless. Then Carl saw through the persona to a man whose faith and under-standing were inadequate for the rigors of his actual life. By then, the fact that his father had a very real capacity for seeing need and responding to it appropriately paled beside his father's failure to have enough aggression, in the eyes of the son, to match the mother's often powerful personality.

The "man-eater" dream contained many of the major themes which constituted Jung's life work: his ambivalent relationship to Christianity, expecially to its neglected dark side; his unremitting exploration of the "underworld" of the unconscious; the strong influence of his mother, with her warning, "This is the man-eater!" (which would be enough to trigger any castration fears that he had not had earlier!); and the importance of a symbolic approach to understanding religion. Indeed, one could see this dream, with its raising of the fundamental question of the dark side of God, as preoccupying Jung his entire life, and putting to him, at age three, a question that he only felt able to address in *Answer to Job*,[81] one of his last works.

Overall, however the dream may be interpreted, it pointed the way for Jung to go, as indeed he did, for the rest of his life: "I descended." Thus, from the age of three on, Jung's strongest experiences were within, and his descent into his own unconscious, to face his experiences of emptiness and learn from them, became his true vocation.

This is not the ordinary direction of childhood development, needless to say. In addition to the young Carl's having an obvious "talent" for dreams, introspection and memory, already active at age three, one must recognize a certain despair about the ability of adult others to match the intensity of his inner experience. Apart from the story of his asking his father the meaning of the Trinity—a test that the father failed—there is no story whatsoever of Jung's ever seeking help or guidance from either parent. Jung "descended," therefore, because it was the only way to go. There, in his inner experience, lay both power and mystery. The attention to and cultivation of his inner life was more real to the young Carl than events in the outer world. Indeed, one might say that the importance of actual people for Jung[82]—from his parents to his wife, Emma, to Freud, Toni Wolfe and others—lay primarily in their role as helpers and enablers of his inner journey.

At the age of three, the young Carl's original experience of his father as powerful in his clergy role and as a caring and nurturing parent was perhaps too threatening for him to acknowledge, especially given his mother's inconsistency. Particularly from the perspective of young Carl's intense inner experience, moreover, his father could not meet him on the ground of inner awareness. Thus, Jung experienced his father as an inconsistent and unreliable model in a way different from his mother, but in a way that nonetheless contributed to his experience of emptiness.

At the age of eleven, the powerlessness of his father in his role as clergy became underscored in another inner experience, this time involving a thought and an image. One day after leaving school, he wandered by the cathedral square and began musing about the beauty of the day, the beauty of the church and the God who made it all, when he felt stopped.

> Here came a great hole in my thoughts, and a choking sensation. I felt numbed, and knew only: "Don't go on thinking now! Something terrible is coming, something I do not want to think, something I dare not even approach. Why not? Because I would be committing the most frightful of sins. What is the most terrible sin? Murder? No, it can't be that. The most terrible sin is the sin against the Holy Ghost, which cannot be forgiven. Anyone who commits that sin is damned to hell for all eternity. That would be very sad for my parents, if their only son, to whom they are so attached, should be doomed to eternal damnation. I cannot do that to my parents. All I need do is not go on thinking."[83]

For three nights, Jung struggled to keep back his unthinkable thought. He wondered where this thing that he did not want to think might be coming from, and decided it was not *he* who brought it about. Neither was it imaginable that it was his parents, or grandparents. He traced his ancestors back to Adam and Eve, who had no choice but to be as they were created, and asked himself how they could have sinned if they were perfectly created. Jung then came to the (for him at eleven years old) revolutionary conclusion that

> *Therefore it was God's intention that they should sin.*
> This thought liberated me instantly....[84]

He went on struggling with the implications of his discovery.

> "Obviously God also desires me to show courage," I thought. "If that is so and I go through with it, then He will give me His grace and illumination."

Journeys into Emptiness

> I gathered all my courage, as though I were about to leap forthwith into hell-fire, and let the thought come. I saw before me the cathedral, the blue sky. God sits on His golden throne, high above the world—and from under the throne an enormous turd falls upon the sparkling new roof, shatters it, and breaks the walls of the cathedral asunder.
>
> So that was it! I felt an enormous, an indescribable relief. Instead of the expected damnation, grace had come upon me, and with it an unutterable bliss such as I had never known. I wept for happiness and gratitude. The wisdom and goodness of God had been revealed to me now that I had yielded to His inexorable command. It was as though I had experienced an illumination. A great many things I had not previously understood became clear to me. That was what my father had not understood, I thought; he had failed to experience the will of God, had opposed it for the best reasons and out of the deepest faith. And that was why he had never experienced the miracle of grace....he did not know the immediate living God....
>
> ...It was obedience brought me grace....One must be utterly abandoned to God; nothing matters but fulfilling his will.[85]

There are a number of remarkable things about this three days' and three nights' process. Quite apart from the content, the *tenacity* and *thoroughness* with which Jung kept exploring his experience, questioning, thinking it through from various vantage points and all the while being aware of his own thoughts about the unthought-thought is extraordinary.

As a psychological drama, it is a marvelous working through of a paranoid position. From the paranoid position, God is the judge who forces one to do something that is against his will, that will provoke his judgment. One is therefore caught in a double-bind. If the only God is the one that occupies a place in the superego, there is no escape. This was Melanie Klein's point: If the mother cannot endure the child's hate and aggression, the child will be forced to keep it inside and it will turn against her. Jung entrusts Being with his destructiveness and experiences wholeness.

The Experience of Emptiness in Depth Psychology

As a theological act, Jung trusts that there is a God beyond his own ego-conception of God who is trustworthy. One obeys God by defying God. This is the trust whereby one calls upon God to be true to the promise made to all humankind, to be pro nobis, no matter what. This is the position taken by Job (which Jung expanded on later, as mentioned) in which Job calls God to account and entrusts himself to God, at the risk of his own life.

> ...leave me to speak my mind, and let what may come upon me!
> I will put my neck in the noose and take my life in my hands. If he would slay me,
> I should not hesitate. I should still argue my cause to his face.[86]

As a working through of an early adolescent's disappointment with his father, it is an empowering act, consonant with the Christian understanding of God as the more real parent than one's genetic ones. One might say in this episode that Jung worked through his father's failures and discovered not only God beyond the father and all the projections of the father onto God, but his own true self mode of being in the world. By the way Jung stayed with his own experience of emptiness as abandoning himself to God, Jung achieved his own integrity. He also experienced a grace that his father never had. His father never experienced it because he did not have the faith to take the risk to put his own understanding of God to the test. The son pushed forward in faith the implications of God's negative side.

From this Jung won a great conceptual prize: the ability to distinguish between a particular notion of God and God's reality, and parallel to that, the ability to distinguish between God and the church. To mix metaphors, these are Archimedean levers in Augean stables, enabling one to cut through and get rid of unnecessary encumbrances to the life of the spirit.

This experience became the basis for much of Jung's later work, but at the time, he was left with a deep ambivalence, because he knew no one who might remotely understand what he had been through. He had discovered that "God could be something terrible," but to share such a thought would have incurred misunderstanding. He was left with the feeling one has any time one has a socially unacceptable thought: shame. At the same time, he knew there was something very real and reliable in his discovery.

The Experience of Emptiness in the Middle of Parents' Marital Conflict

> I was suffering, so my mother told me afterward, from general eczema. Dim intimations of trouble in my parents' marriage hovered around me. My illness, in 1878, must have been connected to a temporary separation of my parents. My mother spent several months in a hospital in Basel, and presumably her illness had something to do with the difficulty in the marriage.[87]

Jung's references to his eczema as an expression of anxiety stemming from his parents' marital difficulties identifies the third component of his experience of emptiness as being the child of parents in conflict, before his memory of his mother's hospitalization. To a degree that we are loathe to acknowledge, infants sense tension not only from an individual parent, but from parents' interactions—or the dearth of them. It is picked up from the tone of voice, from bodily tensions in the parents, from differing kinds and amounts of energy parents manifest, from the twinkle in their eyes or the furrowed brow or tight lips. Before we learn words, our bodies already have a history of satisfaction, safety and pleasure and their counterparts: tension, constriction or lack of strength, nervousness or pain. Whenever such tension exists, infants suffer. They may suffer from an inappropriate overattention as much as from a deprivation of attention, when one parent seeks compensatory attention from the child for what isn't coming from the spouse. Thus, Jung's third aspect of his experience of emptiness in a world of inconsistent and unreliable models was manifested in the somaticization of his own anxiety triggered by his parents' marital conflict.

Carl missed out on the support that comes from parents who have a strong bond of intimacy based on their own true selves, just as his parents had missed out on similar support from their parents. His parents' marriage was riven by the crossed transferences of them both.

By marrying a man who became a pastor, Emilie increased the likelihood of a father transference to her husband, but probably more for its negative aspect (being used once again, to support the pastor's work) than for its positive effect (e.g., a feeling of being special). Johann Paul Jung had none of the powers of ghostly encounters that Samuel Preiswerk had. Johann Paul did evince, however, toward his son, a maternal quality, which might well have been there for Emilie as well, when she was in her "conventional" state of mind. When she was in her "unexpectedly powerful" and "unassailable authority" side, however, one wonders how Johann Paul would likely have responded—from his irritable, angry side, or his nurturing, tolerant side. To some extent he may have thought it imprudent to meet Emilie's power with an equal intensity for fear of exacerbating her own illness.

By marrying a woman who had some degree of mental illness, Johann Paul increased the likelihood of a transference from his grandmother, Sophie Ziegler, including the effect of her illness on his mother, Sophie Frey.[88] If memories of Johann Paul's grandmother were triggered by his wife's illness, his feelings of "powerlessness" may have been increased, which would not have been helpful for Emilie.

In Jung's own view, his parents' effort to be good, as commonly understood in Christian churches, created the opposite effect at home.

> He did a great deal of good—far too much—and as a result
> was usually irritable. Both parents made great efforts to live
> devout lives, with the result that there were angry scenes
> between them only too frequently. These difficulties, under-
> standably enough, later shattered my father's faith.[89]

As illustrated in Jung's image of the turd smashing the cathedral, his father's faith had no room for the shadow, the unwanted
or untoward thoughts, feelings and needs of the true self.
Somewhat similarly, Jung described his mother as conventional in
one part of her personality, and thus like her husband—her striving to be good. As Jung himself saw, whatever is suppressed ultimately comes up, however, and he lived as a child of a troubled
marriage.

Marriage requires a crucifixion in any case, because it requires
the sacrifice of the ego's urge to be center stage and to have things
organized around its own, to-some-degree-neurotic, pattern. In a
healthy marriage, such a sacrifice can be managed because it leads
to transformation without real harm (as distinguished from pain)
to the partners, leading to a fuller, deeper life for both. In an
unhealthy marriage, the crucifixion is not transformative, but is an
unending infliction of pain, a determined, even if passive,
endurance. For Jung, his parents' marriage seemed to be of the
latter kind.

In addition, as mentioned at the beginning of this chapter, an
apparently unspeakable shadow lay across the entire marriage, the
shadow of the death of their firstborn. That experience had to
have been extremely wounding to both parents and to their marriage, as well as to Johann Paul's faith. Yet there is no indication
that anyone ever talked about it. It was, from Jung's point of view,
precisely his parents' inability to accept their own darker sides that
created conflicts both within themselves and between each other.
His mother dissociated her dark side, so that it depressed her and
sent her to the hospital.[90] His father lived largely at a distance from
his dark side, and even when he manifested it in irritability, he

could not accept his own feelings. Jung may even have seen their conflicts as fights over whether to allow irrational and "not-nice" aspects of their personalities into their relationship, with the shadow sides of both Johann Paul's clergy persona and Emilie's conventional, "kindly, fat old woman" side[91] vying for a place in their world. Whatever the exact nature of their marital conflict, it created continuing distress for Jung and became part of his own work to resolve, first in personal terms of his own life, then professionally, in his view of "Marriage as a Psychological Relationship."[92]

A marriage serves as a container, a net or holding environment,[93] not only for the couple but for the children, that is larger than the sum of its parts. Whatever personal idiosyncracies or difficulties children may experience with individual parents can often be mitigated if there is a sense that the marriage itself is reliable and stable. Throughout his youth, from at least the age of three when he developed eczema, however, Jung experienced the emptiness of living with his parents' marital conflicts, a world not only of individually unreliable and inconsistent models, but of the unreliability and inconsistency of the holding environment itself.

FORMATION OF THE PSYCHE IN A WORLD OF INCONSISTENT AND UNRELIABLE MODELS[94]

Personalities No. 1 and No. 2

> ...it occurred to me that I was actually two different persons. One of them was the schoolboy who could not grasp algebra and was far from sure of himself; the other was important, a high authority, a man not to be trifled with...an old man who lived in the eighteenth century.[95]

●

> ...meanness, vanity, mendacity, and abhorrent egotism—all qualities with which I was only too familiar with from myself, that is, from personality No. 1, the schoolboy of 1890. Beside his world there existed another realm...[where] lived the "Other," who knew God as a hidden, personal, and at the same time suprapersonal secret....
>
> ...At such times I knew I was worthy of myself, that I was my true self. As soon as I was alone, I could pass over into this state. I therefore sought the peace and solitude of this "Other," personality No. 2.[96][97]

Carl Jung's experience of emptiness in a world of inconsistent and unreliable models before he was three stemmed from at least three sources: 1) his mother, who was "there" and "not there" simultaneously, and who left him to go to a psychiatric hospital for an extended stay; 2) his father, whom he experienced as "powerless"; and 3) the tension-ridden marriage of them both. The combination of these three factors resulted in the structural formation of his own psyche as "divided" into what he called his personalities No. 1 and No. 2.

This division within the psyche, while caused by experiences of emptiness, was itself an experience of emptiness insofar as one can never feel entirely "whole," "real," or "present" in any situation as long as the bifurcation continues. No pleasure or accomplishment fully satisfies, nor is any trauma entirely comprehended, because the other side is always lurking in the background as either threat or escape.

The experience of the world as consisting largely of polar opposites (male/female, positive/negative, inner/outer, powerful/powerless, etc.) is endemic to such a personality structure and therefore becomes a structuring factor in subsequent experiences, insuring further experiences of emptiness as loneliness, isolation, difficulty with authorities and peers, and decreased energy and enthusiasm for the ordinary tasks of social and psychological development. Thus, during Jung's childhood, he often had anxiety dreams about his mother,[98] suffered from depression[99] and psychosomatic illnesses, including not only eczema but falling[100] and self-induced fainting spells in the service of a school phobia.[101]

On the creative side, Jung's experience of psychological dividedness contributed to his development of several theories involving the role of opposites in psychological dynamics,[102] including enantiodromia,[103] *complexio oppositorum*[104] and the transcendent function.[105]

It was this division within his own psychic foundations that constituted the most comprehensive experience of emptiness in Jung's life. The overcoming of this split within his self constituted his entire life's work. Motivated to heal this experience of emptiness as a basic inner division, Jung spent all his years paying attention to the psyche. Out of his effort came his entire oeuvre, the school in depth psychology known as analytical psychology. In essence, Jung developed a mental illness of his own from his mother's illness, just as she had from her father, and, by attending to his own experiences of emptiness that stemmed from it, he turned it into what Henri Ellenberger has called a "creative illness."[106]

Reviewing Jung's *Memories, Dreams, Reflections*, Donald Winnicott wrote:

> Jung in describing himself, gives us a picture of childhood schizophrenia, and at the same time his personality displays a strength of a kind which enabled him to heal himself. At cost he recovered, and part of the cost to him is what he paid out to us, if we can listen and hear, in terms of his exceptional insight. Insight into the feelings of those who are mentally split. I must ask the reader at this stage to

understand that I am not running down Jung by labeling him a "recovered case of infantile psychosis."[107]

Similarly, Robert Smith reports that Michael Fordham was asked by Jung his opinion of the first draft of the childhood chapter of the memoirs:

> Fordham replied that Jung had been "a schizophrenic child, with strong obsessional defenses....He did not contest my blunt statement."[108]

The variety of diagnostic terms used or refused in assessing Jung's personality by different writers is reflective not only of the attempt to draw conclusions on the basis of relatively little data and differing conceptions of diagnostic categories, but also, and more importantly, of differing valences given to personal history and the understanding of both symptoms and symbols between those who tend to favor Freud and those who favor Jung. Everyone, obviously including Jung himself, agrees, however, that Jung experienced his psyche as deeply divided and yet was able to make the division within himself productive, resulting in the astounding achievement of analytical psychology.

Secrets and Survival

But before one can reach a point of dealing creatively with one's own illness, one must survive. Survival consisted in Jung's case, as with most people, in the bifurcation of his self. Jung saw the division, as mentioned above (p. 226 in terms of personality No. 1 and personality No. 2. Although his personality No. 1 was not considered in any way "false" by Jung, it served the same function Winnicott ascribes to the false self, namely, managing the demands of the outside world so that the true self can survive by hiding. Personality No. 2, for Jung, certainly had the sense of being more "real" for him than No. 1, and in this way parallels Winnicott's true self, which has the qualities of reality and spontaneity. But Jung's

The Experience of Emptiness in Depth Psychology

personality No. 2 allowed an access to the deeper layers of the collective unconscious, the place from which archetypes arose, the objective psyche, and thus gave him access to a realm largely unknown to Winnicott's true self. Further, Winnicott's true self, though repressed, is in principle accessible by analysis or introspection, but in Winnicott's view, Jung's true self was not thus accessible, because Jung remained "split."[109]

Jung repressed his true self all the more because there was no one with whom he could share it to help it live in the outer world. He "knew" he had to keep what he most deeply thought and felt a secret. Beginning with the episode mentioned above (p. 200) where Jung "hided" a neighborhood child, was chastised and then interpreted his mother as siding with him, he kept his secret awareness to himself:

> But I also knew, even at that age, that I must keep perfectly still and not come out triumphantly with: "You see, you think as I do!" She would have repudiated the idea indignantly: "You horrid boy, how dare you pretend such a thing about your mother!" I conclude from this that I must already have had earlier experiences of a similar nature which I have forgotten.[110]

One way a child "knows" that such things cannot be talked about is by the experience of a parent reacting very strongly and negatively to similarly associated events in the past. Thus, young Carl's identification with his mother acquired a secret dimension, and it was by keeping it secret (and therefore unassailable) that it was preserved. The role of having a secret became a determining factor in Jung's personality formation, as he himself acknowledged:

> This possession of a secret had a very powerful formative influence on my character; I consider it the essential factor of my boyhood.[111]

The maintenance of this secret is in the service of forging a union with the mother. Another way a child learns to keep a secret is when the parent reverses generational authority and turns to the child as a confidante. Thus Jung knew that it was his job to hear out his mother, who "would talk to me as to a grown-up. It was plain that she was telling me everything she could not say to my father."[112] To maintain the secret is to maintain the alliance by identification, including the way in which mother and son "secretly" think and feel the same thing.

> I knew of no one to whom I might have communicated... except, perhaps, my mother. She seemed to think along simi-lar lines as myself. But I soon noticed that in conversation she was not adequate for me. Her attitude toward me was above all one of admiration, and that was not good for me. And so I remained alone with my thoughts.[113]

The cost of the secret was twofold. The first was an inner split between the wounded self and the stronger self that linked young Carl to his mother by identification. That inner split was experienced by Jung as two distinct aspects of his own personality, personality No. 1 and personality No. 2.

The maintenance of secrets—thoughts, dreams and images—was also a way by which Jung preserved his own ability to function in the world. Insofar as Jung's "secrets" were of a dissociated character, they would too easily have been minimized or negated by other people's ordinary consciousness, and to have had such inner experiences invalidated would have completely destroyed the young Carl. What Jung did with his "secret self" was more creative and life-serving than is often the case. Jung maintained a place for his secret self in the form of a "fire that had to burn forever,"[114] and a yellow pencil case in which he placed a little manikin that he carved:

The Experience of Emptiness in Depth Psychology

...about two inches long, with frock coat, top hat, and shiny black boots. I colored him black with ink, sawed him off the ruler and put him in the pencil case, where I made him a little bed. I even made a coat for him out of a bit of wool. In the case I also placed a smooth, oblong blackish stone from the Rhine....All this was a great secret....I felt safe, and the tormenting sense of being at odds with myself was gone.[115]

This manikin became something to which Jung could turn for solace, for confirmation and a sense of being whole whenever outer events produced trauma, turmoil or confusion. It functioned much as what D. W. Winnicott, the British object relations psychoanalyst and pediatrician, has termed a transitional object,[116] which mediates psychological space and gives a feeling of wholeness and well-being. Such an object functioned, like teddy bears and dolls do for others, as something onto which Jung could project his true self, and, by giving it physical form and place, keep it in consciousness. By giving a literal "place" in which a split-off part of the self can be projected, maintained and accessed, the sense of wholeness and the possibility of integrity of self is sustained. By keeping certain thoughts and feelings to himself, Jung cultivated his inner life, validating it rather than repressing it, and thereby saved himself from a complete dissociation that would have incapacitated him.

For some people, God is able to carry such split-off pieces of the self, and thereby to keep an essential part of the self, the true self, surviving.[117] Lacking such a transitional object or space, people who suffer psychological splitting are likely to put the unacceptable part of the self, which is identified with the true self as the "regressed ego," into what Winnicott has termed "cold storage,"[118] where it is perhaps completely outside of the person's awareness. By Jung's ingeniously devising this method of keeping the fragile, true self alive and visible, he could remember it, keep it in a protected space and thus manage the outside world, because his basic wholeness was being honored and had been given a symbolic place.[119] It is perhaps because Jung was able to make a place for his own split-off self that it could evolve into a major aspect of his personality, what he called personality No. 2.

The second cost of maintaining his secret was essentially related to the first. Jung experienced himself as, at root, alone in the world.

> My entire youth can be understood in terms of this secret. It induced in me an almost unendurable loneliness....Thus the pattern of my relationship to the world was already pre-figured : today as then I am a solitary, because I know things and must hint at things which other people do not know, and usually do not even want to know.[120]

Here is an experience of emptiness of a very special kind, intrinsically connected, perhaps, to those who, in pursuing the meaning of their own experiences of emptiness, become mentors, teachers, psychotherapists or leaders of others. Such an experience of emptiness as loneliness appears to be implicit in such vocations. This is not the loneliness of solitude per se, but the loneliness of those pioneers and explorers of the inner life who find no one to share their knowledge, their language, their *weltanschauung*— all the more when it is still in incubation.

Insofar as Jung experienced his loneliness as rooted in the maintenance of his "secret," he is referring to the psychological state of his "secret" identification with his mother and the consequent psychic division within himself. Here is where the repressed true self of Winnicott lived in Jung's (Freudian-type) unconscious. To this author's knowledge, Jung never explored, in psychoanalytic fashion, the issues of his identification with his mother, which lay at the root of his personality divisions into 1 and 2. The only conceivable person with whom he could have done that was Freud, and beyond the fact of their breaking apart, even Freud would have considered the depth level of Jung's conflict beyond the scope of analysis.[121] There is an important issue, still debated today, of the status of Jung's images from the collective unconscious as they relate or do not relate to his personal life experiences.

> ...although [Jung] rightly concluded that such images could not be understood in terms of Freud's theory of the repression of sexual fantasies, he did not open himself to the possibility that they might still have had a basis in personal experience. He did not raise the question whether these experiences might be developmentally earlier than the oedipal conflict....Instead, Jung assumed that...they were collective and nonpersonal.[122]

Not surprisingly therefore, Jung minimized the impact that his own mother had on his personality formation.

> I attribute to the personal mother only a limited etiological significance. That is to say, all those influences which the literature describes as being exerted on the children do not come from the mother herself, but rather from the archetype projected upon her, which gives her a mythological background and invests her with authority and numinosity.[123]

As was pointed out above when Jung used the word *woman* rather than *mother,* and as Robert Smith agrees, this interesting and revealing statement further confirms Jung's own need and desire to distance himself from his actual mother.[124]

The maintenance of a secret that one feels cannot be told to anyone is *eo ipso* a self-isolating act. The reasons for keeping something secret are usually related to fear of loss or fear of shame. As Jung acknowledged, had he told his mother, she would have denied it and chastised him severely.

With enormous ramifications for his subsequent career and thought, Jung followed where his personality No. 2 led, and it proved a valuable tool for exploring the unconscious and for avoiding having to deal directly with the secret tie to his mother, which his own divided self was based upon. His loneliness was therefore not that of someone who had no friends nor people to talk to, but the loneliness of a man who, lifelong, carried a secret that constituted important, unfinished psychological business where his hidden true self was stored.

The maintenance of secrets within oneself constitutes another form of the experience of emptiness. While his subsequent explorations of the experiences of emptiness resulted in valuable contributions to the world, his neglect of this core piece of inner division may well have precluded him from attaining the inner unity he sought. On the other hand, his pursuit of that experience of emptiness through his personality No. 2 opened up the entire dimension of impersonal, archetypal life from the objective psyche, which no one seemed to know about before him (except for shamans and seers in religions too "primitive" for Western recognition). His father had rejected his own possibilities of such knowing, and his mother, though she expressed it in her own dissociated No. 2 state, could not talk about it.

LATER CHILDHOOD

This focus on his inner life made the young Carl into what he later termed an introvert, one who finds his orientation in life primarily by attention to his subjective psychological experience. As is common, Jung experienced a great deal of conflict with his school peers because of this basic attitude of self-reflection and his tendency to be a loner. Outwardly, the conflict came in the form of actual fighting. Similiarly Jung's interior world caused its own kind of anguish, because merely being with other people who do not share one's inner world, especially when that world is filled with powerful images and feelings, can be painful.

Between seven and nine years of age, Jung discovered that he was different when he was with his peers than when he was home alone. "...they alienated me from myself,"[125] he reported, and he found something in that wider world of his peers that was

> in some obscure way, hostile....I had a premonition of an inescapable world of shadows filled with frightening, unanswerable questions which had me at their mercy. My nightly prayer did, of course, grant me a ritual protection since it concluded the day properly and just as properly ushered in night and sleep. But the new peril lurked by day. It was as if I sensed a splitting of myself, and feared it. My inner security was threatened.[126]

Once again, Jung was experiencing a timeless, archetypal world and felt alienated from peers because neither they nor anyone else seemed to know the world he was experiencing. The disparity between his inner experience of the archetypal world, associated with the dark night, and the experience of the daylight world of others induced a splitting that was terrifying. One might imagine standing as the ground divides between one's legs, leaving only a deep emptiness into which one may fall. Jung handled this threat with rituals he devised not only with the manikin, but with fire and stone. He found a place in an old stone wall and would build a fire that

> had to burn forever...No one but myself was allowed to tend this fire. Others would light other fires in other caves, but these fires were profane and did not concern me. My fire alone was living and had an unmistakable aura of sanctity.
> In front of this wall...a stone jutted out—my stone....The question then arose: "Am I the one who is sitting on the stone, or am I the stone on which *he* is sitting?[127]

In these two rituals, Jung demonstrated a remarkable ability to deal with the very permeable boundaries of his ego in quite different but equally creative ways. In the ritual of fire, he found a way to stay related to peers and simultaneously preserve his own boundaries in the fire that only he could tend. In the stone ritual, he was able to imagine himself as completely nonhuman and to take a position from the stone in relation to his own human self. As Ann and Barry Ulanov note,

> Such people, at peace with their changing borders…possess true originality. Precisely because their ego is without clear borders and because they have the multiple view from many islands, they can, as the rest of us cannot, stand outside of any boundaries—of family, culture, social class or religious tradition.[128]

From the age of eleven, Jung was greatly occupied with questions about God, Christianity and the church. Instructed by his pastor father for confirmation, the son found these parental instructions boring. Worse, when Carl asked his father about the meaning of the Trinity, an idea that intrigued his young mind, father dismissed the question as something he himself did not know the answer to, nor did he find it important. Greatly disappointed, Carl nonetheless maintained his hope of encountering the numinous upon his first communion, but instead he found an experience of emptiness.

> …I was empty and did not know what I was feeling…nothing had happened. I knew that God could do stupendous things to me, things of fire and unearthly light, but this ceremony contained no trace of God.…this communion had been a fatal experience for me. It had proved hollow; more than that, it had proved to be a total loss.[129]

The young Carl's disappointment led him to feel pity for his father for having dedicated his life to something he neither understood nor believed in. In a way parallel to his not telling his mother what he understood after hearing her mumble, the son felt he could not hurt his father by pointing out the great tragedy of the situation. Thus, once again, young Carl isolated himself in his self-knowledge and accepted the frailty of his parent as a fact of life that sent him back upon himself, into himself, for succor.

The Experience of Emptiness in Depth Psychology

As if to drive home the point that other people were not trust-worthy, at one point in his schooling, probably in his early teens, Jung wrote a paper that he thought would win him high marks. He'd had a fairly mediocre record up to this point. The teacher was impressed so much by the writing that he accused Jung of plagiarism. Jung was as incensed at the accusation as the teacher was at what he thought was true. Bewildered and humiliated, Jung raged for days over the incident until finally he came to regard the teacher with the same attitude with which he viewed his mother and father: He understood the teacher as a flawed human being who was too stupid to know Jung's true ability. One may under-stand his paper as coming from his personality No. 2, and thus, yet again, he experienced rejection whenever he gave voice to what he heard. Inwardly, he returned to his personality No. 2, where he found respite, reassurance and calm. Nevertheless, it spelled an increased general distrust of people, in sharp contrast to the world he knew as unified in God, among nature and animals.[130]

Jung reported in his autobiography that from sixteen to nine-teen he became less depressed and his No. 1 personality emerged with greater strength. At the same time, and continuing into his medical studies, he began to read philosophy avidly, and was par-ticularly intrigued by Schopenhauer and Kant. When, however, he dared to put himself fully into the writing of an essay, he was greeted with a criticism of equal vehemence, if not moral judg-ment, from the teacher. His ideas were credited as "brilliant," but the essay was written so well that it was considered to have been done with "little serious effort," and a "slap-dash attitude."[131] Once again, Jung was greatly offended, though not as hurt as before. The effect, though, was to drive him even further into realizing that the world that was so wonderful and real to him, the world of science, the world of the philosophers, God's world, was not something he could share with others. Thus the division between his No. 1 and No. 2 personalities deepened, and the conviction that his true self would not be mirrored, much less appreciated, in the outer world was strengthened.

When, therefore, Jung neared his graduation from the gymnasium and found himself being asked what he wanted to do with his life, he did not know how to answer. He experienced the options, naturally, as polarized as his own psyche. On one hand, in line with No. 1 personality, he enjoyed science, especially zoology, paleontology and geology; on the other hand, he was interested in religion and the humanities, especially Graeco-Roman, Egyptian and prehistoric archaeology.[132] The problem was that science left out the question of meaning; and in religion, the clergy and theologians Jung met seemed to know nothing about the actual experience of God (recall the vision of the turd dropping down on the cathedral), but rather to be absorbed in details of biblical and historical scholarship and academic theology. Neither field actually resonated with his deepest passions.

The First Half of Life: Vocation, Marriage and Establishing a Foundation

As Jung later formulated in his own view of psychological development, the first half of life (very roughly considered to be into the late thirties or early forties) is usually spent establishing a foundation for survival—a home, marriage, a career and children. The emphasis is on establishing a viable way of living in the outer world, the work of Jung's No. 1 personality, to which he later gave the more universal term, *persona*.[133]

Barring unpredictable tragedy, great difficulty in functioning, or unusual circumstances (such as living at a monastery or going to war), the psychological agenda for the period between early childhood development (up until, say, eight years of age) and midlife is focused on the developing persona, that is to say, on coping with the outer world. Inner issues tend to be relegated into the background so that attention and energy can be given to external needs. Developmentally, therefore, experiences of emptiness tend to be experienced in the first few years of life, around the middle of life and afterward.

Needless to say, one's choices in the first half of life are nonetheless informed, consciously or not, by the earlier experiences of emptiness and the attitude one has taken toward them. One may have a great interest or dream, for example, in a field that is contrary to family, gender or societal expectations, or that requires a substantial investment of money that one does not have. Without support, the dream may languish, and one may spend the first half of life building a structure that is pragmatic but lifeless. This was the case, evidently, with Jung's father. Carl Jung did not intend to—one might say, he could not—make the same mistake. He had experienced too much passion to be satisfied with nominal security.

It was only after many months of pondering and reflecting that the idea of going into medicine dawned on Jung. In spite of his namesake's renown as a doctor of medicine (because of it?— "'Only don't imitate' was my motto."[134]), Jung said he had never before considered medicine, with the possibility it offered of specializing later on.

Though he was uneasy with what seemed to him a compromise, the decision seemed to him thenceforth irrevocable, in spite of his having no idea how he would afford it. His father applied to the University of Basel for financial assistance for Carl, and Carl was both shamed and shocked when it was granted. It countered his general belief that everyone in the world found him unlikeable; and the fact that it had been obtained through his father's intervention suggested that Carl was not as independent as he saw himself to be. His father's "goodness," which Carl distrusted because he knew its other side, had resulted in something good for Carl.

In 1895, Carl Jung began attending the University of Basel, studying the natural sciences and medicine. During this time, he continued to live at home, and it soon became apparent that his father was ill. Carl sensed that his father's increased irritability over the past two years had been caused by his faith crisis: "...how hopelessly he was entrapped by the Church and its theological thinking."[135] Carl felt outrage at how abandoned his father felt and, at the same time, concluded that God had abandoned the church and disavowed theology.

In early 1896, when Carl was twenty-one, his father died, and Carl moved into his father's room and took over the running of the family finances. He began giving his mother specified amounts of money to run the household each week, because "she was unable to economize and could not manage money."[136] Carl's sister, being only twelve, was still too young to assume adult responsibilities.

Jung does not indicate, in his memoirs, that he had any particularly strong reaction to his father's death, except that twice he dreamed of his father returning, which prompted him to begin thinking about life after death. One would find this unusual and indicative of denial were it not for the fact that there is continual reflection on the meaning of his father to him from the earliest pages of *Memories, Dreams, Reflections*. The strongest and most important part of the grieving process is, perhaps, the evaluation of the inner meaning a person has for one, and coming to terms with the clash between what one wished the deceased to be and who he or she actually was. Jung had been engaged in this process for years before his father actually died, so there was perhaps less of the process to go through.

It took a great deal more reflection and dreams before Jung decided to specialize in psychiatry. He was put off from both professions—religion as well as science and psychiatry—by what he saw of the people in them. No one he saw carried the kind of interest in inner experience that he himself had and felt compelled to explore further. Similar to Merton's reading of Cardinal Newman's letter to Gerard Manley Hopkins (above, p. 124), Jung was suddenly struck with the realization of his life direction upon

The Experience of Emptiness in Depth Psychology

reading the preface to the textbook in psychiatry by Krafft-Ebing.[137]

> ...the author called the psychoses "diseases of the personality." My heart suddenly began to pound. I had to stand up and draw a deep breath. My excitement was intense, for it had become clear to me, in a flash of illumination, that for me the only possible goal was psychiatry. Here alone the two currents of my interest could flow together and in a united stream dig their own bed. Here was the empirical field common to biological and spiritual facts, which I had everywhere sought and nowhere found. Here at last was the place where the collision of nature and spirit became a reality.[138]

Jung's choice was met with shock and dismay. His teachers and peers shared his own earlier assessment of the state of psychiatry, based as it was on what he knew from his father's work at Friedmatt, as a horrible, hopeless enterprise, devoted to containing madness, not dealing with persons. It was the hope engendered in Jung by Krafft-Ebing's phrase, "diseases of the personality," with the implication that there was an actual person still dynamically living within psychiatric illness, that so inspired him and motivated his choice. Perhaps there was hope, he may well have felt unconsciously, for his mother—and for himself.

On December 10, 1900, at the age of twenty-five, Jung began studying psychiatry as an assistant physician under Eugen Bleuler, at the Burghölzli mental hospital outside Zurich. The Burghölzli hospital was one of the most prestigious psychiatric hospitals in Europe, and Bleuler had already established a reputation as its head. The hospital was, for Jung, "the monastery of the world," for there the intense singularity of his focus precluded all else, and he felt "life took on an undivided reality."[139] He spent extensive time in the library, reading fifty volumes of the history of psychiatry in six months, as a result of which Jung said he once again alienated himself from his colleagues. Jung's labeling Burghölzli a "monastery" may be seen as entirely consonant with the discussion in the previous chapter on the healing function of monastic life for Merton. Although nominally Jung's time was spent studying psychiatry for his career purposes, one may also see that, when he refers to it as a time of "undivided reality," he is expressing the depth experience that occurs when a person undertakes the actual labor of the psyche, the conscious attention given to understanding all of the pieces of inner experience. In Jung's case, he was studying the full range of knowledge available on mental illness in its various manifestations, which began to lay a foundation for a viable *weltanschauung* large enough to include all of his experiences of emptiness up to that time: those of his mother, grandfather and great-grandmother's and his own mental peculiarities, as well as those of the inmates at the hospital. By actually studying mental processes, Jung began making a place for both sides of his own personality and thus constructing a bridge that would lead, ultimately, to his own healing.

In 1902 he finished his M.D. dissertation on occult phenomena, inspired by experiments he conducted with his cousin, Helene Preiswerk, in spiritualism. He then studied one semester with Pierre Janet in Paris, with whom Freud had also studied.

On February 14, 1903, Carl married Emma Rauschenbach, who came from a wealthy Swiss-German family.[140] She had turned down his first proposal, waiting, perhaps, for him to prove himself. She accepted the proposal in 1902, after he received his M.D. and was appointed to the staff of Burghölzli. She was an attractive and intelligent woman, evidently, who served Jung's personality No. 1's needs for effective dealings with the world very well.[141] Over time, in addition to raising their children, she studied psychology, nearly completed a book on the search for the holy grail, contributed to the development of Jung's ideas on anima/animus and became increasingly active as a lecturer and psychotherapist. She displayed great insight and diplomatic skill in trying to mediate between Jung and Freud. When Jung's later involvement with other women became apparent, she bore it well without surrendering her position. In sum, she seems to have been a remarkable woman and a wonderful wife, and Jung manifestly loved her very much. Together they had three daughters and one son. For a man with a divided psyche, however, even she was not enough.

SEARCH FOR WHOLENESS,[142] PART I

In 1902, Jung began his position as psychiatrist at Burghölzli.
On February 14, 1903, he married Emma.
On December 26, 1904, their first daughter, Agathe, was born. Their second daughter, Gret, was born in February of 1906.[143]
Sometime during the year between his marriage and the birth of their daughter in 1904, Carl Jung became involved with a patient at Burghölzli named Sabina Spielrein.[144] The initial relationship began professionally, then took on a more personal and romantic dimension.

In April of 1906, Jung sent Sigmund Freud (1856–1939) a copy of his *Diagnostic Association Studies*, to which Freud replied in gratitude in a letter of April 11. Jung's reply was dated October 5. Freud's next letter was dated October 7. In Jung's next letter to Freud, dated October 23, 1906, he wrote:

> At the risk of boring you, I must abreact my most recent experience. I am currently treating an hysteric with your method. Difficult case, a 20-year-old Russian girl student, ill for 6 years.
>
> First trauma between the 3rd and 4th year. Saw her father spanking her older brother on the bare bottom. Powerful impression. Couldn't help thinking afterwards that she had defecated on her father's hand. From the 4th–7th year convulsive attempts to defecate on her own feet in the following manner: she sat on the floor with one foot beneath her, pressed her heel against her anus and tried to defecate and at the same time to prevent defecation.

> Often retained the stool for 2 weeks in this way....Later this
> phenomenon was superseded by vigorous masturbation.[145]

Jung's involvement with both Spielrein and Freud may be
seen as two aspects of his true self seeking evocation in ways that
had not happened with his parents.

Although his wife Emma met his personality No. 1's needs
very well, there remained for Jung a need for a deeper erotic
connection that matched the experience he had had with the
maid when his mother was hospitalized. Sabina Spielrein both
elicited and returned Jung's deepest eros, initially as a patient,
and then as a lover.

Similarly, Jung still needed a model of active intelligence,
stature and power to match, evoke and confirm his own abilities
in a way that his "powerless" father had not. Sigmund Freud,
already known as the founder of psychoanalysis, met this need.

Split anima

When, in one's early life experience, the mothering person
exhibits strong polarities of presence—alternately nurturing and
withholding, for example, comforting and critical, reliable and
unavailable or, as in Jung's case, there and not there, what is
taken in and formed is a split anima, divided into the two aspects
of the mothering person as experienced. As has been seen, Jung's
mother, Emilie, was indeed "there" and "not there," not only in
the sense of present versus absent, but of being mentally absent
oftentimes when physically present. Out of his experiences with
his mother, therefore, Jung developed a split anima. The split
mother was introjected as a split anima.[146]

> I was deeply troubled by my mother's being away. From
> then on, I always felt mistrustful when the world "love" was
> spoken. The feeling I associated with "woman" was for a

long time that of innate unreliability. "Father," on the other hand, meant reliability and—powerlessness.[147]

When Jung refers to the feeling associated with the words love, and woman, it is not to be assumed that he made the verbal connection to the feelings when he was three years old, but is the association that later, on reflection, came to his consciousness as he recalled the events from which the feelings originated.

Interestingly, and perhaps proving his point, *woman* and *father* are not parallel terms. There is still distancing and abstraction in his associated memory of his mother when Jung related his story seventy-nine years later! She still appeared as a class of persons, not as a person.

He says he remembers being cared for by an aunt and a maid. He remembers the maid in detail:

> I still remember her picking me up and laying my head against her shoulder. She had black hair and an olive complexion, and was quite different from my mother. I can see, even now, her hairline, her throat, with its darkly pigmented skin and her ear. All this seemed to me very strange and yet strangely familiar. It was as though she belonged not to my family but only to me, as though she were connected in some way with other mysterious things I could not understand. This type of girl later became a component of my anima. The feeling of strangeness which she conveyed, and yet of having known her always, was a characteristic of that figure which later came to symbolize for me the whole essence of womanhood.[148]

In the case of Thomas Merton, his primary anima figure was his distant, critical mother, a mother who—until she died when he was six—was "there" (especially as writer/observer), but in a disapproving, judging way. In the case of Carl Jung, his anima image was divided, at least from the age of three, on two levels: first of all, between the mother who was "there" physically, including the mothering figure who was there when Emilie was *not* there, in the form of the maid with black hair and dark skin; and secondly, between the mother who was "there" physically but "not there" mentally, because she was in an unrelated state of mind.

In the opening pages of his autobiography, Jung himself made the connection between his experience of the maid during his mother's absence and his subsequent experience of "mysterious things" and "strangeness"—in other words, numinosity—as the "whole essence of womanhood." There is, in the *quality* of the experience of his maid, an association with that which is dark, strange and mysterious as also being comforting and supportive. What is dark can perhaps be trusted in a way that what is light cannot be.[149] Even later, when he had his heart attack in 1944, Jung dreamed of "an old Jewish woman" who prepared him "ritual kosher dishes" for a wedding, which was himself. ("I was the marriage.")[150]

Sabina Spielrein

Sabina Spielrein had dark hair. Born in 1885, the oldest child of a wealthy Jewish Russian family, she was sent to Burghölzli in Zurich for treatment of what Jung labeled "psychotic hysteria,"[151] including not only the symptoms detailed above in Jung's letter to Freud, but hallucinations that the entire room was filled with excrement. After nearly a year there, she continued in private treatment with Jung at least through the time he wrote to Freud about her in 1906. In the course of her treatment, she recovered from her symptoms and began medical school.

Carotenuto suggests that Jung did not realize the extent to which he had fallen in love with Sabina until the beginning of 1908 and began trying to separate emotionally from her sometime in 1909.[152] In a letter Jung wrote to Spielrein dated December 4, 1908, he opened up to her in defenseless surrender:

The Experience of Emptiness in Depth Psychology

> I am looking for a person who can love without punishing, imprisoning and draining the other person; I am seeking this as yet unrealized type who will manage to separate love from social advantage or disadvantage, so that love may always be an end unto itself, not just a means for achieving another end.[153]

Such a paragraph expresses Jung's fears, and therefore, one may surmise, his negative view of what his own marriage meant to him as he had come to construct it. His marriage to Emma was in fact exactly the kind of upwardly mobile move he was decrying to Spielrein. Like Peter Peter Pumpkin Eater, Jung had put her in a box and kept her there very well. He was only disturbed by the fact that she wanted more of him. Emma was in fact a very intelligent woman who stayed acquainted with and understood Jung's psychology as it developed, and could have served as an intellectual partner as well as his wife. But at this point in his life, Jung consigned his wife to the role he needed her to play, as someone safe and stable. That left a big gap of erotic and creative need, which he found was met by Spielrein.

On June 10, 1909, Spielrein wrote to Freud, asking that he mediate between her and Jung. The next day she wrote, "Four and a half years ago Dr. Jung was my doctor, then he became my friend and finally my 'poet,' i.e., my beloved."[154] Then she records the letter Jung sent to her mother in which he tried to justify his relationship with Sabina on the grounds that he took no money from her and therefore was not under professional obligation to maintain objectivity. The next day, June 12, she records Jung's second letter to her mother:

> I have always told your daughter that a sexual relationship was out of the question and that my actions were intended to express my feelings of friendship.

In her diary dated September 21, 1909, Spielrein wrote,

> Friendship! Can it alter so suddenly?
> Mother says it is impossible for my friend and me to remain friends once we have given each other our love. A man cannot sustain pure friendship in the long run.[155]

Bruno Bettleheim, reviewing Carotenuto's book, felt Carotenuto had "protested too much" in his insistence that the relationship remained platonic.[156] David Fisher, in his review of the book, was even more direct.

> Spielrein's diary and letters reveal that the Jung/Spielrein connection exceeded the boundary and propriety of the patient-physician relationship. All the available evidence suggests a passionate love affair, almost certainly one that was consummated sexually.[157]

What happened between the romance and Jung's need to distance himself from Spielrein was the increased urgency and excitement she expressed to him about their liaison, and her desire to have a full relationship with him, including having a son by him who would be named "Siegfried," who would symbolize "the union of your and Freud's theories."[158] Referring to her paper on "Destruktion," she wrote to Jung in 1912,

> Dear one,
> Receive now the product of our love, the project which is your little son Siegfried.[159]

For Spielrein, her own wholeness would have been confirmed in a full relationship, including marriage, to Jung.

For Jung, however, his wholeness at the time consisted not in simply trading in a traditional wife for an erotic one, but in having both separately.

> Jung could give himself to her in direct proportion to her degree of independence, which protected him from her ever needing him.[160]

The Experience of Emptiness in Depth Psychology

Jung's split anima required two women in his life. Because his own psyche was divided in a fundamental way and psychoanalytic theory had not yet caught up with the level of wounded narcissism Jung had, he was unable to work through his split anima to achieve a satisfactory relationship with only one woman. He therefore needed Emma to match the traditional side of his mother as manager of the external world's affairs and to remain stable (no more hospitalizations!), his solid anchor. The other, Sabina Spielrein, was needed to evoke and feed his erotic and creative side. These two never came together in Jung's lifetime. Insofar as he achieved a psychological unity toward the end of his life in the writing of *Memories*, as Winnicott suggests,[161] he did it after all the important women in his life had died.

When Jung sought indirect consolation from Freud regarding the affair with Spielrein, he wrote,

> Meanwhile I have learnt an unspeakable amount of marital wisdom, for until now, I had a totally inadequate idea of my polygamous components despite my self-analysis.[162]

It would have been also to the point if Jung had written,

> *I had a totally inadequate idea of how intransigent the divisions within my own psyche are and how they resist coming together in a relationship with one woman.*

The breakup between Jung and Spielrein was psychologically inevitable, therefore, because she wanted a complete and comprehensive relationship, whereas Jung wanted—and could only tolerate—a relationship that enhanced the stability of his marriage and could live right alongside it. As is often the case, erotic countertransference usually represents only a piece of the analyst's psyche and can rarely be the basis for a complete relationship in the world outside the analytic setting.

Journeys into Emptiness

Jung's management of the moving away from Sabina was not handled with much honor or sensitivity. However much of a cad he may have been in the manner in which he ended his personal relationship with Spielrein, Bettleheim reminds us that Jung did, in fact, cure her,[163] and that, given the severity of her hallucinations and acting out, was no mean feat. Largely by her persistence, Spielrein and Jung sustained a professional relationship, including correspondence, for several years.

Spielrein continued to study and work in psychoanalysis, allying herself with Freud, and becoming an analyst in her own right after finishing medical school. She contributed to Jung's understanding of the anima and shadow, and to Freud's idea of the death instinct; indeed, some of her own writings precede the publication of these ideas by either man.

In 1912, she married a physician named Paul Sheftel. In 1923, she returned with her husband and their two daughters to Rostov-on-Don, her hometown in Russia, where she helped to introduce psychoanalysis in Russia, translated several of Freud's works into Russian, wrote some thirty papers and founded a home for infants and children. In 1936, Stalinist Russia outlawed psychoanalysis,[164] and the home for children had to be abandoned. John Kerr reports that during the Nazi occupation in 1941, she and her two daughters were taken to a synagogue and shot:

> Escape was no doubt impossible, but it is said that Spielrein hastened her end by accosting a Nazi officer and rebuking him in German. A long time before, she had lived in Berlin. She disbelieved that the people she had once lived among could be capable of atrocity.[165]

Toni Wolff

The fact that Jung managed to disentangle himself from Spielrein did not rid him of his need for an energizing anima presence. Toni Wolff came to Jung for treatment of depression in 1911, when she was twenty-three years old.[166] Like Jung's maid and

The Experience of Emptiness in Depth Psychology

Sabina Spielrein, Toni Wolff was dark. Also like Spielrein, Wolff was intuitive, very bright and had a knack for understanding psychology, philosophy and religion.[167]

The point at which Jung's relationship with Wolff became more personal than that of patient/therapist is not known. She does appear, however, in the group picture of the Weimar Congress on psychoanalysis in September 1911,[168] which would indicate a shift had already taken place that included her being considered a colleague.[169]

Their relationship became very intimate on both the personal and professional levels. After an initial period when Wolff wanted Jung to marry her, just as Spielrein had, she backed off from her demand and fell into a pattern of consistent involvement that did not require Jung to leave his marriage. This was the flexibility that Jung wanted from his anima figure—to be there when he needed solace and inspiration, but not to threaten the stability of personality No. 1's marriage to Emma. Wolff went to Jung's house on a regular basis every Wednesday afternoon for several years. She also is reported to have spent time with him at the Tower, his Bollingen retreat, especially during the summer months.[170] She was a crucial presence to Jung during his "creative illness,"[171] and was probably the basis of the Salome figure in his dreams of that time. Wolff became an analyst in her own right.[172] Their relationship continued in some variation of professional and personal ways until her death in 1953.

Jung's wife, Emma, evidently went through various stages of anger and acceptance of his involvement with Toni Wolff and her presence among the family.

Ultimately, Emma was able to acknowledge the value Wolff had for her husband, and since it became clear that Jung had no intention of replacing Emma with Toni, Emma accepted the terms of the arrangement. In this author's view, Emma Jung comes out of these stories a very noble and generous woman. Her attitude was not, in the long run, one of even stoic acceptance. It contained a recognition of the reality of her husband's deep need, her own limits in meeting them and from that basis an ability to generously make room for whatever was required. The fact that she may have had her own "needs," which were being ignored, had to have been a source of suffering for her.

In effect, Emma Jung served the ultimate function of a maternal wife: she was able to create a home that could contain all that her husband needed, including another woman. There is heroic realism here, and it is a heroism that is rooted in the particular, rather than based on principle.

Psychologically, it was impossible for Jung at that time to overcome his split anima in order to be monogamously faithful to Emma alone. To his credit, he also knew himself well enough to know he would not have been satisfied with either Wolff or Spielrein alone, so he didn't throw away his marriage. There is, in sum, an extraordinary knowledge of and acceptance of husband, wife and the third party—of one another by each party— *in their particularity*. Such a resolution defies not only moral categories, but common assumptions about the goal of monogamy in marital counseling. It is at once more grand and more humble.

Powerless Father

In Freud's first letter to Jung, dated April 11, 1906, Freud stipulated the basis on which he was interested in Jung:

> Of course your latest paper, "Psychoanalysis and Association Experiments," pleases me most, because in it you argue on the strength of your own experience that everything I have said about the hitherto unexplored fields of our discipline, is true.[173]

Jung's first letter to Freud, in reply, dated October 5, 1906, declares a difference in their perspectives:

The Experience of Emptiness in Depth Psychology

...though the genesis of hysteria is predominantly, it is not exclusively, sexual. I take the same view of your sexual theory.[174]

The next letter from Freud makes it clear that Freud has understood the fact that Jung has a difference of perspective and insists, nonetheless, that the direction of their future lies in Jung's surrendering the difference and coming to agree entirely with Freud.

Your writings have long led me to suspect that your appreciation of my psychology does not extend to all my views on hysteria and the problem of sexuality, but I venture to hope that in the course of the years you will come much closer to me than you now think possible.[175]

In these initial exchanges, like the opening moves of a chess game and like the first interactions of any relationship, the limits and scope of the relationship were laid down. Jung needed the strength and paternal interest of someone more knowing to heal his experience of his father as "powerless." Freud needed disciples, especially gentile ones, for his growing psychoanalytic movement. Jung needed to be able to relate to Freud without completely being in agreement with him. Freud insisted on agreement, even if it took time for Jung to reach it. Even more deeply, Jung needed the recognition and confirmation of his true self from the mentor. Freud demanded false self-compliance. They neither agreed to agree, nor agreed to disagree, either of which would have left things open-ended. Therefore the termination of their relationship was implicit in its beginning, and the only question was what would happen, how much they could actually give to each other, between the beginning and the end.

Freud and Jung did become deeply involved with each other both professionally and personally, with Freud assuming the mentoring father role, and Jung finally able to experience the idealization of a father figure.[176] Children need to idealize their parents, because it gives them hope in facing the many unseen and unknowable powers that can threaten one in childhood. Jung's experience of his father as powerless left him, therefore, without hope in anything more than his own experience and understanding. This may well have strengthened, de facto, his reliance on his inner world, but with Freud Jung began to experience a new level of energy that comes from an idealization that is certainly a kind of falling in love.[177] In October of 1907, writing in reply to Freud's complaint that Jung was being lazy in writing, Jung confessed,

> ...my veneration for you has something of the character of a "religious" crush. Though it does not really bother me, I still feel it is disgusting and ridiculous because of its undeniably erotic undertone. This abominable feeling comes from the fact that as a boy I was the victim of a sexual assault by a man I once worshipped....I find psychological insight makes relations with colleagues who have a strong transference to me downright disgusting. *I therefore fear your confidence.*[178]

Freud's accusation that Jung was lazy in writing clearly shows how much Freud needed Jung's engagement and adulation. Jung's delay must be seen, in addition to his expressed inhibition toward intimacy based on an experience of abuse and betrayal in childhood, as a reflection of the fact that Freud's need for Jung's support superseded Freud's support for Jung's own true self needs—which is of the essence of sexual abuse. In other words, Freud was already reenacting, nonsexually, Jung's experience of being taken advantage of by an older man without regard for Jung's own developmental needs. Jung was responding by putting more time in between letters.

Nevertheless, Jung wrote Freud on February 20, 1908, saying:

> The undeserved gift of your friendship is one of the high points of my life...[I] ask you to let me enjoy your friendship not as one between equals but as that of father and son.[179]

The Experience of Emptiness in Depth Psychology

In a letter of January 17, 1909, Freud promised a reward for Jung's allegiance:

> ...if I am Moses, then you are Joshua and will take possession of the promised land of psychiatry, which I shall only be able to glimpse from afar.[180]

For most of the next four years, Freud and Jung enjoyed a rich relationship of mutual respect and support, including the interpretation of each other's dreams. They traveled to America together, compiled a psychoanalytic journal called the *Jahrbuch*, which Jung edited, and they worked together to build the International Psychoanalytic Association, of which Jung was president until their differences prompted his resignation. Their relationship was never, however, without tension. Freud twice had fainting spells, which he interpreted as a reaction to Jung's wish to kill him.[181]

At a very specific point, Jung's looking to Freud as the more knowing one, and therefore the higher authority, came to a crashing halt. Freud had a dream for whose interpretation Jung asked for more details about Freud's personal life. Freud responded, "But I cannot risk my authority!"

> At that moment he lost it altogether. That sentence burned itself into my memory; and in it the end of our relationship was already foreshadowed. Freud was placing personal authority above truth.[182]

One way the shift in their relationship may be traced is by the changing greeting Freud used in his letters to Jung. In Freud's first letters, he addressed Jung as "Dear Colleague." His letter of November 15, 1907, shifts the greeting to "Dear Friend and Colleague," and by February 17, 1908, Freud addresses Jung simply as "Dear Friend." This continued to be the greeting until Freud's letter of November 14, 1912, which began "Dear Dr.

Jung." On Jung's part, he never wavered from greeting Freud as "Dear Professor Freud."[183]

One may see the breaking away between Freud and Jung as having at least three dimensions interacting simultaneously. On the theoretical level, they disagreed fundamentally on the nature of the psyche, the libido and the unconscious. This was signaled in Jung's first letter to Freud, and the difference between them only grew as Jung became more confident in his approach. On the interpersonal level, the relationship lasted as long as Jung needed Freud to be a supporting and encouraging father figure for him, and ended when Freud refused to let his "son" grow in his own unique way. At stake for Freud was the solidarity of the psychoanalytic movement (as depending on the centrality of the oedipal complex in the genesis of neurosis and the sexuality of the libido) and his authority in it. At stake for Jung was the choice between being true to what he believed or engaging in a false self-compliance, refusing to listen to what was only dimly beginning to form in his mind.

Sabina Spielrein tried to intervene to convince each of them of their value to the other. To Jung she urged he acquiesce to his elder. To Freud, she wrote:

> In spite of all his wavering, I like J. and would like to lead him back into our fold. You, Professor Freud, and he have not the faintest idea that you belong together far more than anyone might suspect.[184]

However true her statement might be—and in terms of what was needed in the world, there can be no question that both men's contributions remain priceless—the men were not able to contain their differences in an ongoing relationship.

Carl Jung's transference to Freud may be seen not just as a father transference, but, insofar as Freud earnestly cultivated Jung's development by taking him under his wing as a son and heir,[185] the transference included the positive mother transference that Jung had experienced with his own father. Insofar as Freud required a false self compliance from Jung, it was a negative mother transference.

In Jung's own account of the change he underwent regarding Freud, he related a dream that he said "presaged the forthcoming break" in which Freud appeared as an "Imperial Austrian customs official" whose "expression was peevish, rather melancholic and vexed."[186] These attitudes are those of Jung's depressed mother, not of his nurturing or sentimental father. Thus, psychologically, Freud must be seen to have served a mothering role as well as a fathering one. When they broke up, therefore, it was a devastating loss for Jung because, intrapsychically, it was the loss of both father and mother; furthermore, in the outside world he was shunned by his former Freudian colleagues. No one was left to support Jung's true self.

Winnicott added a third level of the conflict, centered in Jung's split psyche.

> *From the time of Jung's dream when he was four years old it was certain that he and Freud would not be able to communicate about the unconscious.* Whatever Freud was, he had a unit personality, with a place in him for his unconscious. Jung was different. It is not possible for a split personality to have an unconscious, because there is no place for it to be....He went down under and found subjective life....From this developed Jung's exploration of the unconscious, and (for me) his concept of the collective unconscious was part of his attempt to deal with his lack of contact with what could now be called the unconscious-according-to-Freud....The only place for his unconscious (Freudian sense) would be in his secret True Self, an enigma wrapped in an enigma...a pencil box....[187]

Jung said that he knew, when he was writing the last chapter of *Symbols of Transformation*,[188] "The Sacrifice," that this essay would cost him his relationship with Freud, and that he would himself, in essence, be the "sacrifice."[189]

Journeys into Emptiness

> For two months I was unable to touch my pen, so tormented was I by the conflict....At last I resolved to go ahead with the writing—and it did indeed cost me Freud's friendship.
> After the break with Freud, all my friends and acquaintances dropped away. My book was declared to be rubbish; I was a mystic, and that settled the matter....But I had foreseen my isolation and harbored no illusion about the reactions of my so-called friends....I had known that everything was at stake, and that I had to take a stand for my convictions.[190]

Their actual break took place over a period of about a year. Jung wrote Freud a stinging letter in December 1912, accusing Freud of persisting in his own neurosis, and requiring that he stop treating Jung and other followers like sons by pointing out "symptomatic actions."[191] In October 1913 Jung resigned editorship of the *Jahrbuch* and correspondence between him and Freud was virtually discontinued. In April of 1914 Jung resigned the presidency of the Psychoanalytic Association and, except for one letter referring a patient to Freud, the men no longer had any contact with each other.

Thus, Jung chose to enter into yet another experience of emptiness, the loneliness and isolation of being misunderstood and rejected. As the process of transformation of the self evolves, to attain deeper levels of realization, one is required, from time to time, to let go, and to "drop" ever more deeply into the experience of emptiness. Jung did not run from this experience of emptiness as loneliness, but stood with and in it until it took hold of him and he took hold of it, so that it yielded the images whose understanding and exploration constituted his life work.

The Experience of Emptiness in Depth Psychology

SEARCH FOR WHOLENESS, PART II
NEKYIA, THE NIGHT SEA JOURNEY

Jung began his "confrontation with the unconscious,"[192] before his actual break with Freud. Indeed, it was what Jung was discovering by nondirected thinking[193] that kept reinforcing his need to follow a path different from Freud. In his nondirected thinking, Jung chose not to impose any preset idea of order on his own inner process.

> I said to myself, "Since I know nothing at all, I shall simply do whatever occurs to me." Thus I consciously submitted myself to the impulses of the unconscious.[194]

Nondirected thinking is thus a Jungian rendering of *wŭ wéi*, the Taoist principle of acting by nonacting.

Jung's break with Freud was, however, extremely traumatic and Jung found himself alone in the world with no map, empty of friends and of markers, and thus suffering from extreme disorientation. Like Dōgen before he went to China and Merton before he entered Gethsemani, Jung found himself without an adequate *Weltanschauung* to contain and give direction to his experience of emptiness. As James Helsig pointed out, this lack of an adequate *Weltanschauung* is an experience of emptiness that functions in the same way as the empty spaces in Chinese painting.

> Like the empty spaces in a Chinese painting, the time when nothing happens is often of the deepest significance.[195]

Jung described his experience:

> I was afraid of losing command of myself and becoming a prey to the fantasies.[196]

He verged on complete psychotic breakdown and felt he was kept sane and intact only by his continuing work with patients, his family life, his working in sculpture, and doing yoga. Unmentioned by him in his memoirs is the crucial support of Toni Wolff during this period.

> It was during Advent[197] of the year 1913—December 12, to be exact—that I resolved upon the decisive step. I was sitting at my desk once more, thinking over my fears. *Then I let myself drop.*[198] Suddenly it was as though the ground literally gave way beneath my feet, and I plunged down into dark depths. I could not fend off a feeling of panic. But then, abruptly, at not too great a depth, I landed on my feet in a soft, sticky mass. I felt great relief, although I was apparently in complete darkness.[199]

Like Dōgen's "dropping off body and mind," like Merton's entering the "dark path," Jung dropped down into his own experience of emptiness as "dark depths...complete darkness."

> In order to seize hold of the fantasies, I frequently imagined a steep descent. I even made several attempts to get to the very bottom. The first time I reached, as it were, a depth of about a thousand feet; the next time I found myself at the edge of a cosmic abyss. It was like a voyage to the moon, or a descent into *empty space.*[200]

Fantasies and images continued to emerge, which Jung carefully wrote down as a way of engaging them consciously, emptying himself of defenses and preconceived notions and thus making an empty space that the unconscious could fill if it so chose.

> I wrote everything down very carefully, following the old Greek maxim: "Give away all that thou hast, then thou shalt receive."[201]

Amid the images that came, Jung acquired two figures as guides to his encounters. The masculine image was Elijah, later evolving into "Philemon," a Logos figure who led Jung to the writing of the

The Experience of Emptiness in Depth Psychology

Septem Sermones ad Mortuos, which begins to put into words Jung's experience of emptiness:

> Harken: I begin with nothingness. Nothingness is the same as fullness. In infinity full is no better than empty. Nothingness is both empty and full....[202]
> This nothingness or fullness we name the PLEROMA. Therein both thinking and being cease, since the eternal and infinite possess no qualities. In it no being is, for he then would be distinct from the pleroma, and would possess qualities which would distinguish him as something distinct from the pleroma.
> In the pleroma there is nothing and everything....
> ...Even in the smallest point is the pleroma endless, eternal, and entire....It is that nothingness which is everywhere whole and continuous....[203]

The female image that emerged was a blind Salome. Jung said she was blind "because she does not see into the meaning of things."[204] She was an anima figure whose factor was Eros. These figures, along with subsequent images, assumed for Jung an objective character, so that he felt they were not coming from his personal imagination, but from a deeper strata of human experience that he named the collective unconscious, later termed the objective psyche. For several years, Jung was preoccupied with the fantasies and images emerging from within.

> It was then that *I ceased to belong to myself alone*, ceased to have the right to do so. From then on, *my life belonged to the generality*.
> *...I dedicated myself to service of the psyche*. I loved it and hated it, but it was my greatest wealth. My delivering myself over to it, as it were, was the only way by which I could endure my existence and live it as fully as possible.[205]

By consenting to a possible psychosis or breakdown, Jung found himself met, right at that point, by the objectivity of the

Journeys into Emptiness

psyche. Emptiness that plagued him in the forms of having a mother who was both "not there," and "not there" when she was "there," a father who was powerless, growing up amid parents' marital conflicts, and the loneliness of not being understood now yielded to him the truth, one so moving that Jung responded by dedicating himself to the psyche.

Jung became so caught up in the writing down and working with what was coming up for him that he resigned his teaching position from the university and found himself incapable of reading any "scientific" books. He wrote very little for publication and felt "struck dumb" by what was coming up from his unconscious.

> Curiously, deliberately then, I abandoned my academic career. For I felt that something great was happening to me, and I put my trust in the thing which I felt to be more important *sub specie aeternitatis*. I knew that it would fill my life and for the sake of that goal I was ready to take any kind of risk.
>
> The consequence of my resolve, and my involvement with things which neither I nor anyone else could understand, was an extreme loneliness. I was going about laden with thoughts of which I could speak to no one: they would only have been misunderstood. I felt the gulf between the external world and the interior world of images in its most painful form. I could not yet see that interaction of both worlds which I now understand.[206]

In that "gulf...in its most painful form" was an emptiness so deep that there could hardly be one deeper for a psychiatrist, watching himself, diagnosing himself as he broke down. And right there, in the pit of that emptiness, Jung discovered an objective reality reaching back to him, just as Dōgen discovered that in the emptiness of emptiness the "ten thousand things," ordinary reality, is given back to one, and just as Merton discovered that in the emptiness of the self that was false and empty, God met him.

The Experience of Emptiness in Depth Psychology

Jung began to emerge from his descent between 1918 and 1919. With the discovery of the image of the mandala, his experiences began to coalesce into usable forms. He clarified his understanding of the self as the goal of psychic development, and began to see the nature of the collective unconscious.

> The years when I was pursuing my inner image were the most important in my life—in them everything essential was decided....It was the prima materia for a lifetime's work.[207]

RETURN FROM THE DEPTHS, TREASURES BROUGHT BACK TO THE WORLD

From Jung's confrontation with the unconscious and his subsequent working through of that form of experience of emptiness, his life's work emerged. It became a school of depth psychology in its own right, called analytical psychology. Its hallmarks were the ideas of the collective unconscious; individuation as psychological and spiritual process; active imagination as a method of engaging the self; the rule of opposites and compensation; archetypes; *mysterium conjunctionis*; alchemical processes as paradigmatic for the process of self development; and the crucifixion as a paradigm for emptiness.

From this brief overview of Jung's early years, several important kinds of experiences of emptiness, in addition to those noted, may be underscored. In contrast to the experiences of emptiness prompted by a parent's death for Dōgen and Merton, Jung's parents both lived into his own adulthood. From all outward appearances, therefore, Jung's life story was a fairy-tale-made-real of a small-town boy who came into his own and achieved great things for which he received fame, fortune and family, complete with a castle built by his own hands and the founding of *the* major alternative school of thought in depth psychology to that of Freudian psychoanalysis. Jung's success, of course, was not in fact so easily attained. Jung's experiences of emptiness, therefore, are all the more important as reminders that some of the most important experiences of emptiness are not obvious to the normal observer.

Experience of Emptiness as Psychological Abandonment

Since Jung described the lasting effect on him of his mother's hospitalization, everyone recognizes this event as determinative for him. It was similar to the No. 1 type of emptiness in Merton as loss or abandonment, except that in Jung's case the mother was not dead and she did return. But, for a three year old, three months *is* forever. For young Carl, his mother *did* die, however much her return was promised. Emotionally and psychologically, he suffered from her absence as if she had gone to heaven (a euphemism that blurs distinctions between temporary absence and death). He experienced the same dynamics of grief, depression and rage that he would have felt had she literally died. His anger continued in the form of his ongoing predisposition to see women—as a class—as unreliable.[208]

Experience of Emptiness as Psychological Dividedness

Just as Jung experienced his mother as having two different personalities, so he considered himself to have two separate personalities: Nos. 1 and 2. He experienced them as differing in relative intensity over time and suffered from them most of all when he broke with Freud and underwent his "confrontation with the unconscious."[209]

Different writers have labeled Jung's dual personalities, as well as his mother's, with different terms, indicating different assessments about the degree of psychopathology Jung manifested. At its worst, Jung himself said, "I was menaced by a psychosis."[210] Following those who see Jung's struggle as creative, Anthony Storr nonetheless wrote, "I think his psychosis or near psychosis was of...the nature of a schizophrenic episode."²¹¹ D. W. Winnicott termed Jung's childhood a "recovered case of infantile psychosis" and "childhood schizophrenia," saying that Jung evolved into a "splitting of the personality."²¹²

The word *dividedness* is chosen to designate Jung's lifelong struggle to bring wholeness, which he saw as the goal of psychological development, to his own divided self, so that the term can encompass the differing degrees of severity of the splitting he experienced over time. It is intended to include, therefore, comparatively small conflicts within the psyche as well as major, structural divisions experienced in psychosis and schizophrenia.

Whereas for Dōgen and Merton the experience of emptiness was triggered by an experience of outer loss that led to a search within the self, with a distrust of the outside world because of its impermanence, in the case of Carl Jung, the experience of emptiness was primarily a *psychological* experience, a split within his own psyche. Thus for Carl Jung, the primary experience of emptiness consisted of the relative powerlessness of the conscious ego to control not only external events, but his own mind. Out of that powerlessness, however, through personality No. 2, Jung discovered the objective psyche and the connection therein to cultures and ages of long ago, giving access to universal themes of human experiences of emptiness, their source and their telos.

The difference between the protagonists in the first two chapters and Jung might be likened to different degrees of problems in driving a car. With Dōgen and Merton the experiences of emptiness precipitated by the deaths of their parents may be compared to running out of gas or having two or more flat tires. With Jung, the experience of emptiness as a structural division within the self is more like having one's vision of the road interrupted by dreams, images and associations of other times, places and people, or like seeing someone on the side of the road and suddenly being struck with an image of them dying from cancer. In the latter case, inner experience becomes more powerful than outer perception, or one perceives in a depth dimension, transcending ordinary space and time, things that others are not yet aware of. While such an experience can be disorienting, it also enriches, deepens and broadens one's experience of life and what life has to offer.

In the experience of emptiness that involves the relative powerlessness of the ego, that is, conscious knowing and willing, to regulate mental life, this emptiness includes mental illness, eruptions from the unconscious. It is an experience in which one cannot trust one's conscious intention and conscious knowledge to carry one through. This is the basis of Jung's grounding the ego in the self rather than putting it over the id as Freud did, and this was Jung's great discovery. This is of the essence of the individuation process. This is the insight and experience it takes meditators a long time to achieve.

As part of his inner dividedness, from his earliest memory Jung experienced things that other people either did not experience or tended to dismiss as unimportant—things for which he felt compelled to find significance. For example, his dream between the ages of three and four was so powerful that it preoccupied him for decades.[213] His vision of the turd dropping down onto the church was an Archimedean discovery not only for him personally, but for the view of religion in relation to the self in analytical psychology.[214] Such dreams and visions were so powerful that ordinary life could hardly compete with his inner life for his interest. Jung's earliest experience of emptiness might therefore be said to have been at that age when he found all existing modes of thought inadequate to deal with what he experienced, and what he experienced was his particular mother and father, his own dreams and his knowledge of others. He had a unique gift, his own *daimon*, which brought him images, dreams, sensations and intuitions of a truth that found no confirmation, much less understanding, in the outside world. While he thus was "filled" with inner experience, it was the lack of any container to hold them, to understand them, to connect them with the rest of life, that constituted his primary experience of emptiness and spurred his search inside himself for what he found missing in the outside world. Things were coming to him from the *inside*, in addition to his difficulties on the outside.

Thus, whereas Shakyamuni was driven to pursue his experiences of emptiness by the question of why there is old age, suffering and death, and Dōgen was driven to pursue his experience of emptiness by the question of why practice is necessary if Buddha-nature is permanent and inherent, and Merton was driven by the question of why everything he experienced was so empty, Carl Jung was driven by the need to unite the divisions within his own psyche, to have things tied together,[215] to discover the hidden wholeness that is the telos for which each being strives.

Experience of Emptiness as Receptivity

Throughout his life, Jung's inner life had more power and reality than external forces. Real power was known by intuition, images, the mind's own associations. Thus another aspect of Jung's experience of emptiness was in his remaining psychologically receptive, like an empty cup, to what came to him from his conscious and unconscious. In order to continue to receive what is coming, one must constantly be emptying the cup, as the Zen master demonstrated to the astonished student by pouring tea overflowing into a cup. Jung continually emptied his cup by working with what came to him. What to Jung was a fact of his life, his way of being in the world, was for most people a scarcely-ever-achieved spiritual process.

Things come to the mind—images, thoughts, feelings—that are more or less clear and cohesive, but that have meaning only when understood in a certain way—for which one goes into analysis, psychotherapy, spiritual direction or a monastery to work with more-knowing others, mentors. For Jung, the more-knowing ones were to be found by assiduous study of many cultures, eras and fields. Emptiness here means the surrender of the ego to let these things have a place—be appreciated and worked with—not merely spat out, acted out, controlled or forgotten. Jung could have simply tossed his dreams and visions aside as scary mental events that were, as Freud would have it, expressions of the "seething cauldron of instincts," but instead, Jung persevered, drawing meaning out of them by working with them and seeing where else they appeared in history and other cultures.

The capacity to have such experiences is a kind of talent, an ability that, like most things, can be cultivated by anyone. Like all creativity, however, some people have more of this ability than others. Jung was a genius in this regard. Shamans, seers, psychics, writers and prophets down through history are people with an above-average capacity for receiving such visions, images and dreams and interpreting them.

The experience of emptiness as receptivity includes experiences usually considered not only illogical and irrational, but absurd. Among these are extrasensory perception, automatic writing and speaking in tongues. The realm of the spirit comes through the realm of the unconscious. To be open to this realm requires a lowering of ego defenses, often producing states of mind that we might clarify as symptomatic of mental illness. Thus, to open to the realm of the spirit is to open to the realm of the unconscious, and the vulnerability of the ego in such experiences makes the presence of a mentor or nonintrusive "other" crucial. Paranoid states, like Freud's accusing Jung of wishing him dead, often contain a truth that is being denied to consciousness, a piece of the psyche that is being disowned, and thus, as it were, flung into the air, which is what the "paranoid" person is intuiting and expressing.

The Experience of Emptiness in Depth Psychology

The Experience of Emptiness as the Loneliness of Not Being Understood

Jung experienced a knowledge of things that others did not know, and kept secrets that he dared not tell but which were essential to his very life. These dreams and visions led him to encounter something utterly new in Western psychology—the objective psyche. This encounter made him, as he said repeatedly throughout his memoirs, extremely lonely and isolated. It took years for Jung to discern the meaning and implications of his inner experience and to be able to share it with others who could thereby resonate with his experience.

The Experience of Emptiness as Fate

Part 1 began with a piece of Carl Jung's prehistory, the story of his elder brother's birth and death and its possible impact on both Carl's parents, their marriage and on Carl himself. Similarly, the stories mentioned about his grandfathers were told to connect important aspects of Carl Jung's lifelong concerns with the foreshadowings of his ancestors. Brief sketches of his parents set the stage for his arrival. There was, in Carl Jung's experience, a "givenness" to his life, just as there is for everyone. That "givenness" is the nature of the stage and of the preexisting characters on it that we enter at birth. The experience of emptiness as fate therefore includes the transgenerational aspects of our lives, from the past and into the future. That "who-we-are" is to a large degree given to us to accept or not, work with or not. We have a psychic as well as a genetic inheritance from families, from society, from the historical era that sets the context of our own possibilities: There are some things we cannot be, not because we lack intelligence, but because there are inherited dispositions—positive and negative—and propensities—a certain amount of a path already having been trod—that influence and set the stage on which we "act."

Journeys into Emptiness

I became aware of the fateful links between me and my ancestors. I feel very strongly that I am under the influence of things or questions which were left incomplete and unanswered by my parents and grandparents and more distant ancestors. It often seems as if there were an impersonal karma with a family, which is passed on from parents to children. It has always seemed to me that I had to answer questions which fate had posed to my forefathers and which had not been answered, or as if I had to complete, or perhaps continue, things which previous ages had left unfinished.[216]

●

Our souls as well as our bodies are composed of individual elements which were all already present in the ranks of our ancestors. The "newness" in the individual psyche is an endlessly varied recombination of age-old components.[217]

●

In the Tower at Bollingen it is as if one lived in many centuries simultaneously....my ancestors' souls are sustained by the atmosphere of the house, since I answer for them the questions that their lives once left behind. I carve out rough answers as best I can. I have even drawn them on the walls. It is as if a silent, greater family, stretching down the centuries, were peopling the house. There I live in my second personality and see life in the round, as something forever coming into being and passing on.[218]

In closing this part of the presentation of Jung's life and work, we note that his profound contribution not only to psychology but to religion stands out all the more for his having opened up ways of exploring and comparing all religions. The question whether Jung was more a psychotherapist or a mystic[219] continues to arise.

The Experience of Emptiness in Depth Psychology

In 1952, Ira Progoff wrote his doctoral thesis on the contribution of Jung's psychology to the social sciences and asked Jung to comment on the text. At one point Progoff mentions "the therapy of individuation..." to which Jung replied:

> Why therapy? It is not therapy. Is it therapy when a cat becomes a cat? It is a natural process. Individuation is a natural process. It is what makes a tree turn into a tree; if it is interfered with, then it becomes sick and cannot function as a tree, but left to itself it develops into a tree. That is individuation.[220]

EPILOGUE

Practicing the Edge

In the lives of the three men treated in this book, we have seen repeatedly that their experiences of emptiness as loss led them to emptiness as a way of living. By letting go of inner and outer attachments they were led to the emptiness of all things, a rich source of unity with all being. However different their cultures, eras and disciplines, their stories exemplify the life-giving value of entering such experiences rather than ignoring or denying them. Paying attention to and entering deeply into our experiences of emptiness is nothing less than a way of increasing and deepening consciousness, being awake in order to penetrate the meaning of reality on its deepest level.

Following the path of our experiences of emptiness turns out, therefore, to be identical with the path urged upon us in Joseph Campbell's famous instruction, "Follow your bliss." The experience of bliss, as Campbell gleaned from his vast cross-cultural studies of myth, religion, symbol and ritual, has the same source as the experience of emptiness we have been exploring in the lives of Dōgen, Merton and Jung. Though the experience of emptiness in its initial stage feels different from the experience of bliss, when one sets out to follow where either experience leads, one is led deeper and deeper into the multilayered, multitextured interconnectedness of life itself, which ultimately results in an experience of mystical union with all. One has thus learned how to tap into the great infinite wellspring of life itself, which includes death and what is beyond both life and death.

Journeys into Emptiness

This fact—that it ultimately doesn't matter whether we begin with one's experience of emptiness or with one's bliss—is a reflection of the Buddhist declaration that "form is exactly emptiness, emptiness exactly form." It exemplifies further Shakyamuni's claim that *dukkha*, suffering, consists in pleasure as well as pain, because the pleasure doesn't last.

To follow one's experience of emptiness and to follow one's bliss have as their common ground, Jung discovered, the experience of the numinous as the source of all, within all, beyond all, yet never apart from the here and now.

Our experiences of emptiness and our experiences of bliss are numinous because they take us to the exact edge of life and death, to that very place where the rich, delicious feast of life meets the inevitability of death and where we are then placed in that existential forced choice about how to live: whether to follow vitality with its attendant risks, struggles and promise, or whether to succumb to the death within life of unconsciousness and refuse to receive and take responsibility for the particular form of life that has been revealed and given to us.

The task is to see all of our experiences in their depth dimension and to forge our lives accordingly. The message of each of our three men is that taking our pain and our bliss seriously is an imperative with a promise, exactly as expressed by Moses' instructions to the recently liberated people of Yahweh as they were about to enter the promised land: "See I set before you life and death, blessing and curse....therefore choose life that you and your descendants may live long..." (Deuteronomy 30:19).

Poignantly, Moses reminds us, our own choices influence others down through history, for better or for worse. Thus there is an added burden to our freedom: the entire world is impacted by our decisions. How we live—our own decisions to enter more deeply into our lives, including death, or to retreat into unconsciousness and irresponsibility—may constitute a decision not only to die, but to be dead before we die.

Epilogue

To practice life at the edge is to dedicate ourselves to being alive and awake, paying attention to the implications and consequences of our choices. To practice life at the edge is simply to be willing to see what is at stake in everything we do, and to take responsibility for our choices with an overarching commitment to the life within life, the particular instance and form that life's vitality is presenting to us in this very moment.

Wake up!

Choose life!

Befriend your unconscious!

Be yourself!

And yet, it is not always easy to know when we're choosing life and when we're choosing death, when we're honoring our false self or true. Nor is it always easy to act according to what we *do* know.

The nature of personal transformation is complex and difficult, and our egos resist change with subtlety and power. This is true of personal journeys in any time and place. There is additionally, and very poignantly, a further complexity to the psychospiritual journey of our time: through the communications media, rapid transportation and the great intermixing of people of all races, cultures and nations, people of today have an unprecedented awareness of cultures other than their own, so much so that we might even say that pluralistic culture is *the* dominant experience of many people around the world. This leaves us acutely aware of the relativity of any inherited psychospiritual tradition, making the pursuit of any single path seem not only arbitrary, but inadequate.

Yet, far from relegating all psychospiritual paths to death by relativity, the multicultural experience of all people today, based on the readings of the lives and work of Dōgen, Merton and Jung, would seem to require that everyone begin with where they are and move into the depths of the personal self, seeing where that leads. It might well lead someone to a different path than their inherited one, or it might lead one to add to and adapt what they know by immersion in an auxiliary tradition.

We are required, in effect, to take responsibility for our own journeys, paying attention to our own unique, personal needs and looking for what is helpful. We are even more acutely in the situation Merton described in his last public talk over thirty years ago: "From now on, everybody stands on his own feet."[1] And yet, by benefit of all that has gone on in the world since Merton's time, we can say, "we are alone…and yet not alone." The vast plenitude of riches of so many traditions assures us that we are part of an infinitely stretching line of people both behind and in front of us, fellow travelers of journeys into emptiness. How one navigates one's personal journey among so many rich options is very much a task of individuation, tuning into the deepest places of resonance for healing and growth.

I believe there are at least four elements required for the long-term psychospiritual journey.

First, we need a *container,* in Winnicott's sense of a holding environment. It is a physical space, with boundaries that hold us like a wise, loving parent, so that we feel safe and receive what we need in terms of nurture and care for our bodies, our minds and our hearts. A container protects us from the outside world so that there is not too much threat, impingement, expectation or demand.

For Dōgen and Merton, the container was a monastery. For Merton, it was only Gethsemani, however much he doubted its sufficiency, and, in the last years, his hermitage. For Dōgen, it was one monastery after another until he built his last one at Eihei-ji. The container can change, but having one is necessary. For Jung, it consisted, first of all, in a stable marriage, without which he would not have been able to be creative at all. Without the reliability of his wife, he would have been caught in a repetition of his earliest experience of his abandoning mother. Had Emilie demanded more of his time and attention, required that he be monogamous or engaged him in endless bouts of fury, he would never have been able to take the risks of psyche, profession and intellect to do the work. With his marriage as a primary container, Jung then built his own container, the Tower, where he could retreat at will.

A container provides a place of "good enough" mothering and fathering to hold one in as well as keep others out. The nature of mind and spirit tends toward unfettered freedom and resists boundaries. The ego would be god omnipotent. Boundaries are imperative to force us to face ourselves, to turn our energy and attention inward, so that even our projections can be seen and worked with.

The second two things we need are interrelated, a *teacher* and a *practice*. Sometimes we become inspired by a teacher and adopt the teacher's practice. Sometimes we have a practice that works, but need mentoring by a more knowing one to help us go further.

Dōgen scoured Japan and was never satisfied with any of his teachers, so he went to China. Even there, after three years, he was about to give up and return to Japan. Only then did he meet the teacher, Rujing, who was able to facilitate Dōgen's full realization.

To a large degree, one might say Merton hardly found a peer, much less a mentor. The abbots of Gethsemani certainly helped, but more as reinforcers of the container than as actual teachers. Even the mentor/psychiatrist Jim Wygal was quickly shifted to being a peer for Merton. Unfortunately, one of the things we most need is someone smart enough in every sense of the word to see through the games we play with ourselves as well as with others, someone who is not dazzled by our wit, intellect, beauty or social standing. Merton rarely found such a person in the Gethsemani environs. He certainly looked to outsiders for help: all the writers, theologians, poets and radical activists from all over the world with whom he corresponded. He also clearly drew from the great classical spiritual guides of the church. But the sum of it all was that Merton's mentors were always mediated by the written word, and never, until his time with "S" was a direct, personal relationship the basis of his learning. And even then, it was with someone who was not even a peer, much less a mentor.

Journeys into Emptiness

Jung had his mentors at Burghölzli and then, of course, the most important mentor, Freud. But after their break, Jung was on his own, and the consequences of what Winnicott pointed to as Jung's continuing split psyche are a continuing subject of debate.

Ultimately, the function of a teacher is to so shape the student that the practice itself becomes one's ongoing mode of learning and growth; then the teacher becomes dispensable. The goal is for both the container and the teacher to become so well internalized that the practice is a way of life and provides the basis for unlimited psychospiritual growth and awareness.

However filled we might be with inspiration on occasion, our egos are by definition devoted to controlling things. Our egos are in general adverse to any form of discomfort or destabilization and are intent on maximizing security, pleasure and anything that looks to us like happiness. We need a teacher who sees that underneath our evasions and manipulations is a true self desperately seeking emergence, a self who is terrified and mistrustful of the real and clueless about how to be simple. A teacher is needed not only to help us through the brambles of our own minds but also to help us learn the language of wisdom, the play of *Hagia Sophia*, the compassion of *Guan Yin*.

It is at this point that the question of the relationship between a psychotherapist and a strictly spiritual teacher arises. Their functions are not the same, though there is much overlapping and ultimately each has an essential role to play in the growth of the individual. From a practical point of view, even though it is possible to train one person in both areas, the responsibilities for the common good and the unique needs of the individual can sometimes conflict. What is important is to have both psychological and spiritual mentors available, each of whom is informed and sensitive to the issues of the other field: spiritual leaders who are psychologically trained and psychotherapists who are spiritually attuned and dedicated.

A *practice* consists of all the things we do to cultivate awareness, manage our lives in accordance with our priorities, deepen our connection to our true self (which is none other than the larger Self of the universe), and eliminate as many of the inessentials as possible. Practice therefore includes prayer, meditation, study, ritual, liturgy, art, body care and ethics. Psychotherapy and psychoanalysis are also forms of practice that are sometimes akin to meditation, as well as study, the study of the self and of relationships. Nondirected thinking and meditative writing are also forms of practice. Practice includes everything that we do intentionally to take care of our lives, our degree of consciousness and the life of the world. Most essentially, practice is our method of orienting our lives in that larger ground of being of which we are a part, from which we gain not only a more cohesive sense of self, but a clearer sense of direction.

The fourth essential is our need for *community*. In all of the traditions we have been engaging here, there is a call away from the collective, the thoughtless, undifferentiated, reactive, unconscious mass and a call to consciousness and personal responsibility in the manifestation and emergence of the true self. But the call to one's true self is never for one's individual benefit alone. It is always on behalf of the larger concerns for compassion, wisdom and responsibility in the larger cosmos. Those who are called to the fullness of life are called to bring back what they have learned for the benefit of all beings, including the air, mountains and waters.

Community is not only where we give back; it is also where we learn to receive, learn to trust, learn to allow ourselves to be loved and cared for. No one grows up alone. No one is healed in isolation. In community, we learn that though we are personally responsible both for what we do and what happens to us, we need others. Community helps us to break through egoism, stoicism and super-mania propensities, because in community we are known with our bumps and warts as well as for our loving ingenuity.

Community serves further to remind us of our primary commitments, and to give support to the absolute value of our psychospiritual journey amid competing demands for allegiance to lesser values. A community of people committed to consciousness, personal growth and the general welfare of all beings is needed to validate choices we make that, by the collective, ordinary world's standards, seem crazy.

With these empowering elements, practicing the edge means constantly paying attention to our hopes, fears and dreams and pushing ourselves to whatever is "next." Practicing the edge requires constantly leaving behind the known, secure and familiar for the unknown that seems, somehow, to beckon.

I am reminded of climbing Mt. Katahdin, the end of the Appalachian Trail in Baxter Park, Maine. My daughter Allison and I have driven to Chimney Pond for a day hike to the top. It is the summer before she goes away to college.

The trail begins to have more climbing places where hands are needed for lifts and curves and ledges. At a point up ahead is all granite rock and boulders, and looking back we can see the vertical ascent we've made from the tree line. At this point I become aware of an alertness to my senses, my body waking up to the need not to take our safety for granted. Increasingly, steps need to be placed deliberately, so that the step after that can be made.

We are soon able to see, up and over to the right, what is called the Knife Edge, a thin line of broken rocks leading from Pamola, the peak we're now ascending ("home of the gods," in Penobscot), to Baxter Peak, the summit, at 5,267 feet, of Mt. Katahdin.

More climbing of hand over hand, of huge granite faces, some too big to see around. Every once in awhile I look back and see Allison's small, thin hands grabbing big gray rocks. We get to what looks like the top, only to see more above.

So much of the path is hidden from view; all I know is the next boulder, ledge or wall. I reach one rock too big to see over, impossible to see around. I see no handhold, nor can I yet see the other side. All I see is one place for my next step, room only for one boot.

I lift myself up. I see over the top of the rock. It is a sheer drop down the other side and I see only one place for a toehold, after which is a huge boulder, seemingly nowhere to go from there.

Why am I here? I suddenly ask myself. If I manage this shift, will Allison? There is no place where I can be secure enough to reach for her. She sees my hesitation.

"Is everything okay?" she asks.

I take a deep breath. "Yeah, sure. How're you doing?" I return the concern.

I am suddenly aware of needing all my energy and acumen for the climb, and acutely aware that my daughter will have to make her next few steps without my help, without my being able to catch her if she falls. As I pull myself over the rock and reach with my toe for the only place left to step, I look down five thousand feet and see myself as vulnerable, as much at risk as I am accustomed to imagining her to be. I describe the step up and the step over to her, in as even a tone as I can muster, trying still to be the guide, the more knowing one.

Ha! I say to myself. There are two edges being approached here: this sheer rock beyond which I cannot see, and the end of my illusion that I could protect her from danger.

I make my move to the last place I can see to go. I shift all my weight to that one ledge at the corner of the rock. Suddenly the beginning of the Knife Edge is clear and I sigh and say, with only too obvious relief, "I can see the rest of the way!"

I look back to watch her leg come over the wall, her toe feeling its way to the ledge. She does well, moves with ease. I am grateful and proud.

We reach the beginning of the Knife Edge. It is not nearly as narrow, looking across it, as it seemed from below. Although it is a drop of a couple of thousand feet of broken rock on either side, the Knife Edge itself is several feet wide, not half as risky as the last few steps we took.

Journeys into Emptiness

Ironic, I think to myself. The danger they tell you about is not the greatest one: by the time you reach the supposedly scary one, you've already passed the hardest part.

It is a walk, not a climb, along Knife Edge. Sometimes we actually leap from rock to rock with confidence.

We reach the peak. We sit and survey the land and lakes and forests for miles in all directions. We taste the water. We take pictures and head home.

ABBREVIATIONS

Full references are given in the bibliography.

AJ   *The Asian Journal*, Thomas Merton

AS   *The Analysis of the Self*, Heinz Kohut

ASFS   *A Search for Solitude*, vol. 3, Thomas Merton

BCPN   *Borderline Conditions and Pathological Narcissism*, Otto Kernberg

BOD   *The Zen Teaching of Bodhidharma*, trans., Red Pine

Brom   *Jung*, Vincent Brome

CP   *Contemplative Prayer*, Thomas Merton

CPT   *The Central Philosophy of Tibet*, Robert Thurman

CW 6   *Psychological Types*, Carl G. Jung

CW 7   *Collected Works*, Carl G. Jung

CW 8   *Structure and Dynamics of the Psyche*, Carl G. Jung

CW 9 i *Archetypes and the Collective Unconscious*, Carl G. Jung

CW 9 ii *Aion, Researches into the Phenomenology of the Self*, Carl G. Jung

CW 10   *Civilization in Transition*, Carl G. Jung

Journeys into Emptiness

Abbreviations

Naga	*The Fundamental Wisdom of the Middle Way,* Nāgārjuna
NSC	*New Seeds of Contemplation,* Thomas Merton
PR	*Playing and Reality,* D. W. Winnicott
RD	*To Meet the Real Dragon,* Gudo Nishijima
RJ	*Road to Joy,* Thomas Merton
RMDR	"Review of *Memories, Dreams, Reflections,*" Donald W. Winnicott
RN	*Religion and Nothingness,* Keiji Nishitani
RTM	*Run to the Mountain: Journals,* vol. 1, Thomas Merton
RU	*Religion and the Unconscious,* Ann and Barry Ulanov
SFS	*A Search for Solitude: Journals,* vol. 3, Thomas Merton
SHO	*Shōbōgenzō, Dōgen,* trans., Nishiyama
SJ	*Sign of Jonas,* Thomas Merton
SL	*Silent Lamp: The Thomas Merton Story,* William Shannon
SMTM	*The Seven Mountains of Thomas Merton,* Michael Mott
SSM	*Seven Storey Mountain,* Thomas Merton
SSSS	*A Secret Symmetry—Sabina Spielrein between Jung and Freud,* Aldo Carotenuto
TB	*Tom's Book,* Thomas Merton
TL	*Transmission of the Light: Zen in the Art of Enlightenment,*
TMR	*A Thomas Merton Reader,* ed., Thomas P. McDonnell

Journeys into Emptiness

NOTES

INTRODUCTION

1. *Dukkha*, the Pali word for suffering in Buddhism, refers to the experience of all of conditioned life. It includes not only pain, but pleasure, since pleasure must end. That all life is dukkha was Shakyamuni Buddha's First Noble Truth.

2. *Wabi* really means "poverty"...not to be dependent on things worldly—wealth, power, and reputation—and yet to feel inwardly the presence of something of the highest value....Stated in terms of practical everyday life, *wabi* is to be satisfied with a little hut, a room of two or three tatami (mats), like the log cabin of Thoreau, and with a dish of vegetables picked in the neighboring fields, and perhaps to be listening to the pattering of a gentle spring rainfall. (Daisetz T. Suzuki, *Zen in Japanese Culture,* Bollingen Series 64 [Princeton: Princeton University Press. 1973], 23.)

3. As will be explored later in this study, although the initial experience with emptiness may bring one to a significant life threshold or doorway, where a decision must be made either to be passive or active in response, subsequent thresholds or doorways involving the experience of emptiness are often encountered in time and may take one further, in different ways, in one's spiritual learning process or the psychological process of individuation.

4. *ETS*, 405.

5. *MDR*, 177.

6. In a study that has many close affinities to this one, Jerome Miller takes the same view of the human propensity to avoid suffering and maps out his view of the transformation that can happen if one follows through on such unsettling experiences, which he calls "crises." Like the major authors explored in this study, Miller concludes with a return to the value of ordinary life. One must underscore, however, that in between the beginning and the end of ordinary life is a transformative middle process. Jerome Miller, *The*

Journeys into Emptiness

Way of Suffering: A Geography of Crisis (Washington, D.C.: Georgetown University Press. 1988).

7. *GG*, Case 5.

8. *CW* 7, Part II "Individuation: The Function of the Unconscious."

9. *GG*, 233.

10. *CW* 8, "On the Nature of the Psyche," par. 428.

11. Freedom is essential to transcendence. For example, "falling in love" happens to one, but loving—in depth consideration of the "other," or over time—is a commitment that takes one beyond oneself and beyond the accident of "falling in love" to a higher, transcendent way of being-in-the-world. Self-realization is a similar process.

12. *SHO*, "Genjokoan."

13. Genesis 32:24 ff.

14. In Zen Buddhism, Self with a capital S refers to the point reached in Enlightenment in which the personal "I" is left behind and one becomes at one with all things. *Self* then means the being of all things, all things in their "suchness."

15. A frequently used Buddhist term to indicate the entire phenomenal universe.

16. *CW* 12, 41, "The [S]elf is not only the centre but also the whole circumference which embraces both conscious and unconscious; it is the centre of this totality, just as the ego is the centre of the conscious mind."

CW 7, 238, "...the [S]elf is our life's goal, for it is the completest expression of that fateful combination we call individuality...."

For both Dōgen, and Jung, therefore, *Self* is usually capitalized to signify its transindividual nature. Throughout this work, since self and ego are used in very different ways by different writers, their meaning in each instance will be articulated in terms of the way it is being used at the time, and contrasts and comparisons with others' usage will be noted when important.

17. See the Ten Ox-Herding Pictures of Master K'uo-an in *The Ox and His Herdsman: A Chinese Zen Text*, trans. M. H. Trevor (Tokyo: Hokuseido Press, 1969). The Ox-Herding Pictures depict the different stages of transformation leading to enlightenment.

18. For Jung, the anima is the contrasexual figure in men that connects them to their unconscious. Thus, the animus is the contrasexual figure functioning similarly for women. Recent Jungian theorists, however, see everyone as having both aspects within themselves, and needing to attend to the inner relationship between them. See *TS*, ch. 1.

Notes

1. EMBRACING EMPTINESS IN THE EAST

1 śūnyatā, in Sanskrit (Sn.), *kō ng* in Chinese (Ch.), *kū* in Japanese (Jp.).These three different languages are given here, as will happen from time to time in this study, to clarify as much as possible the derivation of, and therefore the meaning of, the chosen word, in English. In studying the history of Zen Buddhism, most terms were originally in Sanskrit or Pali, then translated into Chinese, then into Japanese. The English word has thus been chosen usually at third or fourth remove from the original language, and has always reflected the then-current Western philosophical categories into which Buddhist terms were forced to fit.

2. See, for example, *CPT*, 5: "There are numerous lists of the four, sixteen, eighteen, and twenty emptinesses. The usual emptinesses are those of (1) the internal, (2) the external, (3) both internal and external, (4) emptiness, (5) the ultimate, (6) the created, (7) the uncreated, (8) eternity, (9) nonrejection, (10) the universal, (11) nature, (12) all things, (13) intrinsic identity, (14) nonapprehension, (15) phenomena, (16) nothingness, (17) both things and nothings, (18) intrinsic reality, (19) intrinsically real nothingness and (20) infinity." It is hard to imagine anything left out. This study consists in moving among these various kinds of emptiness as articulated by our chosen major writers.

3. For example, see Arthur Lovejoy, *The Great Chain of Being* (Cambridge: Harvard University Press, 1964).

4. For a fuller treatment of this problem, see "dualism" p. 58.

5. Actual facts about the lives of Shakyamuni, Nāgārjuna and Bodhidharma are often difficult to discern and separate from myth, fiction or error. The figures that emerge from these stories are thus to a large degree archetypal, with features that reflect not so much historical fact as psychological and spiritual truth.

6. In this study, *Shakyamuni* will be used, rather than *Śakyamuni*. It literally means "the sage (muni) from the Śakya tribe." Siddhartha was his given name. *Gotama* is the Pali, and *Gautama* is the Sanskrit word for his family name. See *ZBH*, 3–12.

7. According to tradition, Shakyamuni's care, including nursing, was immediately taken over by his mother's sister, so that, especially in contrast to Dōgen and Merton, there was no loss of actual human contact and caring for Shakyamuni. Robert Paul nevertheless asserts an important psychodynamic impact on Shakyamuni that affected his resolution of his Oedipal conflict. (See Robert Paul, *The Sherpas of Nepal in the Tibetan Cultural Context* [Delhi: Motilal Banarsidass, 1989]. The point of view expressed in this study makes a different point: while Shakyamuni may have suffered no lack of genuine care and contact, as part of his later (adolescent/postadolescent) development, he experienced a need to know what was *real*. This search for the real was an inner and an outer process:

Journeys into Emptiness

as an outer process, it is what led him outside the gates of the palace; as an inner process, it led him on his spiritual quest. The search for what is real underlies the search of adopted children for their real, i.e., genetic, parents.

8. "For adoptees, the birth of a child has special meaning....Having, keeping, and raising a child of one's own is likely to stir up old and new feelings about birth parents." ("Growing Up Adopted," in Elinor R. Rosenberg, *The Adoption Life Cycle: the Children and Their Families Through the Years* [New York: MacMillan, 1992], 89 –122.) Shakyamuni's home departure was right after the birth of his son.

"...the majority of searching adoptees described their relationships with their adoptive parents as average or better than average." Julia Tugendhat, *The Adoption Triangle: Searching and Uniting* (London: Bloomsbury, 1992), 33 –44. A search is thus not prompted by inadequate care, necessarily.

"...the adopted adult may suddenly and unexpectedly experience an acute longing for her birthparents at particularly momentous times—the birth of a child, the death of a spouse or adoptive parent, a child's graduation or marriage, an illness."

"The theme of the orphan, severed from her roots, lost and then found, is archetypal and symbolic, appearing in the myths and religions of many countries. It speaks to all of us, not just those who have literally been orphaned, of a state of being vulnerable and lost, longing for roots that cannot be found....At some psychic level we are all orphans. Is it not likely that adoptees who pursue their own fate, searching for their origins, are involved in a metaphorical as well as literal search? Is this searcher so different from those of us who seek the wellsprings of our being in meditation, who visit the hometowns of our grandparents for clues about ourselves....On this level, our children's searching...is something to be respected. It goes far beyond us, and we are fortunate if we can witness some of it." Mary Watkins and Susan Fisher, "Adoption and the World of the Young Child," in *Talking with Young Children about Adoption* (Binghamton, N.Y.: Vail-Ballou Press, 1993), 92 –93.

9. Some Buddhists may object, asserting that the "breaking up of inner soil," the predisposition to a spiritual path, was accomplished by the good karma accumulated in previous lives, rather than a significant personal loss in their current life. Depth psychology would see such "previous lives'" experience, along with ancestors, as active in the person's unconscious, but would nonetheless look for current life events on the basis of which such predispositions from the unconscious arise. Depth psychology would hold Buddhism to its own assertion of cause and effect and assert that compassion cannot develop without some experience of suffering.

10. In chapter 3, "The Experience of Emptiness in Depth Psychology," we will go into more detail about the connection between an early, deep experience of

emptiness as loss or neglect, and a subsequent spiritual search. What we are here underscoring is the fact that abiding spiritual pursuits usually have a significant experience of emptiness underlying them as part of the person's concrete history.

11. Francis Thompson's poem "The Hound of Heaven" articulates the common view of spiritual vocation originating from a divine call from "heaven." The point of this study is to note the "earthly," concrete, historical and psychological experiences of emptiness that predispose one to pay attention to the "heavenly" dimension.

12. It should be further noted that Shakyamuni's response to his encounter with old age, suffering and death was not simply to do works of compassion. That would be the reaction of someone who simply saw a job that needed doing and did it. Rather, he felt forced to look inside himself for what he experienced as a fundamental existential, or human, problem. From a depth psychological point of view, the draw inward was prompted by the unresolved, unconscious experience of emptiness in the loss of his mother.

13. See, for example, Thomas Merton, *The Wisdom of the Desert* (New York: New Directions, 1970). Also, *Late Medieval Mysticism*, vol. 13, Library of Christian Classics (Philadelphia: Westminster Press [no date given: ca. 1960]).

14. In analytical psychology, the school of depth psychology developed by Carl Jung, the "collective" usually refers to the consciously held assumptions about reality, what is considered common sense, including assumptions about what is good and bad, right and wrong.

15. Individuation is the process noted by Carl Jung in which a person sorts through the inherited, "collective" assumptions about himself and reality, to reach a deeper truth in which his/her unique self is discovered. Such a discovery also brings new perspective for the larger human community.

16. *Bodhi* comes from the same root word as *Buddha*, which means "awakened one," and is used to indicate the place where Shakyamuni experienced enlightenment. The actual tree was a pippala tree, which has large leaves and branches out like a banyan tree.

17. In accepting the needs of his body without entirely being devoted to pleasing the body's appetites, Shakyamuni took the first step in what came to be called "the Middle Way" in Buddhism, which is to avoid extremes of any kind, whether of satiation or deprivation.

18. John Daido Loori, *The Eight Gates of Zen* (Mt. Tremper, N.Y.: Dharma Communications, 1992), 13–14. This particular formulation of Shakyamuni's exclamation upon enlightenment reflects the Zen emphasis on the suddenness of the experience.

19. Sources disagree. Compare, *ZBH*, 6 with *EEPR*, 333.

20. *EEPR*, 46.

21. *ZK,* 38.
22. *CPT,* 23.
23. *CPT,* 24.
24. Nicene Creed.
25. Robert Thurman acknowledges his departure from translators' convention in his choice of the word *Centrism* for *Mādhyamika* in order to make the point that it is the central philosophy of Buddhism. See *CPT,* 6.
26. *ZBH,* 28.
27. *ZK,* 107-8.
28. See, for example, *RN.*
29. *ZK,* 124.
30. Nāgārjuna thus comes back to a place similar to that of Jerome Miller in his *The Way of Suffering: A Geography of Crisis,* especially the epilogue, "The Holiness of the Ordinary" (Washington, D.C.: Georgetown University Press. 1988).
31. Naga, ch.24, v. 18.
32. Naga ch. 24, v. 8, 296.
33. Naga, 305.
34. "When Bodhidharma arrived in China...there were approximately 2,000 Buddhist temples and 36,000 clergy in the South. In the North, a census in 477 counted 6,500 temples and nearly 80,000 clergy." *BOD,* x.
35. An Shih-kao is credited with being the first known teacher and translator of Buddhism in China, *ZBH,* 64.
36. *TL,* ch. 29.
37. *Prajna* is Sanskrit for wisdom.
38. *TL,* 120.
39. See *BOD,* introduction, ix-xvii. Compare with *TL,* 121, who says Bodhidharma arrived in 527. Despite this fifty-two-year discrepancy, all sources agree the trip to China took three years!
40. *ZBH,* 91.
41. Serious Buddhist students generally, but Zen students especially, use the word *practice* to refer to the ways in which they deliberately engage in conscious activity as part of their intention to follow the Buddha Way. Practice includes preeminently the activity of *zazen,* which is sitting meditation, but it also includes chanting, doing art, doing one's work, noncompetitive physical sports and academic study, all of which are part of the Eightfold Path. Since the goal of practice is full awareness in everything one does, anything can be part of one's practice insofar as it is engaged for the sake of self-realization.
42. Bodhidharma's "Bloodstream Sermon," *BOD,* 44-45.
43. *BOD,* 29.

Notes

44. Although, once understood, seeming paradoxes are only so in the way we use language, not in the reality of whatever is described. "There's no such thing as a paradox," says Abbot John Daido Loori in Dharma talks at Zen Mountain Monastery. "Paradox is a limitation of language, not a statement about reality."
45. *BOD*, 49.
46. *BOD*, 59.
47. *BOD*, 65.
48. Galatians 3:28.
49. The only given name by which Dōgen is known is Dōgen, the name given him upon receiving the Bodhisattva precepts and shaving his head under Koen, at the age of thirteen. As continues to be common, the name given upon receiving precepts carries a special meaning and significance. Dōgen's name consists of two characters, *Dō* and *gen* (Jp.). *Dō* means "the Way," which is how the Chinese introduced Buddhism into their Taoist world, and therefore means the Buddha Way. *Gen* means source of all things, all life, all truth. Thus *Dōgen* means "the Buddha Way is the Source of Life, or of all things." Only much later, in 1248 C.E., after he made a trip to Kamakura, did he add the name *Kigen* to himself in *Eihei-ji koin seiki*. Thus, Hee Jin Kim's biography gives him the name *Dōgen Kigen*.
50. *DFYC*, 17. Kodera offers the most detailed examination of Dōgen's family background in English.
51. *DKMR*, ch. 2.
52. Discrepancies about Dōgen's age in accounts of his parents' deaths and other events in his life vary according to whether or not one uses the Chinese system, according to which one is one year old at birth. In this study, the Western mode will be used, in which one becomes one year old at the end of the first year.
53. *DKMR*, 17.
54. *RD*, 25.
55. Michichika was father of Michitomo by another woman, making Michitomo Dōgen's elder half-brother. Through other links, Moroie and Dōgen are also half-brothers, and Motofusa and Michichika are brothers-in-law. See *DFYC*, 23 and footnotes Nos. 15 and 46.
56. Exodus 1–3.
57. For Joan Stambaugh, "Impermanence" is the central category for understanding Dōgen's thought. See her *Impermanence is Buddha-nature* (Honolulu: University of Hawaii Press, 1990).
58. According to Robert Thurman (personal comment to this author), in the first appearance of śūnyatā in monastic Buddhism it was formulated as having four aspects: impermanence, suffering, emptiness and selflessness. With Mahāyāna developments, śūnyatā became equal to avērtnatā, meaning "self-

Journeys into Emptiness

lessness" in the personal sense. That meaning was continued, but also included "objective selflessness," or the "selflessness of things," in other words, no fixed identity, insubstantiality of all things, including persons. In overarching terms, one might say that this study moves from the subjective experience of emptiness as some form of suffering to an objective experience of the emptiness of all things.

59. *DKMR*, 17.

60. "The continual experience of impermanence (*mujo*/Jp.), which commenced at his mother's death and was intensified by the circumstances of his family, eventuated in his decision to renounce the world and to become a monk." *DFYC*, 23.

61. *Hōkyōki*, Annotated Translation, Kodera, 117.

62. Dōgen, *Eihei shosō gakudō yōjin shū*.

63. *RD*, 33.

64. Daniel Stern, *The Interpersonal World of the Infant* (New York: Basic Books, 1985), 10 –11. The "sense of self" Stern studies is not the same as the self that is refuted in Buddhism. This will be clarified in more detail in chapter 3, on depth psychology.

65. "Yahweh, the Lord...punishes sons and grandsons to the third and fourth generation for the iniquity of their fathers!" (Exodus 34: 7). Similarly, see Exodus 20:5, Numbers 14:18 and Deuteronomy 5:9.

Stern appears open to the possibility of the sense of self being affected by prenatal conditions. See his parenthetical remark, p. 6.

67. *DFYC*, 24.

68. *DFYC*, 25.

69. *DFYC*, 25.

70. Philip Kapleau summarizes the Zen requirements for enlightenment as consisting of Great Doubt, Great Faith and Great Determination. See *Three Pillars of Zen* (New York: Anchor Books, Doubleday, 1980).

71. See also ch. 1, "The Importance of Faith," by Francis Cook in his *How to Raise an Ox* (Los Angeles: Zen Center Publications, 1978). Cook argues that faith is an essential aspect of Buddhism at least until one reaches the point of direct experience and confirmation of Buddhist truth.

72. See note 69, above.

73. *DFYC*, 25.

74. Also known and spelled as *Eisai*.

75. *DFYC*, 26 –29.

76. The Buddha, Dharma and Sangha are the Three Treasures in Buddhism. The Buddha is both the historical Shakyamuni Buddha and all other Buddhas. The Dharma is both the teachings of the Buddha and the entire phenomenal universe. The Sangha is the community of practitioners, both in a given historical point in

time, and the community that extends throughout all space and time. There are interesting and fruitful comparisons to be made with the Trinity in Christianity.

77. *DFYC,* 117.

78. *DFYC,* 36.

79. *DFYC,* 36.

80. *DKMR,* 251.

81. *Shikantaza* may be understood as "single-minded intense sitting." It implies absolutely no movement of the body and complete concentration of the mind.

82. The *Shōbōgenzō* is, firstly and unless otherwise noted, the primary collection of Dōgen's writings, containing lectures given, primarily to monks, called fascicles. *Fascicles* refers to the way books were traditionally bound, in small pamphletlike sections that were stored in larger boxes or binders constituting volumes. Depending on the particular collection, it may have 75, 93 or 95 such fascicles. *Shōbōgenzō* means "Treasury of the true Dharma eye," which was part of Shakyamuni's announcement when he transmitted to Mahakasyapa, and was the title originally used by Ta-hui Tsung-kao (1089–1163) for his collection of koans. It is also the name Dōgen gave to his collection of 300 koans, written in Chinese, and the name give by Ejō to his collection of Dōgen's talks (*Shōbōgenzō zuimonki*).

83. In Buddhism, especially in the Hinyana tradition, an arhat is one who has attained the highest degree of enlightenment, and has thus been liberated from repeating the cycle of life and death. The arhat thus epitomizes the ideal of personal salvation, in contrast to the Mahayana ideal of deferring exemption from the cycle of life and death in order to save others.

84. *DFYC,* 51.

85. A document of succession lists all the traditional Buddhist patriarchs through one's lineage up to the point of one's own receipt of transmission, the official acknowledgment of one's teacher that one has attained enlightenment and is thus qualified to teach the true Dharma.

86. *Hōkyō-ki, DFYC,* 117.

87. *DFYC,* 55.

88. See Jung's essay, "Synchronicity: An Acausal Connecting Principal," in *CW,* 8.

89. Psalm 42:7.

90. *DFYC,* 56.

91. *Ango* (Jp.) is one of the two three-month periods of intensive training in Buddhism, originally set aside according to the rainy seasons in India, during which monks would retreat from their wandering mendicancy into a common living area. *Ango* means "peaceful dwelling."

Journeys into Emptiness

92. *DFYC*, 61.

93. For discussions about the relationship between the psychological ego and the spiritual ego, see Roger Walsh and Frances Vaughan, eds., *Paths Beyond Ego, The Transpersonal Vision* (Los Angeles: Tarcher/Perigee, 1993).

94. See, for example, Melanie Klein, *The Psychoanalysis of Children*, and Otto Kernberg, *Borderline Conditions and Pathological Narcissism*. The relationship between splitting and dualism will be elaborated in chapter 3.

95. Genesis 3. This is also the story adduced to account for the doctrine of original sin. What many people fail to realize, but people such as Matthew Fox have been recently underscoring, is that the opening chapters of Genesis are about the original goodness of creation. The divided self that is the condition from which sin springs is an event in human historical life. Depth psychology offers some tools for identifying this psychological event.

96. *DFYC*, 62–63 (italics for emphasis).

97. Philip Yampolsky, trans., *The Platform Sutra of the Sixth Patriarch* (New York: Columbia University Press, 1967), 132.

98. *DFYC*, 107.

99. Sitting erect with each foot resting on the opposite thigh. This posture is varied sometimes to accommodate people who have not grown up accustomed to extended cross-legged sitting, so that one may place only one foot up (half-lotus), sit in some form of kneeling (*seiza*, Jp.), lower legs parallel (Burmese) or sitting upright on a chair. The purpose is to achieve independence, stability and optimal comfort for ease of breathing. See Shunryu Suzuki, *Zen Mind, Beginner's Mind*. part 1, "Right Practice" (New York: Weatherhill, 1975).

100. See *Cultivating the Empty Field: The Silent Illumination of Zen Master Hongzhi* (San Francisco: North Point Press, 1991).

101. At the same time, it needs to be said that all forms of meditation require energy for sustained attention.

102. See the "Shinji Shōbōgenzō" in *Dōgen Zenji Shihōshū* (in Japanese), Nishijima Wafu, ed. (Tokyo: Kanazawa Bunko, 1990).

103. The Great Death is thus sometimes regarded as the Great Enlightenment. In practice, most people consider enlightenment a neverending process after an intial breakthrough, according to Abbot John Daido Loori of Zen Mountain Monastery, Mt. Tremper, N.Y.

104. *DKMR*, 35.

105. *DFYC*, 68. Note the continuing prejudice in spite of the obvious esteem and affection. Although the balance of status may have shifted in the last seven hundred years between China and Japan, their continuing competitiveness is striking for its longevity.

106. *DFYC, 77 –78.* The Four Mountains are birth, old age, sickness and death; that they are low means suffering is overcome. (Kodera notes, 162 –63).

107. Kannon Bodhisattva is said to have 10,000 eyes throughout every part of her/his body by which she sees and hears the cries of humankind and responds appropriately to the need. *Guan* means "seeing"; *Yin* means "sound".

108. *MD,* 21ff.

109. *MD,* 70.

110. *DS,* 135.

111. *DS,* 138 –41.

112. *MD, Sansui-kyō,* "Mountains and Waters Sutra," 106 –7.

113. *DS, Sansui-kyō,* quoted in Hee-Jin Kim's "The Reason of Words and Letters," 57.

114. *DS,* 58.

115. *DKMR, Gabyo,* "Painting of a Rice-Cake."

116. *MD,* from *Uji,* "Being-Time."

117. Luke 10:25–37.

118. Luke 3:11.

119. *MD,* from *Bendōwa,* "On the Endeavor of the Way."

2. EMPTINESS AS HOMELESSNESS AND THE SEARCH FOR THE TRUE SELF

1. In a conversation (10/4/96) with this author and Zen teacher Bonnie Myotai Treace, Kaz Tanahashi, gifted translator of Dōgen, suggested that the best word for understanding the meaning of emptiness (*Sunyatā* Sn./ *kū,* Jp./*kòng,* Ch.) in vivid, contemporary terms was "homelessness."

2. Boldface type in these quotes are this author's, used for emphasis.

3. *SSM,* 49.

4. *ETS,* 43, 48.

5. *AJ,* 235–36.

6. In Greek mythology, Ariadne was given a ball of thread by Daedalus to enable her to enter and leave the Labyrinth by tying one end to the entrance door, unrolling it as she descended, and retracing it to return. She actually gave the thread to Theseus for him to make the journey to kill the Minotaur. In this context, note that Merton himself wrote an unpublished novel called *The Labyrinth.* (The application of the "thread" metaphor to Merton is, however, this author's.) See David Adams Leeming, *Mythology: the Voyage of the Hero* (New York: Lippincott, 1973), 138–39. This parallel from Greek mythology is a reminder that to pursue the experience of emptiness entail's a classical hero's journey. See also,

Journeys into Emptiness

Joseph Campbell, *Hero with a Thousand Faces* (Cleveland: Meridian Books, 1956).

Kenosis is the Greek word used for God's act of emptying himself out into Jesus as the Christ, as described in Philippians 2:5ff. It is put forth as the model for how Christians should empty themselves of all concern for self in order to be like Christ in the world.

8. Merton's opening line in his autobiography, *Seven Storey Mountain*, declares he was born "under the sign of the Water Bearer," that is, Aquarius, which Carl Jung sees as representing the self. *SSM*, 3; *MDR*, 339.

9. Most information about Merton's life and background will be drawn, unless otherwise stated, from Michael Mott's authoritative biography, *SMTM*.

10. *SMTM*, 7.

11. It is commonly assumed that the name *Tom* was taken from a family friend in England, the physician, Dr. Thomas Bennett. Bennett was Tom Merton's godfather, into whose care Merton was left when his father died.

12. *NSC*: Merton wrote, "For me to be a saint means to be myself. Therefore the problem of sanctity and salvation is in fact the problem of finding out who I am and of discovering my true self" (p. 31).

13. *SMTM*, 7. See also Ed Rice, *The Good Times and Hard Life of Thomas Merton, The Man in the Sycamore Tree* (Garden City, N.Y.: Doubleday, 1970), and *A Catch of Anti-Letters*, by Merton with Robert Lax (Mission, Kans.: Sheed, Andrews and McMeel, 1978).

14. The front page reads, "TOM'S BOOK—TO GRANNY With Tom's best love, 1916" (*TB*). It was to have been sent to Owen's mother in New Zealand.

15. Mott translates this phrase as "What a wide-awake kid!" (*SMTM*, 7). Since *Buddha* means "the awakened one," the peasant might well have said, "What a Buddha!" The appellation would certainly fit, since Merton was obviously evincing an exceptional alertness from such an early age. His powers of attention and observation were an essential part of his writing talent.

16. *SMTM*, 17.

17. Kohut cites the difficulty going to sleep as evidence of the lack of psychic structures needed to neutralize "oral (and oral sadistic) narcissistic tensions." These structures are introjected by the mother's soothing and holding presence. The lack of them is therefore an indication of deficits in the mothering process. See *AS*, 233–35.

18. *SMTM*, 17.

19. Alice Miller, *Prisoners of Childhood: The Drama of the Gifted Child and the Search for the True Self* (New York: Basic Books. 1981), 34–35.

20. For anecdotal pictures of Merton, see *Thomas Merton, Monk: A Monastic Tribute*, ed. Patrick Hart (New York: Sheed & Ward, 1974).

21. Robert E. Daggy, "Thomas Merton and the Ground of Birth," a talk given at Southampton Conference, May 1996. Unpublished manuscript given to this author.

22. *SSM*, 5.

23. Monica Furlong, *Merton: a Biography*. (Liguori, Mo.: Liguori Publications, 1995), 7.

24. *SMTM*, 16.

25. Quoted in Daggy, 8.

26. Daggy, 9.

27. Mahler and Bowlby were among the first to study mother/infant interactions systematically and to correlate their observations with psychological developmental theory. See Margaret Mahler, *The Psychological Birth of the Human Infant* (New York: Basic Books, 1975); John Bowlby, *Attachment and Loss: Vol. 1, Attachment* (New York: Basic Books, 1969). Also see the work of Daniel Stern, cited above, p. 54, which follows their work with more precise research.

28. One of the reasons Merton gave himself for not going to Harlem to work and choosing Gethsemani instead was because "being with girls....is, to me personally, intolerable" (*RTM*, Nov. 29, 1941, 464–65). Twenty-four years later, in August of 1965, he wrote in his journal about "the refusal of woman which is a fault in my chastity" (*FTE*, 31).

29. Merton apparently had little sense of his own body in space: Early in Gethsemani, he lost control of a truck and never drove again. He also suffered greatly from numerous physical ailments, from early loss of teeth, chronic arthritis, dermatitis and finally a spinal problem that required surgery. What relation might these physical symptoms have had to emotional dynamics that never got articulated?

30. Merton entered Gethsemani wondering whether he should have gone somewhere else and spent the rest of his twenty-seven years constantly asking to be sent elsewhere or wondering whether he should be elsewhere. See below.

31. *AS*, 16.

32. *BCPN*, 213. See chapter 7, "The Subjective Experience of Emptiness."

33. *SMTM*, 17.

34. *SMTM*, 18.

35. *SSM*, 8.

36. John Paul came to the monastery to see his brother in July of 1942. John Paul was killed in April 1943, when Merton was twenty-eight. See *SMTM*, 221–22.

37. *SSM*, 10.

38. Emphasis added.

39. *SSM*, pp. 13–16.

40. See Ernest Becker, *The Denial of Death* (New York: Free Press, 1973); Elizabeth Kubler-Ross, *Death and Dying* (New York: Macmillan, 1969) and *Death: The Final Stage of Life* (Englewood Cliffs, N.J.: Prentice-Hall, 1975); and Ernest Grollman, *Explaining Death to Children* (Boston: Beacon Press, 1967).

41. This statement is based on Merton's own description of the event and constitutes the psychological, if not the literal, truth of what happened. In fact, it is possible that someone was trying to comfort him during this time, but the inner experience of emptiness, which is the primary focus of this study, was of utter abandonment and loss. In one's ongoing development, it is events as remembered that comprise the basis for self-understanding and motivation. When, for example, in analysis, new details emerge that provide contrary information to the memory, a fundamental shift in one's way of seeing self or others can happen.

42. See Murray Stein, *Jung's Treatment of Christianity: The Psychotherapy of a Religious Tradition* (Wilmette, Ill.: Chiron, 1985). Also see chapter 2, "The Personal and Mythic Father" in Robert C. Smith, *The Wounded Jung* (Evanston, Ill.: Northwestern University Press, 1996).

43. Reported by Timothy Kelley, O.C.S.O., in "Epilogue: A Memoir," *The Legacy of Thomas Merton*. ed. Br. Patrick Hart (Kalamazoo: Cistercian Publications, 1986), pp. 217–25.

44. Quoted from "Restricted Journals," 1966, in *SMTM*, 25. These journals were restricted in accordance with the terms of the Thomas Merton Trust and his will so that no publication or public access was possible for twenty-five years after his death. They are only recently being published, as noted in the bibliography.

45. *FTE*, 123.

46. *SMTM*, 26.

47. *SSM*, 69.

48. Ibid., 71–72.

49. Ibid., 83.

50. It is worth considering the impact of the proximity of his father's death to his own birthday. Such a proximity can cast a pall over the would-

be enjoyment and celebration of one's own entrance into the world for a long time.

51. *SSM*, 85.

52. *SL*, 9.

53. Ibid.

54. *HWSF*: The title is borrowed from T. S. Eliot, "East Coker," from the *Four Quartets*.

55. *TPP*, "Aggression in Relation to Emotional Development," 212.

56. *SSM*, 85.

57. *SMTM*, 83.

58. *SSM*, 126–27. (italics are this author's).

59. *RTM*, 34.

60. *SMTM*, 78 ff.

61. Typescript of *SSM* manuscript at Boston College, quoted in *SMTM*, 80.

62. *SSM*, 121.

63. Erik Erikson, *Identity and the Life Cycle* (New York: Norton, 1965).

64. The identity of the woman Merton impregnated has never been discovered. It was assumed that she was one of the maids in Merton's dormitory at Clare College, Cambridge. Merton's silence and flight from this situation must be seen as lurking, nonetheless, within him, exacerbating his adolescent tendencies toward self-destruction and inducing an unspoken guilt, which he compulsively revealed to the Franciscans when he applied to their order in 1940.

65. *The Collected Poems of W. B. Yeats* (New York: Macmillan, 1960), 184–85. This poem was Yeats's vision of the twentieth century. Merton saw himself as carrying within himself the issues at stake in the twentieth century, thus linking the personal and global issues in a way also consonant with Jung.

66. See *SMTM*, 90.

67. Ibid., 58.

68. His first trip had been taken with his father two years before.

69. *SMTM*, 67.

70. Mott summarizes Merton's reflections in the unpublished "Labyrinth." *SMTM*, 67.

71. *SMTM*, 68.

72. *SSM*, 111.

73. *SSM*, 114.

74. Quoted from *The Labyrinth*, in *SMTM*, 67–68. It may be obvious from these several quotes from *The Labyrinth* that this unpublished novel was a

fictionalized autobiography in which Merton expressed much of his life experience that never got into *Seven Storey Mountain*. It contains much material that reveals his personal feelings and attitudes, most instructive of all when he crossed out passages even in that manuscript.

75. *SSM*, 177.

76. Private conversation with this author, November 1996.

77. *SMTM*, 101.

78. *SSM*, 178.

79. *SMTM*, 115.

80. Mott considers the work "poor," and notes that Merton blithely skipped over the visual aspect of Blake's work to focus on the verbal and cognitive. See *SMTM*, 116.

81. Later he revised this position. See David Cooper, *Thomas Merton's Art of Denial: The Evolution of a Radical Humanist* (Athens, Ga.: University of Georgia Press, 1989), 120 ff.

82. *SMTM*, 117.

83. *WCT*.

84. *SSM*, 73.

85. *SSM*, 161.

86. Emphasis added.

87. *SSM*, 163–65.

88. Ibid., 204.

89. Ibid., 207.

90. It is very telling that Joyce's novel, which is primarily about his doubts and conflicts regarding Catholicism, was experienced by Merton, who had never experienced Catholicism as an active, assumed part of his life, as opening up an unforeseen possibility, a deeply felt connection to the Catholic Church!

91. Ibid., 215.

92. In interview with this author at the Abbey of Gethsemani, June 1996.

93. *SMTM*, 155.

94. *SSM*, 238.

95. Colossians 3:4.

96. Philippians 2:5–11.

97. The only reason Merton expressed for *not* joining the Carthusians was because, at that time (1941), none existed in the United States. While he considered those in Europe beyond his reach because of the war, his decision is nonetheless a very strong statement about the importance to

Merton of remaining here. He became a U.S. citizen in 1951, ten years after entering Gethsemani, and noted in his journal, "...the country is worth loving...and is full of very good people" (*ETS*, 2/28/51).

98. *Prima materia* is the undifferentiated material out of which elements emerge into their distinctive identity by alchemical transformation. Jung applied this concept to the individuation process in human development, as he experienced it in his own life (*MDR*, 199).

99. Dante, *Divine Comedy*.

100. In a letter to "Bill W.," the cofounder of Alcoholics Anonymous, Jung wrote about "Roland H.," an alcoholic who had gone to Jung for help: "His craving for alcohol was the equivalent, on a low level, of the spiritual thirst of our being for wholeness, expressed in medieval language: the union with God. [Jung quotes Psalm 42:1: "As the hart panteth after the water brooks, so panteth my soul after thee, O God."]...You see, *alcohol* in Latin is '*spiritus*' and you use the word for the highest religious experience as well as for the most depraving poison. The helpful formula therefore is: *spiritus contra spiritum*" (Letter quoted in full in *AA Grapevine*, New York, January 1963, 6–7).

101. In a disastrous and terribly unprofessional meeting arranged by the Abbot between Merton and Gregory Zilboorg, a prominent psychiatrist who had recently converted to Catholicism, Zilboorg analyzed Merton on the basis of reading some of Merton's writings, including an essay on psychology. This meeting was arranged to coincide with a conference on psychiatry and religion in Minnesota. Zilboorg's verbal delivery of his analysis, while largely valid, was made in a devastating, critical, belittling and manipulative way in obvious conspiracy with Abbot Dom James to dissuade Merton from his wish for a more hermitic life. In bombastic fashion, Zilboorg declared, "You want a hermitage in Times Square with a large sign over it, saying "HERMIT" (See *SMTM*, 290–98).

Narcissism in those days (1956), especially by non-analytically trained psychiatrists, was considered unanalyzable and requiring moral or social controls. This study assumes a very different position about the nature of narcissism and its productive possibilities, as the next chapter will make clear.

102. *SMTM*, 182.

103. Inspired by his actual experience in St. Anthony's Hospital in July 1960, Merton began ruminating about the figure of Sophia, the Wisdom of God, important in Russian mysticism. "Hagia Sophia" was published in a special edition by Victor Hammer, in 1962. In 1966, when he was in the

hospital again, Merton experienced an *embouleversement* when a living *Hagia Sophia* figure entered his life and he fell in love.

104. To what degree it is possible to work through specific complexes in meditation without dealing directly with specific personal history is a very important question, for which no definitive answer can be given at this point. For example, based on Merton's writings (mostly in the *Journals*), his image of his father as the very talented, creative and loving presence in his life never changed. But the image of his mother as the dominant anima figure underwent noticeable revisions, as will soon be spelled out.

105. *SSM*, 372.

106. For a brief account of Merton's method of contemplative prayer, see his letter to Abdul Aziz, 2/1/66, in *HGL*, 63–64. The fullest understanding of Merton's view is in the collection of discourses entitled "Inner Experience," officially unpublished by his own request, but available through Cistercian Publications. Also, of course, see *CP*.

107. *ETS*, 8/26/49, 362. Emphasis added.

108. *ETS*, 8/17/47, 99.

109. *ASFS*, October 18, 1958, 225.

110. *TS*, 214.

111. *SSM*, 97–99.

112. *ETS*, 436–39.

113. Late in his years at the monastery, Merton's dermatitis and eczema were diagnosed as stemming from allergies to milk products, such as cheese, which the monastery made and which constituted a large part of the monks' diet. The first milk, of course, is from one's mother's breast. See below, ch. 3, p. 197 for Jung's early childhood experience of eczema. Jung made direct connections between such physiological symptoms and their psychological origins.

114. *FTE*, 41.

115. *ETS*, March 25, 1950, 424.

116. See, for example, Kōshō Uchiyama's autobiographical story of his neglecting an infection in his toe (!) and the consequences, in *Refining Your Life: From the Zen Kitchen to Enlightenment* (New York: Weatherhill, 1990), 79–81. It is interesting that the lesson he drew from the experience was not about caring for his body, but his attitude toward the pain.

117. Ann Ulanov, *The Functioning Transcendent* (Wilmette, Ill.: Chiron Publications, 1996), 20.

118. *RJ*, 118.

119. Merton wrote a novel entitled *The Labyrinth* between graduation

from Columbia and teaching at St. Bonaventure's. It was never published, though he sent it to numerous publishers. Whatever its virtues, it represented Merton's earnest desire for acceptance as a writer in the secular world, and the repeated rejections he received had to have played a role in his developing identity, representing, in retrospect perhaps, his false self in contrast to his true self. This is one of those points where it is interesting to speculate how a life might have been different with a different outcome. What, for example, if his novel had been published and had succeeded?

120. *SSM*, 49.

121. *RTM*, 34.

122. *SSM*, 126–27.

123. Ibid., 163–65.

124. Merton seriously considered working directly with people in Harlem with the Baroness rather than staying at St. Bonaventure's. With benefit of hindsight, of course, it is easy for us to see how inappropriate it would have been for him to have worked there: he was too much of an introvert and intellectual, not a direct, person-to-person individual. On the other hand, given Merton's difficulties with women, it certainly would have been interesting. He decided against going there, largely because he could not tolerate the feelings aroused in him in the presence of young women. He felt both very excited by them and puzzled as to how to relate to them.

125. *SSM*, 352.

126. See the section on Dōgen, chapter 1.

127. *RTM*, 232.

128. Ann Ulanov, personal comment to this author.

129. From tapes in the library of the Thomas Merton Studies Center, Louisville, Kentucky.

130. *ETS*, 11.

131. *VC*, 143.

132. *ETS*, 49.

133. Now available through Cistercian Publications.

134. *RTM*, 470.

135. *CP*, 22.

136. Ibid., 24–25.

137. See David Cooper's Prologue, *Thomas Merton's Art of Denial* (Athens, Ga.: University of Georgia Press, 1989).

138. It should be remembered, however, that Merton was appointed master of scholastics in June 1951, and was therefore occupied with preparing conferences on scripture, the Rule, monasticism and liturgy. Over

time, the notes for teaching the scholastics comprised twelve volumes (noted to this author by Jonathan Montaldo).

139. *ETS*.

140. *ASFS*.

141. New York: New Directions, 1953.

142. *The Last of the Fathers: Saint Bernard of Clairvaux and the Encyclical Letter, "Doctor Mellifluus"* (New York: Harcourt, Brace. 1954).

143. *Exile Ends in Glory* (Milwaukee: Bruce, 1948).

144. *CP*, 70. Emphasis added.

145. "...you died; and now your life lies hidden with Christ in God" (Colossians 3:3) New English Bible (New York: Oxford University Press, 1970).

146. *CP*, 88.

147. *CP*, 98. Emphasis added. Compare also, in "Hagia Sophia," 4, "A homeless God, lost in the night, without papers, without identification, without even a number, a frail expendable exile lies down in desolation under the sweet stars of the world and entrusts Himself to sleep." *A Thomas Merton Reader*, ed. T. P. McDonnell (New York: Doubleday Image, 1989), 511.

148. *CP*, 101.

149. Ibid., 110.

150. *IE*, 40–41.

151. In this author's view, it was never entirely resolved: witness the multiple possibilities Merton continued to mention in the *Asian Journal* about where to live as he traveled in California, Alaska and Asia.

152. "It seems to me that what I am made for is not speculation but silence and emptiness, to wait in darkness and receive the Word of God entirely in His Oneness and not broken up into all His shadows" (*SJ*, 160–61; quoted in *SL*, 139).

153. *IE*, 54–55.

154. *SFS*, 181–82.

155. *FTE*, 40.

156. *AJ*, 143.

157. See above, p. 89.

158. *SSM*, 88 ff.

159. Recall his impregnating the young woman in England and leaving both her and the baby.

160. *TS*, 4.

161. *SMTM*, 295.

162. Ibid., 307.

163. *ASFS*, 101–2.

164. For the role of *Sophia* as an anima figure of divine wisdom, see Ann Belford Ulanov, *The Feminine in Jungian Psychology and in Christian Tradition* (Evanston, Ill.: Northwestern University Press, 1971), 189–92.

165. Jung, *CW* 11, 458 ff.

166. Above, p. 156.

167. *ASFS*, 176.

168. Jung would call this letter a work of active imagination.

169. *SMTM*, 322–25.

170. See Mott's recounting of this period, *SMTM*, 361–71.

171. *TMR*, 506 ff.

172. See Jung, *CW* 11, 438 ff., regarding the role of the "sun-woman" in the birth of the son who unites in himself the *collectio oppositorum*.

173. *NSC*, ch. 23.

174. Ibid., 29–47.

175. One may recall the importance of Merton's mother's soothing voice, reported in "Tom's Book," above, p. 89.

176. An assumed name. Merton usually refers to her in his journals as "S."

177. A small "cabin" built of cinder blocks less than a mile from the main monastery halls. Merton continued to keep the monastic schedule of liturgy, including going to bed between 7 and 8 P.M. and rising by 2:30 A.M. Supposedly designed to meet Merton's demand for greater solitude, the hermitage was quickly beset by numerous visitors from around the world, often at his own invitation, thus proving the point above that the issue was more the quality of presence enabling his true self to flourish, than solitude per se. Sometimes Merton was given permission to have visitors; sometimes he invited people without permission. Merton's increased freedom to be with people, including his propensity to include alcohol, was problematic for his spirituality. For twenty-four years his boundaries had been set by his superiors. Now he had to devise them on his own.

178. *FTE*, 31.

179. Ibid., 40.

180. Ibid., 41.

181. Ibid., 50.

182. Ibid., 51.

183. Ibid., 58.

184. Ibid., 59.

185. Ibid., 59.

186. All the evidence points to the relationship as one in which both felt strongly in love with each other. Her story, however, has never really been told. Out of deference to her own privacy, this author supposes, she has not been asked to tell it. That it may have greatly complicated her life seems not only likely, but is consonant with hearsay.

187. *FTE, 67.*

188. *SMTM, 436.*

189. *FTE, 74.*

190. Ibid., 78.

191. Ibid.

192. Reported to this author by Jonathan Montaldo, (editor of volume 2 of the *Journals, ETS*), in a private note, 1/97.

193. *FTE, 87.* Note that this is Griffin's interpretation.

194. *LAL, 25–38.*

195. Merton had a lifelong preoccupation with "wires" and "cables," as well as images of burning. See "Cables to the Ace," in *The Collected Poems of Thomas Merton* (New York: New Directions, 1977). Kohut relates the theme of electrical wires with vicissitudes of narcissistic development (Kohut, 1974, 245 ff.). Merton also was preoccupied with images of burning as a consequence of proximity to God. Recall the last line in *SSM*, "That you may become the brother of God and learn to know the Christ of the burnt men" (423). Also, "I know well the burnt faces of the Prophets and Evangelists...for they looked at God as into a furnace..." (*ETS*, 362). Merton apparently believed that love, whether divine or human, was a "hot wire"! This must be seen as another view of the experience of emptiness.

196. *AJ, 235–36.*

197. *MD*, "Mountains and Waters Sutra," 97.

198. See C. W. Huntington, *The Emptiness of Emptiness* (Honolulu: University of Hawaii Press, 1989).

199. *SMTM, 93.*

200. David D. Cooper, *Thomas Merton's Art of Denial: the Evolution of a Radical Humanist* (Athens, Georgia: University of Georgia Press, 1989).

201. Part of his problem was one which is shared by all people who are bright, talented and famous: It takes a person of not only similar intelligence, but one who has no narcissistic need of their own to be entertained by one's performance, to see through one's evasive maneuvers. One suspects this may have happened with Dr. Wygal.

202. John Wu, *The Golden Age of Zen* (New York: Doubleday, 1996). See Merton's "Introduction."

203. *HGL*, 170–74.

204. *FTE*, 123.

205. *WCT*, 24.

206. Proprioceptive writing workshops are given by Toby Simon, Ph.D., and Linda Metcalfe, Ph.D. (New York, N.Y.). Emphasis is placed on the "proprioceptive sense" in using writing to access deep levels of knowing that are in the body.

207. Merton was granted permission to receive psychiatric help from James Wygal, M.D., of Louisville on December 31, 1959, alluding to the "neurosis" he had been charged with. He and Wygal became good friends, and by July, Merton was going there to listen to jazz records! See *SMTM*, 345. Tellingly, both the doctor and the psychiatrist at Gethsemani considered Merton well able to "analyze" and "correct" himself: The first is impossible and the second is not the point. Wygal continued to give Merton advice during the episode with the nurse.

208. *FTE*, 63 and throughout.

209. Heinz Kohut's *Analysis of the Self* was published in 1971.

210. *SL*, 2.

211. *SMTM*, 345.

212. *MDR*, 297.

213. Anthony Padovano, *The Human Journey—Thomas Merton: Symbol of a Century* (Garden City, N.Y.: Doubleday, 1982).

3. THE EXPERIENCE OF EMPTINESS IN DEPTH PSYCHOLOGY

1. "The psyche consists of energy, consciousness, the personal, unconscious, and the collective unconscious or the objective psyche" (*CW* 7, 151).

2. Jung sent Freud a copy of his *Diagnostic Association Studies* in 1906, which Freud acknowledged in a letter of April 11 and to which Jung replied in October of the same year. From the time of their actual meeting in 1907, they worked together intensely until riven by conflict on several levels (see below, E2) until their final break in 1914. See *FJL*, 552.

3. "I use the term 'individuation' to denote the process by which a person becomes a psychological 'in-dividual,' that is, a separate, indivisible unity or 'whole.'" *CW* 9, i, 275. "…it also implies becoming one's own self. We could therefore translate individuation as 'coming to selfhood' or 'self-realization.'" *CW* 7, 171.

4. Jung's use of the word *collective* refers to the ways in which humans

form groups that behave as a whole, in the same way an individual constitutes a whole. The collective is usually some identifiable group of society, nation, race or culture. For Jung, all individuals and groups are psychologically interconnected in time as well as space. The largest collective "whole," therefore, would be humankind all over the world throughout history. Compare this understanding with the Christian "communion of saints," and the Zen Buddhist idea of "all Buddhas and Boddhisatvas throughout space and time." Jung's theories preceded the articulation of general systems theory (see G. Bateson, *Steps to an Ecology of Mind*, 1972), but when he defines the individual and a given collective in terms of their functioning as "wholes," he is referring to the same dynamics later called systems. There are systems within systems, and they interact and affect each other, without end.

5. "...the human psyche is not a self-contained and wholly individual phenomenon, but also a collective one....insofar as differentiations exist that correspond to race, tribe, or even family, there exists also a collective psyche limited to race, tribe, or family over and above the 'universal' collective psyche." *CW 7*, "The Relation between Ego and the Unconscious."

"...the objective psyche...functions according to its own laws of contiguity, similarity, association, and simultaneity, and expresses the great range of archetypes from the physical to the spiritual." (Ann and Barry Ulanov, *Transforming Sexuality: The Archetypal World of Anima and Animus* (Boston: Shambhala, 1996), 34. The word *objective* is used to denote the fact that the contents are not subjective, but "other," deriving from one of the collective groups of which one is a part. Racial prejudice and gender stereotypes, as well as what is understood by "courtesy" or "manners," for example, are thus parts of the objective psyche.

6. The realm of the spirit is larger than that of the psyche and transcends it. "Jung...sees spirit as a reality that transcends the whole psyche as well as the ego, as energy that can attach itself to any complex (so that we can speak, for example, of the spiritual aspect of the anima); he sees it as directly related to religion but not necessarily to be named in clinical work as belonging to a specific religious tradition." *FT*, 4.

7. The converse, a person's failure to take responsibility for her own psyche and the consequences of that refusal, is more obvious. Thus, for example, the failure of a parent to learn to control frustration or impulses may result in violence or incest, with damaging consequences that extend for generations.

8. "...an intermediate area of *experiencing*, to which inner reality and

external life both contribute….a resting-place for the individual engaged in the perpetual human task of keeping inner and outer reality separate yet interrelated" (*PR*, 3).

9. "[Donald W. Winnicott] introduced the terms 'transitional objects' and 'transitional phenomena' for designation of the intermediate area of experience, between the thumb and the teddy bear, between the oral erotism and the true object-relationship, between primary creative activity and projection of what has already been introjected, between primary unawareness of indebtedness and the acknowledgement of indebtedness ('Say: *"ta"*')" (*PR*, 2).

10. For example, music and alcohol (or a particular drug) may both be used for their soothing and inspirational powers, but when used to the point of addiction, psychological growth is arrested.

11. There was one earlier Carl Jung, the grandfather to this one, a "Dr. med. et. jur. Carl Jung" from Mainz, Germany, who died in 1654. The ability to trace one's lineage back over centuries, whether it serves as a source of pride or a burden, gives one at least a strong sense of continuity of self and a connection to others that goes beyond one's immediate circumstances. See *MDR*, 233.

12. *WI*, 10.

13. Wehr, 15.

14. *WI*, 12.

15. Ibid.

16. Though it is a topic worth considerable discussion, it would not be amiss to say that what depth psychology offers, especially in the analytical psychology of Jung, is a restoration of what Protestantism lost: a restoration of the felt connection to the supra-rational aspects of religious and human experience, most frequently conveyed in images and symbols, rather than logic and thought.

17. Brom, quoting from Jung, *Letters*, vol. 2, Dec. 30, 1960, to Ewald Jung, 23.

18. *WI*, 12.

19. *TWJ*, 14.

20. See below, p. 250ff.

21. "It is a curious fact about this century that so many of its seminal thinkers in depth psychology and theology lived in a split-anima situation….In cases of this kind, a split invariably exists between the feelings, attitudes, dreams and fantasies engendered or not engendered by the 'regular' partner—usually, as in these cases, a wife—and the outsider, the

'irregular.'...The split-anima condition reflects in its sexual triangles a man's effort to unite in himself what has been split apart, the tending, holding maternal and the exciting, transforming feminine." *TS*, "Barth, Freud, Jung, Tillich and the Split Anima," 159–67.

22. Brome, 28; Wehr, 9; Jung's brother's birth and death are not even mentioned in *TWJ*.

23. What associations might this name have had for Carl's father: that of the conquering warrior or that of the vulnerable soldier who barely survived his lover's death?

24. See below, p. 208ff.

25. *MDR*, 7.

26. *MDR*, 6–7.

27. Recall Erik Erikson's first stage of life, Trust vs. Mistrust, in *Childhood and Society* (New York: Norton, 1963). The view expressed in this study derives more from Object Relations and Self Psychology theory, which places the dynamics of trust in the earliest weeks of life, and offers a finer microscopic view of early infancy than Erikson's developmental ego psychology.

28. This author's translation, "All is quiet, everyone is turning in."

29. Recall, above, Merton's experience of his mother's voice soothing him, chapter 2, p. 89.

30. Also recall Merton's chronic skin ailments, including eczema. Winnicott notes the importance of the skin as a container of the developing self, the barrier that first enables distinctions between inner and outer, self and other, introjected from the mother as holder. Diseases of the skin may thus be seen as reflective of environmental failure, as well as the eruption into the skin of unconscious rage. See *HWSF*, 45. See also Anne Clancier and Jeannine Kalmanovitch, *Winnicott and Paradox from Birth to Creation* (London: Tavistock, 1987), 11–13, 27–29.

31. Vincent Bronte reports that it has been impossible to confirm the exact hospital and dates of Emilie Jung's hospitalization because records were destroyed. He further speculates that the hospitalization was prompted by the family's move to Klein-Hüningen, but that would have happened a year later than Jung's report. See Vincent Bronte, *Jung* (New York: Atheneum, 1978), 30.

32. *MDR*, 8.

33. Ibid.

34. *TWJ*, 18, 179, regarding deletions made from the original manuscript of *MDR*.

35. See above, chapter 2, p. 95.

36. Smith specifically mentions the deletion of many details about his mother's "mental aberrations" from the original manuscript before publication. *TWJ*, 17.

37. *MDR*, 48–49.

38. See above, chapter 1, p. 57ff.

39. *MDR*, 49.

40. *TWJ*, ch. 1, "Mother No. 1 and Mother No. 2."

41. *MDR*, 52.

42. *TWJ*, 28. This description, without previous history, might be seen as an organic problem related to aging. The earlier episodes of dissociation, however, make this report simply one more in a long history of Emilie's mental peculiarities.

43. Self psychology and object relations theories, because they focus on the earliest months of an infant's life, see all infant's psyche as being not only impacted, but formed by the mothering figure/infant unit. See D. W. Winnicott, "There's no such thing as a baby"—in other words, in the beginning, the two are really one. It is an important new stage in psychological development when a baby acquires "unit" status, according to Winnicott.

44. "As in religion, so in depth psychology, the past lives in the present. It has given identifying shape to the present and continues to do so through the influence of superego models long ago introjected from outside object into inside image, and through identification with archetypal objects and images long ago concretized in living encounters with parents and siblings." *RU*, 16–17.

45. Self-objects are "objects which are not experienced as separate and independent from the self" (*AS*, 3). This does not preclude Jung's experience of her as having "hearty animal warmth, humor, etc. (*MDR*, 48).

46. *MDR*, 48, 52.

47. Ibid., 8–9.

48. *TWJ*, 27.

49. Quoted above, *MDR*, 48–49.

50. Underlining for emphasis.

51. *MDR*, 96.

52. *MPFE*, 142–43.

53. See below, section 5, p. 225ff.

54. See below, C 2, p. 228.

55. Paralleling her father's unresolved grief over his first wife's death,

which resulted in regular dissociative states acted out in his conversations with her in the reserved chair.

56. As recently as 1972, Ivan McLaughlin, M.D., consultant at Augusta State Hospital in Augusta, Maine, reported to this author his belief that a large percentage of women admitted for "hysteria" were driven to such extreme emotions by the lack of attentive husbands and sexual engagement in the marriage. Such husbands would exacerbate the problem by viewing their wives' emotionality as "irrational" and "crazy," thus justifying the husbands' further distancing from their wives and institutionalizing them.

57. *CW* 6.

58. Above, p. 95.

59. *MDR*, 8.

60. Brome shares this author's puzzlement about Jung's meaning of "powerless": "Powerless to replace the missing mother, powerless to control the events which had removed the mother, or powerless to control the boy's distress and illness?" Brom, 30.

61. Wehr, 20.

62. From a depth psychological perspective, every decision has an inner dynamic, as well as an outer one. Just because someone opens a door doesn't mean you have to walk through. Was there something he saw in his pastor-father-in-law that he thought worth emulating? What it meant to Johann Paul to choose to be a pastor remains unclear. How *he* understood the issues that life was presenting him in his parish and at home, from the standpoint of his calling, we have no real clue. To what extent his decision was practical and realistic, rather than a failure to go after what he most wanted, cannot be determined either. In either case, he suffered a crisis of faith in his vocation, according to his son.

63. *MDR*, 91–92.

64. *MPFE*, "On Communication,"181ff.

65. Animosity comes from the root word for animus and anima, and tellingly manifests the outbreak of emotion under the influence of a negative animus. See *FEM*.

66. The issues of the meaning of mental illness and theodicy (Why is there suffering if God is good?) remain difficult even today, after fifty years of sophisticated psychological training and theological reflection.

67. See Anton Boisen, *Out of the Depths*, for his description of his experience of psychotic illness and its implications for his Christian faith.

68. Given Johann Paul's father's conversion to Protestantism under

Schleiermacher, who so emphasized the importance of *experience* in religious faith, it is all the more ironic that the later Carl experienced his own father's religious faith as arid and lifeless.

69. *MDR*, 93.
70. *TWJ*, 13, 32.
71. *MDR*, 18.
72. Ibid., 75.
73. Ibid., 56.
74. Ibid., 31.
75. Ibid., 77–78.
76. Ibid., 11–12.
77. *MDR*, 9.
78. Ibid.
79. Jung's age at this observation is unclear, but is in a context of very early childhood events, from three until seven. *MDR*, 9.
80. A screen memory is a memory associated to some aspect of a dream that actually covers over a deeper, even more frightening, memory of the original trauma, which the dream is reflecting in code or symbolic form.
81. *CW* 11, ch. 6.
82. Compare this tendency in Jung to Merton above, p. 134.
83. *MDR*, 36.
84. *MDR*, 38.
85. Ibid., 39–40.
86. Job 13:13–15.
87. *MDR*, 8.
88. Interestingly, Carl I married a woman (his third marriage) with his mother's name. The later Carl married a woman named Emma, which is quite close to Emilie, his mother's name.
89. *MDR*, 91.
90. Depression is often seen as rage turned against the self. "…conflict in depression roughly speaking has to do with the individual's personal task of accommodating his or her own aggression and destructive impulses. When someone who is loved dies, the mourning process belongs to the working-through within the individual of the feeling of personal responsibility for the death because of the destructive ideas and impulses that accompany loving." *MPFE*, 221. One wonders to what degree Emilie experienced Carl's birth as another loss.
91. *MDR*, 48.

92. *CW* 17, *The Development of Personality.*

93. "Satisfactory parental care can be classified roughly into three overlapping stages: (a) Holding. (b) Mother and infant living together. Here the father's function (of dealing with the environment for the mother) is not known to the infant. (c) Father, mother and infant, all three living together. The term 'holding' is used here to denote not only the actual physical holding of the infant, but also the total environmental provision prior to the concept of *living with.*" "Parent-Infant Relationship" (*MPFE*, 43).

94. It should be noted that the observations made in these opening sections about Jung's history and development are based primarily on the years preceding his sister's birth when he was nine years old. By then, the foundations of his own personality were already in place. The good relationship he had with her took several years of her own growth and development before it could happen.

95. *MDR*, 33–34.

96. Ibid., 45.

97. Compare Jung's personality no. 2 with the Zen notion of *daishin*, "big mind." See Dōgen and Uchiyama, *Refining Your Life*, ch. 11, "Living Through the Life of the Self" (New York: Weatherhill, 1990). What Jung called his "natural mind," "archaic and ruthless, ruthless as truth and nature" (*MDR*, 50), which he identified with his no. 2 personality, has important affinities with the Zen mind.

98. *MDR*, 50.

99. Ibid., 42.

100. For Jung, his falling suggested "an unconscious suicidal urge or, it may be, [due] to a fatal resistance to life in this world" (*MDR*, 9).

101. Ibid., 30.

102. The general index of *CW* 20 lists 120 pairs of opposites used throughout Jung's corpus, 496–98.

103. *CW* 6, 708–9.

104. See especially "Answer to Job," *CW* 11, 358ff.

105. In the process of individuation, conflict inevitably arises between the individual and collective standards. The transcendent function mediates the conflict by a process of symbolization, aided by dreams and images. See *CW* 6, 51, "Symbol." See *FT*, 55, ix–x.

106. Henri Ellenberger, *The Discovery of the Unconscious* (New York: Basic Books, 1970), 672ff. Ellenberger's idea of the creative illness follows

much the same patterns as those of Dōgen, Merton and Jung in their experiences of emptiness.

107. *RMDR.*

108. *TWJ*, 22.

109. *RMDR*: "What we cannot find in the material Jung provides is imaginative destruction followed by a sense of guilt and then by constructions....the thing that was repressed in Jung's early infancy, that is, before the infantile breakdown, was primitive aggression—precisely this primitive destructiveness that is difficult to get at when an infant is cared for by a mother who is clinically depressed....Jung himself spent his life looking for his own self, which he never really found since he remained to some extent split..." (454).

110. *MDR*, 50.

111. *MDR*, 22. In addition, for an important study of the importance of "secrets" in the development of a sense of self, see M. Masud Khan, *Hidden Selves: Between Theory and Practice in Psychotherapy* (New York: International Universities Press, 1983), especially chapter 6, "Secret as Potential Space." Comparing space based on "secret" to the transitional space of Winnicott would be fruitful. Jung seemed to lack enough coming toward him from his mother to have this experience. See also Ann Ulanov, "A Shared Space," *Quadrant* (Spring, 1985).

112. *MDR*, 52.

113. Ibid., 48.

114. *MDR*, 20.

115. Ibid., 21.

116. *PR*, chapter 1, "Transitional Objects and Transitional Phenomena."

117. This is the import, psychologically, of Colossians 3:4: "...now your life lies hidden with Christ in God." The true self survives in a space protected by divine power and divine sanction. This also underscores the importance of the doctrine of God's omniscience: God knows about the true self that other people do not see or know. (Compare with Merton, chapter 2, p. 163.)

118. Winnicott quoted in Harry Guntrip, *Psychoanalytic Theory, Therapy, and the Self* (New York: Harper Torchbooks, 1973), 152.

119. Insofar as the experience of ghosts represents split-off aspects of the psyche, Carl Jung's own dissociative personalities as exemplified by Nos. 1 and 2 would seem to be a clear line from his mother's father to his mother to himself, at least a three-generational phenomenon. It might

also suggest that the difference between 1 and 2 for Jung was not only a reflection of Emilie's personality, but a reflection of the Jung vs. Preiswerk sides of Carl's grandfathers.

120. *MDR*, 41–42. Jung elaborates more fully on the role of secrets in individuation, the experience of loneliness and the importance of following one's *daimon* toward the end of the memoirs (342–44, 356).

121. This is so because issues of narcissism antedate the oedipal complex on which psychoanalysis was based, for Freud.

122. Peter Homans, *Jung in Context* (Chicago: University of Chicago Press, 1995), 84.

123. *CW* 9, 1, para. 159.

124. *TWJ*, 94.

125. *MDR*, 19.

126. Ibid.

127. *MDR*, 20. David Rosen has noted the parallel between Jung's experience with the stone, and Chuang Tzu's reflection on dreaming of a butterfly: "Did Chuang Tzu dream he was a butterfly, or did the butterfly dream he was Chuang Tzu?" See Rosen, *The Tao of Jung* (New York: Viking Arkana, 1996), 19. Jung acknowledged the connection. See *CW* 8, para. 923.

128. *TS*, 275.

129. *MDR*, 54–55.

130. MDR, 63–67.

131. Ibid., 71.

132. Ibid., 72.

133. "The persona is...the individual's system of adaptation to, or the manner he assumes in dealing with, the world. Every calling or profession, for example, has its own characteristic persona....One could say, with a little exaggeration, that the persona is that which in reality one is not, but which oneself as well as others think one is." *CW* 9, i, 122 f.

134. *MDR*, 86.

135. MDR, 93.

136. Ibid., 96.

137. *Lehrbuch der Psychiatrie*, 4th ed. (1890), noted in *MDR*, 108.

138. *MDR*,108–9.

139. Ibid., 112.

140. *TWJ*, 82.

141. Wehr, ch. 8.

142. Jung used the word *wholeness* to describe the psyche's direction

and intention. It must be understood, however, that it is the search—the reach and extension of ego toward Self—as a process that is unending that is important. The self for Jung is, like the mind in Zen Buddhism, boundless, with no edge, no end or stopping point. It parallels, in its endless extension, the notions in two daily Zen vows: "Vast is the robe of liberation, a formless field of benefaction," and "The Dharmas are boundless, I vow to master them."

143. The inclusion of the dates of his first two children's births is prompted by a consideration not noted elsewhere: there is a particular psychological reaction common to newly married men upon the birth of the first and—perhaps even stronger—their second child. The man is forced to surrender his need for the maternal dimension from his wife to the needs of the child (even while in the womb, with an often accompanying attenuated sexual activity). To have an affair during such a time is not unrelated to the pregnancies and births.

144. "...by the year 1904 Sabina had entered the Burghölzli and was being treated by Jung. Indeed, the present director of the Burghölzli has confirmed that Sabina Spielrein was a patient there from 17 August 1904, to 1 June 1905. Probably the treatment was still going on in 1906" (*SSSS*, 140). Author's note: This book is excellent not only for the well-researched details relating to these three people, but for Carotenuto's sensitive and careful exploration of the many dimensions of erotic transference and countertransference. Every analyst should read it.

145. *FJL*, letter 4J. The fact that this letter is referring to Sabina Spielrein is supported by hospital records, Spielrein's letters to both Jung and Freud, and Jung's letter to Sabina's mother regarding his treatment of her daughter.

146. It is not assumed, here, however, that Jung's Nos. 1 and 2 personalities exactly paralleled his mother's dual personality. See *TWJ*, ch. 1, for an elaboration of the interconnection between Jung's divided psyche and his mother's.

147. *MDR*, 8.

148. Ibid., 8–9.

149. One is reminded also that Merton's beginning transformation of his anima was with his dream of Proverb, a young Jewish girl, "mysterious and strange." There is something important here (a) about the origins of Jung's notion of the shadow and its connection with racial

difference; and (b) about the meaning of an anima that begins as "alter," as other than the one that was supposed to be there.

150. *MDR*, 294.

151. So designated in Jung's report to the First International Congress of Psychiatry and Neurology, according to Carotenuto (1982), 159.

152. *SSSS*, 167.

153. Ibid., 168.

154. Ibid., 92–93.

155. Ibid., 6.

156. Bruno Bettelheim, "Scandal in the Family," *New York Review of Books*, June 30, 1983.

157. *TWJ*, 83–84.

158. Bettelheim, as above.

159. *SSSS*, 48.

160. Aedo Carotenuto, "Jung's Shadow Problem with Sabina Spielrein," in *Proceedings of IAAP Conference of Analytical Psychology*, 1986, 241ff.

161. *RMDR*, 450ff.

162. *FJL*, 133J, 7March, 1909, 207.

163. Bettleheim, 44.

164. *SSSS*, 196.

165. John Kerr, *A Most Dangerous Method* (New York: Alfred Knopf, 1993), 478.

166. *TWJ*, 84.

167. Wehr, 94.

168. *FJL*, insert.

169. It should be kept in mind, when considering the significance of Jung's relations with Spielrein and Wolff, that the time we are talking about is in the earliest days of psychoanalysis, and Jung's experience was used by Freud, in addition to his own, as the basis for the first grapplings with issues of transference and countertransference. They were both pioneers in uncharted territory, at least in terms of psychotherapy. Their medical code would not have been adequate to discuss the psychodynamics.

170. *TWJ*, 86.

171. See below (G: Search for Wholeness, part 2). Jung's "creative illness" as it was called by Ellenberger, covered the period from approximately 1913 to 1919.

172. See, for example, Irene Champernowne, *A Memoir of Toni Wolff* (San Francisco: C. G. Jung Institute, 1980).

173. *FJL*, 1F.

174. Ibid., 2J.

175. Ibid., 3F.

176. See Homans, 50–51.

177. Robert Smith's interpretation that "Jung voluntarily took a vow of submission and subservience to Freud" (*TWJ*, 47) seems to this author a failure to distinguish between the feelings of adoration that Jung experienced as part of his own healing and the consistent stand that his view of psychology was never entirely the same as Freud's.

178. *FJL*, 49J, Jung's italics.

179. Ibid., 72J.

180. Ibid., 125F.

181. *MDR*,156–57.

182. Ibid., 158.

183. *FJL*, ad hoc.

184. Written in 1914, exact date unclear. Quoted in *SSSS*, 112.

185. "…if I am Moses, then you are Joshua and will take possession of the promised land of psychiatry, which I shall only be able to glimpse from afar" (letter from Freud to Jung, Jan. 17, 1909; FJL, 125, F). See also Hans Loewald, M.D., "Transference and Countertransference: the Roots of Psychoanalysis: book review essay on *The Freud/Jung Letters*," *Psychoanalytic Quarterly* (46): 514–27, 1977.

186. *MDR*, 163.

187. *RMDR*, 450–55.

188. *CW* 5, originally published as *Wandlungen und Symbole der Libido* in 1912. The German title underscores the crucial issue between Freud and Jung more precisely than the English title, indicating the symbolic basis of the libido.

189. *MDR*, 167–68.

190. Ibid.

191. *FJL*: In letter 335J, Jung wrote, "Even Adler's cronies do not regard me as one of theirs." Freud replied (337F) that Jung should consider that he made a slip in writing "Even Adler's cronies do not regard me as one of yours." The difference in German is the difference between *Ihrigen* and *ihrigen*. Jung must have experienced Freud's noting of Jung's verbal slip as similar to his mother's "nitpicking" every

time he would go out of the door as a child (*MDR*, 26), thus further indicating the "mother" aspect of Jung's transference to Freud.

192. *MDR*, ch. 6.

193. Recall the loose associations Jung's mother demonstrated, which he, as a child, learned to follow.

194. *MDR*, 173.

195. James Heisig, *Imago Dei: A Study of C. G. Jung's Psychology of Religion* (Lewisberg, Pa.: Bucknell University Press. 1979), 29. For an excellent study of this principle, see François Cheng, *Empty and Full: The Language of Chinese Painting*, Ch. 2, "Emptiness in Chinese Painting" (Boston: Shambhala, 1994).

196. *MDR*, 178. One must imagine the terror of a psychiatrist trained in disorders contemplating the possibility of his own psychological disintegration. He knew what he was up against!

197. Advent is the time in the Christian calendar of darkness, preparatory to the coming of the "light," i.e., Jesus as divine logos which "shines in the darkness and the darkness cannot put it out" (John 1:5). December 12 is also just a week before winter solstice, the longest, darkest day of the year.

198. Emphasis added.

199. *MDR*, 179.

200. Emphasis added.

201. *MDR*, 186. Compare this to the Zen story quoted above about the empty tea cup.

202. Recall that Dōgen's experience of emptiness led to the ten thousand things, and Merton's emptiness was met by the presence of God as nothingness. Thus, the testimony of all three writers is that the experience of emptiness leads to a certain kind of fullness.

203. Quoted in appendix 5, *MDR*, 379.

204. *MDR*, 182.

205. Emphases added.

206. *MDR*, 194.

207. *MDR*, 199.

208. Recall Jung's statement, *MDR*, 8.

209. Ibid., ch. 6.

210. Ibid., 176.

211. Brom, letter from Storr to Brome, 301.

212. *RMDR*.

213. *MDR*, 11.

214. Ibid., 36–41.

215. Religion comes from *religāre*, "to bind together," or *religēre*, "to bind back." *Compact Edition of the Oxford English Dictionary* (London: Oxford University Press, 1987).

216. *MDR*, 233.

217. Ibid., 235.

218. Ibid., 237.

219. See Aniela Jaffé, *Was C. G. Jung a Mystic? and Other Essays* (Einsiedeln, Switzerland: Daimon Verlag, 1989).

220. *C. G. Jung Speaking: Interviews and Encounters*, ed. William McGuire and R. F. C. Hull, Bollingen Series 97 (Princeton: Princeton University Press, 1977).

BIBLIOGRAPHY

Chapter I. Dōgen and Zen Buddhism

PRIMARY SOURCES

A. In Japanese

Dōgen Zenji Shihōshū: Fukan Zazengi, Gakudō yōjinshū, Hōkyōki, & Shinji Shōbōgenzō (Dōgen Zenji's Four Treasure Collection). Nishijima Wafu, ed. Tokyo: Kanazawa Bunko, 1990.

Gendaigoyaku Shōbōgenzō (Shobogenzo in Modern Japanese). Nishijima Wafu, ed. 13 volumes. Tokyo: Kanazawa Bunko, 1970 –89.

Shōbōgenzō (in original classical Japanese). Edited and annotated by Mizuno Yaeko. 4 vols. Tokyo: Iwanami Bunko, 1990–93.

B. In English

Dōgen. Dōgen's Pure Standards for the Zen Community: A Translation of Eihei Shingi. Trans. Taigen D. Leighton and Shohaku Okumura. Albany: SUNY Press, 1996.

————. Eihei-kōroku. Trans. Yūhō Yokoi. Tokyo: Sankibo Buddhist Bookstore. 1987.

————. Flowers of Emptiness. Selections from Dōgen's Shōbōgenzō. Trans. Hee-Jin Kim. Lewiston, N.Y.: Edwin Mellon Press. 1985.

————. Master Dōgen's Shōbōgenzō, Book 1. Trans. Gudo Nishijima and Chodo Cross. Surrey: Windbell Publications,1994.

————. Master Dōgen's Shōbōgenzō, Book 2. Trans. Gudo Nishijima and Chodo Cross. Surrey: Windbell Publications, 1996.

————. Moon in a Dewdrop, Writings of Zen Master Dōgen. Ed. Kazuaki Tanahashi. San Francisco: North Point Press, 1985.

Journeys into Emptiness

————. *Record of Things Heard: Shōbōgenzō-zuimonki.* Trans. Thomas Cleary. Boulder: Prajna Press, 1980.

————. *Shōbōgenzō: The Eye and Treasury of the True Law.* Trans. Kōsen Nishiyama. Tokyo: Nakayama Shobō and Japan Publications, 1975.

Kodera, Takashi, *Dōgen's Formative Years in China: An Historical Study and Annotated Translation of the Hōkyōki.* San Francisco: Prajna Press, 1980.

SECONDARY SOURCES

Abe, Masao. *Buddhism and Interfaith Dialogue.* Honolulu: University of Hawaii Press, 1995.

————. *A Study of Dōgen: His Philosophy and Religion.* Albany: SUNY Press, 1992.

————. LaFleur, William, ed. *Zen and Western Thought.* Honolulu: University of Hawaii Press, 1985.

Bielefeldt, Carl. *Dōgen's Manuals of Zen Meditation.* Berkeley: University of California Press, 1988.

Blofeld, John. Zen *Teaching of Instantaneous Awakening of Master Hui Hai.* Devon, U.K.: Buddhist Publishing Group, 1995.

Collcutt, Martin. *Five Mountains: The Rinzai Zen Monastic Institution in Medieval Japan.* Cambridge, Mass.: Harvard East Asian Monographs, 1981.

Conze, Edward. *A Short History of Buddhism.* Oxford: One World, 1995.

Cook, Francis Dojun. *How to Raise an Ox.* Los Angeles: Zen Center, 1978.

Dalai Lama. *The Buddhism of Tibet.* Ithaca, N.Y.: Snow Lion Press, 1987.

Dumoulin, Heinrich. *Zen Buddhism: A History.* Vol. 1: *India and China.* New York: MacMillan, 1988. Vol 2: *Japan.* New York: Macmillan, 1990.

Faure, Bernard. *La Vision Immediate: Nature, Eveil et Tradition Selon Le Shōbō-genzō.* France: Editions Le Mail, 1987.

Fundamental Wisdom of the Middle Way: Nāgārjuna's *Mūlamadhyamakakā-rikā.* Translation and commentary by Jay L. Garfield. New York: Oxford University Press, 1995.

Heine, Steven. *Dōgen and the Koan Tradition—A Tale of Two Shō-bōgenzō Texts.* Albany: State University of New York Press, 1994.

Hongzhi. *Cultivating the Empty Field: The Silent Illumination of Zen Master Hongzhi.* San Francisco: North Point Press, 1991.

Hopkins, Jeffrey. *Emptiness Yoga: The Tibetan Middle Way.* Ithaca, N.Y.: Snow Lion Press, 2nd Edition, 1995.

Bibliography

Hui-Neng, The Diamond Sutra & the Sutra of Hui-Neng. Boston: Shambala, 1990. *The Platform Sutra of the Sixth Patriarch, text of the Tun-Huang Manuscript.* Trans. Yampolsky. New York: Columbia University Press, 1967. ————. *The Threefold Lotus Sutra.* Tokyo: Kosei Publishing Co., 1990.

Huntington, C. W. *Emptiness of Emptiness.* Honolulu: University of Hawaii Press, 1989.

Inquiry into the Origin of Humanity. An Annotated Translation of Thung-mi's Yuan jen lun, with a Modern Commentary. Translation and commentary by Peter Gregory. Kuroda Institute. Honolulu: University of Hawaii Press, 1996.

Kapleau, Philip. *The Three Pillars of Zen.* New York: Anchor Books, 1989.

Kasulis, T. P. *Zen Action/Zen Person.* Honolulu: University of Hawaii Press, 1981.

Keizan, Zen Master. *Transmission of the Light: Zen in the Art of Enlightenment.* Trans. Thomas Cleary. San Francisco: North Point Press, 1990.

Kim, Hee-Jin. Dōgen *Kigen, Mystical Realist.* Tucson: University of Arizona Press, 1987.

LaFleur, William, ed. *Dōgen Studies.* The Kuroda Institute: Studies in East Asian Buddhism, no. 2. Honolulu: University of Hawaii Press, 1985.

Loori, John Diado. *The Eight Gates of Zen.* Mt. Tremper, N.Y.: Dharma Communications, 1992.

————. *The Ghost Cave—Emptiness in the Zen Tradition.* A Dharma Discourse audiotape. Boulder, Colo.: Sounds True Recordings, 1989.

————. *The Heart of Being—Moral and Ethical Teachings of Zen Buddhism.* Rutland, Vt.: Chas. Tuttle, 1996.

————. *Mountain Record of Zen Talks.* Boston: Shambala, 1988.

————. *Two Arrows Meeting in Mid Air: The Zen Koan.* Rutland: Chas. Tuttle, 1994.

Lopez, Donald S., Jr. *Elaborations on Emptiness: Uses of the Heart Sūtra.* Princeton: Princeton University Press, 1996.

Murti, T. R. V. *Central Philosophy of Buddhism.* London, Boston: Unwin Paperbacks, 1980.

Nagao, Gadjin. *Madhyamika and Yogacara.* Albany: SUNY Press, 1991.

Nhat Hanh Thich. *The Diamond That Cuts Through Illusion.* Berkeley: Parallax Press, 1992.

————. *For a Future to be Possible: Commentaries on the Five Wonderful Precepts.* Berkeley: Parallax Press, 1993.

————. *The Heart of Understanding.* Berkeley: Parallax Press, 1988.

————. *Interbeing.* Berkeley: Parallax Press, 1984.

————. *Living Buddha, Living Christ.* New York: Riverhead Books, 1995.

————. *Our Appointment with Life.* Berkeley: Parallax Press, 1990.

Journeys into Emptiness

————. *The Sutra on The Eight Realizations of the Great Beings*. Berkeley: Parallax Press, 1987.

————. *Zen Keys*. Garden City, N.Y.: Doubleday, 1995.

Nishida, Kitaro. *An Inquiry into the Good*. New Haven: Yale University Press, 1987.

Nishijima, Gudo Wafu. *To Meet the Real Dragon*. Surrey, England: Windbell Publications, 1992.

Nishitani, Keiji. *Religion and Nothingness*. Berkeley: University of California Press, 1982.

Porter, Bill. *Road to Heaven: Encounters with Chinese Hermits*. San Francisco: Mercury House, 1993.

Roberts, Bernadette. *The Experience of No-Self, A Contemplative Journey*. Albany: State University of New York Press, 1993.

————. *The Path to No Self*. Boston: Shambala, 1985.

Roland, Alan. *In Search of Self in India and Japan*. Princeton: Princeton University Press, 1989.

Ryu, Kee Chong. *Nagarjuna's Emptiness and Paul Tillich's God—a Comparative Study for the Dialogue Between Christianity and Buddhism*. Madison, N.J.: Drew University Ph.D. thesis, 1984.

Shaner, David. *Bodymind Experience in Japanese Buddhism*. Albany: SUNY Press, 1985.

Shapers of Japanese Buddhism. Yusen Kashiwahara and Koyu Sonoda, eds. Tokyo: Kosei Publishing Co., 1994.

Sheng-yen, Master. *Getting the Buddha Mind*. Elmhurst, N.Y.: Dharma Drums Publications, 1982.

————. *Faith in Mind*. Elmhust, N.Y.: Dharma Drums Publications, 1987.

Soto Zen in Medieval Japan. William Bodiford, ed. The Kuroda Institute: Studies in East Asian Buddhism, no. 8, 1993.

Stambaugh, Joan. *Impermanence is Buddha-nature: Dōgen's Understanding of Temporality*. Honolulu: University of Hawaii Press, 1990.

Streng, Frederick J. *Emptiness, A Study in Religious Meaning*. New York: Abingdon, 1967.

Studies in Ch'an and Hua-Yen. Robert Gimello and Peter Gregory, eds. The Kuroda Institute: Studies in East Asian Buddhism, no. 1. Honolulu: University of Hawaii Press, 1983.

Suzuki, D. T. *An Introduction to Zen Buddhism*. New York: Grove Press, 1964.

————. *Zen and Japanese Culture*. Bollingen Series. Princeton: Princeton University Press, 1959.

————. *The Zen Koan as a means of Attaining Enlightenment*. Rutland, Vt.: Chas. Tuttle, 1994.

Thurman, Robert. *Central Philosophy of Tibet.* Princeton: Princeton University Press, 1991.

————. *Essential Tibetan Buddhism.* San Francisco: Harper, 1996.

————. *The Holy Teaching of Vimalakirti: A Mahayana Scripture.* University Park, Penn.: Pennsylvania State University Press, 1976.

Uchiyama, Kosho. *Opening the Hand of Thought: Approach to Zen.* Trans. Okumura and Wright. New York: Penguin, 1993.

————. *Refining Your Life: from the Zen Kitchen to Enlightenment.* New York: Weatherhill, 1990.

Wu, John C. H. *The Golden Age of Zen.* New York: Doubleday, 1996.

Yokoi, Yuho. *Zen Master Dōgen.* New York: Weatherhill, 1976.

Zen Teaching of Instantaneous Awakening by Master Hui Hai. Trans. John Blofeld. A complete translation of the *Tun Wu Ju Tao Yao Men Lun* and the *Tsung Ching Record.* Devon, U.K.: Buddhist Publishing Group, 1987.

Chapter 2. Thomas Merton and Christianity

PRIMARY SOURCES

Merton, Thomas. *Asian Journal.* New York: New Directions, 1975.

————. *Conjectures of a Guilty Bystander.* New York: Doubleday, 1989.

————. *Contemplative Prayer.* New York: Doubleday, 1989.

————. *Entering the Silence—Becoming a Monk and a Writer—The Journals,* vol. 2. Ed. Jonathan Montaldo. Harper: San Francisco, 1995.

————. *The geography of lograire.* New York: New Directions, 1968.

————. *Hidden Ground of Love: Letters.* Farrar, Straus and Giroux, 1985.

————. *Honorable Reader.* New York: Crossroad, 1989.

————. *Love and Living.* Ed(s). Naomi Burton and Bro. Patrick Hart. New York: Harcourt, Brace, 1979.

————. *The Monastic Journey.* Cistercian Publications, 1992.

————. *The New Man.* New York: Farrar, Straus and Giroux, 1961.

————. *Mystics and Zen Masters.* New York: Farrar, Straus and Giroux, 1967.

————. *New Seeds of Contemplation.* New York: New Directions, 1961.

————. *Raids on the Unspeakable.* New York: New Directions, 1966.

————. *Run to the Mountain—The Story of a Vocation—The Journals,* vol. 1. Ed., Patrick Hart. San Francisco: Harper, 1995.

Journeys into Emptiness

————. *School of Charity: Letters of Thomas Merton on Religious Renewal and Spiritual Direction.* Ed., Patrick Hart. New York: Farrar, Straus and Giroux, 1990.

————. *A Search for Solitude–The Journals,* vol. 3. Ed., Lawrence Cunningham. San Francisco: Harper, 1996.

————. *The Sign of Jonas.* New York: Harcourt, Brace, 1953.

————. *Thomas Merton in Alaska.* New York: New Directions, 1989.

————. *The Way of Chuang Tzu.* New York: New Directions, 1965.

————. *Thomas Merton: Preview of Asian Journey.* Ed. Walter Capps. Crossroad, 1989.

————. *Thoughts in Solitude.* New York: Farrar, Straus and Giroux, 1958.

————. *Turning Toward the World–The Journals,* vol. 4. Ed., Victor Kramer. San Francisco: Harper, 1996.

————. *Woods, shore, desert: Notebook, May, 1968.* Santa Fe: Museum of New Mexico Press, 1982.

————. *Zen and the Birds of Appetite.* New York: New Directions, 1968.

SECONDARY SOURCES

Carr, Anne. *A Search for Wisdom and Spirit: Thomas Merton's Theology of the Self.* Notre Dame, Ind.: University of Notre Dame Press, 1988.

Cooper, David. *Thomas Merton's Art of Denial: Evolution of a Radical Humanist.* Athens, Ga.: University of Georgia Press, 1989.

Dupre, Louis. *Transcendent Selfhood.* New York: Seabury Press, 1976.

Finley, James. *Merton's Palace of Nowhere: A Search for God through Awareness of the True Self.* Notre Dame, Ind.: Ave Maria Press, 1978.

Forest, James. *Living with Wisdom: a Life of Thomas Merton.* New York: Orbis Books, 1991.

Furlong, Monica. *Thomas Merton: a Biography.* Liguori, Mo.: Liguori Publications, 1980.

Griffin, John Howard. *Follow the Ecstasy: the Hermitage Years of Thomas Merton.* Orbis Books, 1993.

Kierkegaard, Soren. *Fear and Trembling/The Sickness Unto Death.* New York: Doubleday, 1954.

————. *For Self Examination.* Minneapolis: Augsburg Publishing House, 1962.

Kylin, Helen. *When Silence Becomes Singing.* Pendle Hill Publishers, 1984.

Lipski, Alexander. *Thomas Merton and Asia: His Quest for Utopia.* Cistercian Society: Cistercian Publications, 1983.

Malits, Elena. *Solitary Explorer: Thomas Merton's Transforming Journey.* Harper & Row, 1980.

Merton, Thomas. *Seven Storey Mountain.* New York: Harcourt Brace, 1978.

Mitchell, Donald. *Spirituality and Emptiness.* New York: Paulist Press, 1991.

Mommaers, Paul and Jan Van Bragt. *Mysticism—Buddhist and Christian: Encounters with Jan van Ruusbroec.* New York: Crossroad, 1995.

Mott, Michael. *The Seven Mountains of Thomas Merton.* Boston: Houghton Mifflin Co., 1984.

Nouwen, Henri. *Thomas Merton: Contemplative Critic.* Harper & Row, 1981.

Padovano, Anthony. *The Human Journey: Thomas Merton, Symbol of a Century.* Garden City, N.Y.: Doubleday, 1982.

Shannon, W. H. *Thomas Merton's Dark Path: the Inner Experience of a Contemplative.* New York: Farrar, Straus and Giroux, 1987.

————. *Silent Lamp.* New York: Crossroad, 1992.

The Merton Annual. New York: AMS Press, 1988ff.

Thomas Merton/Monk. Ed., Patrick Hart. New York: Sheed and Ward, 1974.

Waldron, Robert G. *Thomas Merton in Search of His Soul.* Notre Dame, Ind.: Ave Maria Press, 1994.

Chapter 3. Depth Psychology

PRIMARY SOURCES

Jung, C. G., *Aion, Researches into the Phenomenology of the Self.* Bollingen Series XX. Vol. 9, II, Collected Works. Princeton: Princeton University Press, 1959.

————. *Alchemical Studies.* Vol. 13, Collected Works. Princeton: Princeton University Press, 1967.

————. *Archetypes and the Collective Unconscious.* Vol. 9, I, Collected Works. Princeton: Princeton University Press, 1959.

————. *Civilization in Transition.* Vol. 10, Collected Works. Princeton: Princeton University Press, 1953.

————. *The Development of Personality.* Vol. 17, Collected Works. Princeton: Princeton University Press, 1964.

————. *Man and His Symbols.* New York: Doubleday, 1964.

Journeys into Emptiness

————. *Memories, Dreams, Reflections.* New York: Vintage Books, 1961.

————. *Practice of Psychotherapy.* Vol. 16, Collected Works. Princeton: Princeton University Press, 1953.

————. *Psychology and Religion: West and East.* Vol. 11, Collected Works. Princeton: Princeton University Press, 1958.

————. *Structure and Dynamics of Psyche.* Vol. 8, Collected Works. Princeton: Princeton University Press, 1953.

The Freud/Jung Letters. Ed., William McGuire, Trans. Ralph Mannheim and R. F. C. Hull. Princeton: Princeton University Press, 1974.

SECONDARY SOURCES

Carotenuto, Aldo. *A Secret Symmetry: Sabina Spielrein between Jung and Freud.* Translated by Arno Pomerans, John Shepley, and Krishna Winston. New York: Pantheon Books, 1982.

Clarke, J. J. *Jung and Eastern Thought: A Dialogue with the Orient.* New York: Routledge, 1994.

Coward, Harold G. *Jung and Eastern Thought.* Albany: SUNY Press, 1985.

Dupre, Louis. *Transcendent Selfhood: Loss and Rediscovery of Inner Life.* New York: Seabury, 1976.

Edinger, Edward F. *Bible and Psyche: The Individuation Process.* San Francisco: Inner City Books, 1986.

————. *The Christian Archetype: A Jungian Commentary on the Life of Christ.* San Francisco: Inner City Books, 1987.

Goldbrunner, Josef. *Holiness is Wholeness.* Notre Dame Press, 1964.

Gruen, Arno. *The Betrayal of the Self.* New York: Grove Press, 1986.

Guntrip, Harry. *Schizoid Phenomena, Object Relations and the Self.* New York: International Universities Press, 1969.

Halligan, Frederica, and John Shea. *The Fires of Desire: Erotic Energies and the Spiritual Quest.* New York: Crossroad, 1992.

Homans, Peter. *Jung in Context.* 2d Ed. Chicago: University of Chicago Press, 1995.

Jacobi, Jolande. *The Way of Individuation.* New York: Harcourt Brace, 1967.

————. *Masks of the Soul.* Grand Rapids, MI.: Eerdmans, 1976.

Bibliography

Jones, James W. *Contemporary Psychoanalysis and Religion*. New Haven: Yale University Press, 1991.

———. *Toward a Relational Psychoanalysis of Religion*. Unpublished manuscript, 1995.

Kerr, John. *A Most Dangerous Method: the Story of Freud, Jung and Sabina Speilrein*. New York: Alfred Knopf, 1993.

Kohut, Heinz. *The Analysis of the Self*. New York: International University Press, 1974.

———. *How Does Analysis Cure?* Chicago: University of Chicago Press, 1984.

———. *The Restoration of the Self*. New York: International University Press, 1977.

———. *The Search for the Self*. Vols. 1 & 2. P. Ornstein, ed. New York: International University Press, 1978.

Kurtz, Stephen. *The Art of Unknowing*. New York: J. Aronson, 1989.

Meckel, Daniel and Robert Moore, eds. *Jung and Christianity in Dialogue: Faith, Feminism & Hermeneutics*. Mahwah, N.J.: Paulist Press, 1990.

———. *Self and Liberation: The Jung/Buddhism Dialogue*. Mahwah, N.J. : Paulist Press, 1992.

Moore, Robert and Murray Stein. *Jung's Challenge to Contemporary Religion*. Wilmette, Ill.: Chiron Publications, 1987.

Odajnyk, Walter. *Gathering the Light*. Boston: Shambala, 1994.

Ulanov, Ann. *Picturing God*. Boston: Cowley Publications, 1986.

Ulanov, Ann and Barry. *The Functioning Transcendent: A Study in Analytical Psychology*. Wilmette, Ill.: Chiron Publications, 1996.

———. *The Healing Imagination*. New York: Paulist Press, 1991.

———. *Primary Speech, a Psychology of Prayer*. Atlanta: John Knox Press, 1982.

———. *Religion and the Unconscious*. Philadelphia: Westminster Press, 1969.

———. *Transforming Sexuality: The Archetypal World of Anima and Animus*. Boston: Shambhala, 1994.

Winnicott, Donald W. *Home Is Where We Start From*. Essays by a Psychoanalyst. New York: W. W. Norton, 1986.

———. *The Maturational Processes and the Facilitating Environment*. New York: International University Press, 1986.

———. *Playing and Reality*. New York: Penguin Books, 1971.

Journeys into Emptiness

———. *The Spontaneous Gesture.* Selected Letters of D. W. Winnicott. Ed. F. R. Rodman. Cambridge: Harvard University Press, 1987.

———. *Through Paediatrics to Psycho-Analysis.* New York: Basic Books, 1975.

About the Author

Robert W. Gunn received his A.B. in Philosophy at Columbia College, New York; his M.Div., S.T.M., and Ph.D. in Psychiatry and Religion from Union Theological Seminary, New York; and his D.Min. from Andover Newton Theological School, Newton, Massachusetts.

He received his training as a pastoral psychotherapist from the Blanton Peale Graduate Institute, New York City. He is a Fellow in the American Association of Pastoral Counselors, a Clinical Member of the American Association of Marital and Family Therapy, and a member of the American Psychological Association and the International Council of Psychologists.

As an ordained minister in the United Church of Christ, for twelve years he was pastor of churches in Maine, Massachusetts and New York.

For the past twenty years, he has been in private practice of psychotherapy in New York City. He is Director of Admissions and on the faculty of the Center for Spirituality and Psychotherapy of the National Institute for the Psychotherapies, New York. He has also been adjunct faculty at Union Theological Seminary and the Postgraduate Center for Mental Health, Pastoral Studies Department, New York.

He is a Master Scuba Diver Trainer with the Professional Association of Diving Instructors, International.

He is a member of the Mountains and Rivers Order of Zen Mountain Monastery in Mt. Tremper, New York, where he received the Buddhist precepts from John Daido Loori, Roshi, and was given the dharma name, Jingen, meaning both "God is the source of my life," and "my life is the source of God."

He has two daughters and four grandsons.

Other Books in the Jung and Spirituality Series

SPIRITUAL PILGRIMS
Carl Jung and Teresa of Avila
by John Welch

FROM IMAGE TO LIKENESS
A Jungian Path in the Gospel Journey
by W. Harold Grant, Magdala Thompson
and Thomas E. Clark

JUNG AND SHAMANISM IN DIALOGUE
Retrieving the Soul/Retrieving the Sacred
by C. Michael Smith

RELIGION AND THE SPIRITUAL IN CARL JUNG
by Ann Belford Ulanov